THOMAS COMPUTER CONSU
33333 W. TWELVE MILE RD
FARMINGTON HILLS, MICH
(810) 489-0707

D1164198

Special Edition

USING
ACTIVEX

THOMPSON CONSULTANTS, INC.
MI, MICHIGAN 48084
(810) 555-0707

Special Edition

USING
ACTIVEX

Written by Brian Farrar

Special Edition Using ActiveX

Copyright© 1996 by Que® Corporation.

All rights reserved. Printed in the United States of America. No part of this book may be used or reproduced in any form or by any means, or stored in a database or retrieval system, without prior written permission of the publisher except in the case of brief quotations embodied in critical articles and reviews. Making copies of any part of this book for any purpose other than your own personal use is a violation of United States copyright laws. For information, address Que Corporation, 201 W. 103rd Street, Indianapolis, IN, 46290. You may reach Que's direct sales line by calling 1-800-428-5331.

Library of Congress Catalog No.: 96-69954

ISBN: 0-7897-0886-8

This book is sold *as is*, without warranty of any kind, either express or implied, respecting the contents of this book, including but not limited to implied warranties for the book's quality, performance, merchantability, or fitness for any particular purpose. Neither Que Corporation nor its dealers or distributors shall be liable to the purchaser or any other person or entity with respect to any liability, loss, or damage caused or alleged to have been caused directly or indirectly by this book.

98 97 96   6 5 4 3 2 1

Interpretation of the printing code: the rightmost double-digit number is the year of the book's printing; the rightmost single-digit number, the number of the book's printing. For example, a printing code of 96-1 shows that the first printing of the book occurred in 1996.

All terms mentioned in this book that are known to be trademarks or service marks have been appropriately capitalized. Que cannot attest to the accuracy of this information. Use of a term in this book should not be regarded as affecting the validity of any trademark or service mark.

Screen reproductions in this book were created using Collage Plus from Inner Media, Inc., Hollis, NH.

Credits

PRESIDENT
Roland Elgey

PUBLISHER
Joseph B. Wikert

PUBLISHING MANAGER
Fred Slone

SENIOR TITLE MANAGER
Bryan Gambrel

EDITORIAL SERVICES DIRECTOR
Elizabeth Keaffaber

MANAGING EDITOR
Sandy Doell

DIRECTOR OF MARKETING
Lynn E. Zingraf

ACQUISITIONS EDITOR
Angela C. Kozlowski

PRODUCTION EDITOR
Maureen A. Schneeberger

COPY EDITORS
Matt Cox
Sherri Fugit
C. Kazim Haidri
Nancy Sears Perry

EDITORIAL INTERNS
Elizabeth Barrett
Kate Givens

PRODUCT MARKETING MANAGER
Kim Margolius

**ASSISTANT PRODUCT
MARKETING MANAGER**
Christy M. Miller

STRATEGIC MARKETING MANAGER
Barry Pruett

TECHNICAL EDITOR
Joel Goodling

TECHNICAL SUPPORT SPECIALIST
Nadeem Muhammed

SOFTWARE RELATIONS COORDINATOR
Patricia J. Brooks

ACQUISITIONS COORDINATOR
Carmen Krikorian

EDITORIAL ASSISTANT
Andrea Duvall

BOOK DESIGNER
Ruth Harvey

COVER DESIGNER
Dan Armstrong

PRODUCTION TEAM
Marcia Brizendine
Jenny Earhart
Brian Grossman
Daryl Kessler
Kaylene Riemen

INDEXER
Kevin Fulcher

Composed in *Century Old Style* and *ITC Franklin Gothic* by Que Corporation.

Thanks to my wife Annie, for putting up with me while I typed furiously into the night on my laptop computer.

About the Author

Brian Farrar received his B.A. from Wabash College in 1985 in English and Economics. He completed an MBA from Indiana University in 1987. He began his career at GTE and progressed through a series of positions until 1994, when he left to start an Internet and intranet consulting practice for Metamor Technologies. Through this consulting practice, Brian has helped some of the largest companies in the world decide on and deploy Internet technologies to solve business problems.

We'd Like to Hear from You!

As part of our continuing effort to produce books of the highest possible quality, Que would like to hear your comments. To stay competitive, we *really* want you, as a computer book reader and user, to let us know what you like or dislike most about this book or other Que products.

You can mail comments, ideas, or suggestions for improving future editions to the address below, or send us a fax at (317) 581-4663. Our staff and authors are available for questions and comments through our Internet site, at **http://www.mcp.com/que**, and Macmillan Computer Publishing also has a forum on CompuServe (type **GO QUEBOOKS** at any prompt).

In addition to exploring our forum, please feel free to contact me personally to discuss your opinions of this book: I'm **akozlowski@que.mcp.com** on the Internet.

Thanks in advance–your comments will help us to continue publishing the best books available on new computer technologies in today's market.

Angela Kozlowski
Acquisitions Editor
Que Corporation
201 W. 103rd Street
Indianapolis, Indiana 46290
USA

Contents at a Glance

Contents

Introduction

To help you turn immediately to the sections that best suit your needs, the following brief summary of each major section is provided. Suggestions for quick starts with each of the various technologies will help you avoid wasting time and turn directly to the pages that will get you started quickly. ■

Part I—ActiveX and Dynamic Web Content

Chapters 1–3 begin by introducing the ActiveX SDK from Microsoft. You'll get a 10,000 foot view of each of the major components of the ActiveX SDK. If you've been away from OCXs for a while, these chapters will treat you to a review the Component Object Model on which OLE 2.0 is built. Reviewing these issues ensures that you are reacquainted with important basic concepts. ActiveX is based heavily on the OLE 2.0 specification. Though this section is not intended to teach you how to build OLE controls, a certain amount of review will reacquaint you with the issues involved in constructing OLE controls. You'll also be introduced to the differences between the OLE 2.0 OCX and the ActiveX Control. The beauty of ActiveX is that ActiveX Controls are, in fact, repackaged OCX controls. The principal difference is not in their conceptual make-up but in implementation. Most developers build OCXs using the OCX wizard in VC++, while ActiveX Controls are constructed using the ActiveX SDK.

Chapters 4–6 guide you through the process of applying ActiveX Controls to Web pages. To round out the discussion, this chapter also provides examples implementing Microsoft provided controls.

The so-called "intrinsic controls" and scripting functions of ActiveX are covered in Chapters 7–10. One alternative to Common Gateway Interface applications for simple applications is the use of a scripting language such as VBScript or JavaScript. This chapter teaches you how to use VBScript to develop dynamic documents. You'll also get a sense of the market dynamic going on related to VBScript and JavaScript. You'll see how Microsoft's VBScript is positioned in the Internet development market space.

Part II—The ActiveX Internet Control Pack

Chapters 11–18 guide you through the process of employing ActiveX Controls in Visual Basic Applications. The Microsoft Internet Control Pack controls will be used to construct Internet-ready applications. Each chapter will employ one the controls providing detailed implementation and step-by-step construction of an application using the control. The properties and functions of each control will be explained and demonstrated.

Part III—The ActiveX Server Framework

Security is always in issue when users are downloading software over a network. In Chapter 19, Microsoft's plans for ensuring security are discussed. This chapter also compares and contrasts features of ActiveX security plans with the Java security architecture.

Chapters 20–24 discuss in detail ISAPI and CGI. ISAPI will be compared and contrasted with the CGI. You will be positioned to make good decisions about which approach is appropriate for your own applications. You will be guided through the process of building ISAPI extensions. You'll also learn how to use ISAPI to develop and extend Web servers. You'll learn the architecture and its comparative advantages and disadvantages to the nearly ubiquitous CGI standard. This section also develops a simple ISAPI filter in a step-by-step manner.

Conventions Used in This Book

Several type and font conventions are used in this book:

- *Italic type* is used to introduce new terms.
- Screen messages, code listings, and script samples appear in a `monospaced typeface`.
- URLs and anything you are asked to type appear in **bold**.

N O T E Notes provide additional information that may help you avoid a problem, or offer advice that relates to a particular topic. ◼

 T I P Tips present short advice on a quick or often overlooked procedure. These include shortcuts that can save you time.

CAUTION

Cautions warn you about potential problems that a procedure may cause, unexpected results, and mistakes to avoid.

ActiveX and Dynamic Web Content

Understanding Dynamic Web Content

Unless you've been sleeping for the past 18 months, (or perhaps trapped under something heavy), you are either convinced that the dynamic rise of the Internet in computing will change life, the universe, and everything; or, like the Beta tape or the Edsel, the Internet is a fad that will blow itself out as fast as it blew itself in. Given the impact of networks on computing in business, the truth is likely somewhere in between. You know that you can't simply chase every new technology that comes out. However, by picking up this book, you already recognize that some software tools are destined to change the way we think about software.

Dynamic documents (a term we will define more carefully in a moment) in the Internet market space are clearly one of those key technological shifts. More specifically, ActiveX enables software developers to easily include dynamic, animated, engaging content in Web pages without significant programming. ActiveX also provides programmers with tools to drag and drop Internet-aware controls into application development environments, such as Visual Basic, adding Internet functionality with the same ease that you add text boxes and list boxes today.

How the World Wide Web works

Briefly review the way that the Web works in terms of the technology employed over the 'Net.

Interaction of TCP/IP and HTTP

HTTP is a protocol that relies on TCP/IP. You must understand how this relationship affects your Web documents.

Common Gateway Interface (CGI) applications

Dynamic content can be generated in a number of ways including through the use of CGI applications.

Static content and the evolution of HTML 1.0 and HTML 2.0

Follow the transition of Web content from its origins to where we are today.

Dawn of dynamic documents including the effect of Java

ActiveX and Java are the beginning of a new era in dynamic content over the Web.

This introductory material is meant to reacquaint you with some of the issues that have affected Web and Internet-based application development prior to the introduction to ActiveX. In some ways, you'll see that ActiveX is an improvement over existing tools. You'll also note that in other ways Microsoft is clearly attempting to muscle into a market they were slightly late in getting to (but more on that later). This introduction is not meant to teach you all there is to know about these technologies, so if you're new to all of this stuff you may want to refer to some other material. ■

How the World Wide Web Works

The World Wide Web is an application that uses the Internet as its transmission medium. The basic unit of transmission on the World Wide Web is the Web page. A Web page can contain text, graphics, sound, and video clips. In addition, a Web page has a very special kind of text called a *hypertext link*. Before the invention of hypertext, reading was always a very linear operation. Say you were reading a general essay on the solar system. Throughout the text, the author might mention various planets like Mars and Venus. In the event that you wanted to read more about Mars, you would have to return to the table of contents, look up Mars, and the flip to the appropriate page.

With the advent of hypertext, a Web page author allows the reader to jump directly to the information on Mars by simply clicking the text itself. Reading is thus, in effect, non-linear. The reader chooses the path he or she will take through the material. If you've used the help files in most MS-Windows applications, you've experienced hypertext. What really makes the World Wide Web powerful is the ability to link from a page in Athens, Ohio, to a related page of information in Athens, Greece. This world wide networked hypertext linking is made possible by a global Internet network.

The Internet is not a single network. Instead, the Internet is a global network of networks all networked together. This worldwide phenomenon grew from an experiment funded by the U.S. government. In 1969, the government of the United States funded an experiment in computer networking. The Advanced Research Projects Agency (or ARPA) wanted to develop robust networking technologies that would allow computers to be linked together on a network. ARPA wanted networks constructed so that adding or removing computers (network nodes) left all other nodes on the network unaffected.

As the government, over time, become more and more reliant on computers and networks, investment in new technology made good sense. This climate was the fertile ground into which ARPANet (the genesis of the Internet) was planted. ARPANet began with the connection of four computing sites on or near the west coast of the United States. Through experimentation and research, a technology called *Transmission Control Protocol over Internet Protocol (TCP/ IP)* was developed. The ARPA research proved that networks based upon the TCP/IP technology could continue to operate under significant duress. In the past 18 months, that duress has been the literally billions of packets of data floating over the Net carrying Web pages, graphics, sounds, video, and various and sundry other cyber goodies.

The World Wide Web is literally "on the Net" (see fig. 1.1). Network protocols are often referred to as *stacks*, one protocol layered on top of the next. The Web actually exists as a layer on top of the network protocol stack. The networking protocol that carries most Internet traffic is TCP/IP, but the language used for communication between Web browsers (such as Netscape or Microsoft Internet Explorer) and Web servers (such as Microsoft's Internet Information Server) is called *HyperText Transmission Protocol* (*HTTP*). An HTTP message is actually carried via TCP/IP between a Web browser and a Web server. So, in a very real sense, the World Wide Web layer rests on top of or "on the Net."

FIG. 1.1

Network protocols are often referred to as stacks, one protocol stacked on top of the next.

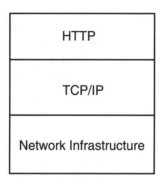

The Web works on a computing paradigm called *client/server* which is perhaps the single most over-used buzzword to ever hit the technology market place (see fig. 1.2). However, in the case of the Web, it is both applicable and accurately used. In the client/server model, the central computers and the desktop computers both contain significant processing power. Thus, the intense work of crunching large amounts of data can be shared by lots of computers over a network.

FIG. 1.2

The Web is based upon the client/server paradigm.

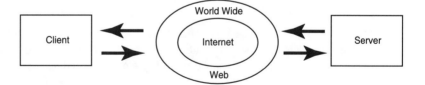

Let's take a quick look at how this client/server model is applied to the World Wide Web. Along the way, you'll be reminded of some of the critical pieces of the technology that make the Web work. The process of serving a Web page to a user on the Internet can be broken into three basic steps as follows:

1. Web browser issues a request for a Web page on a specific Web server.

2. Web server receives the request for Web page, searches the document space for specified Web page, and sends the requested page to the Web browser.

3. Web browser receives and renders the Web page content.

As you can see, the computing tasks are divided such that the client (most often, the *Web client* is referred to as a *Web browser*) renders the look and feel of the Web page, and the server processes the Web requests by serving up the requested data. Let's walk through each step again and break it down a little further.

Step One

The first step is that the Web browser issues a request for a Web page. This request is typically in the form of a HTTP GET request or an HTTP POST request. Static pages, graphics, and other Web objects (such as sound files and video clips) are retrieved by a GET request. A Web browser may also request that the Web server run a program that dynamically generates Web page data. These applications are often referred to as *Common Gateway Interface* (or *CGI*) *applications* because they use the CGI interface to communicate parameters (for instance, data entered in a text box by the user prior to issuing the page request). Most application requests generated by the Web browser are HTTP POST requests.

Step Two

The Web page request is now transmitted over the Internet to the appropriate server for processing by the Web server. This transmission is connected to the appropriate server using a TCP/IP socket. The desired server is indicated by the domain name portion of the *Uniform Resource Locator* (*URL*) (see fig. 1.3).

FIG. 1.3
Examine the structure of
Uniform Resource
Locators.

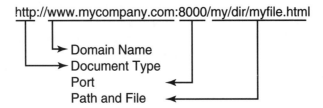

http://www.mycompany.com:8000/my/dir/myfile.html

Domain Name
Document Type
Port
Path and File

The URL is a now nearly pervasive item on everything from magazine ads to city bus billboards. The Web server searches the *document space* (a specific set of directories on a disk accessible by the Web server application) for a file corresponding to the file and path indicated in the URL. If the file is found, the Web server transmits the file to the Web browser. In order to help the browser to understand the type of content being transmitted, the server passes a *content type* header. The content type header will be especially important to you when we get to CGI and ISAPI programs later, because a program that dynamically generates HTML must supply a content type header as part of its output.

ON THE WEB

http://hoohoo.uiuc.ncsa.edu/cgi   If you are looking for a good resource on Common Gateway Interface applications development, check out for this URL an excellent and in-depth introduction to CGI.

Step Three

The Web server now receives the file and renders the page as directed by the HTML (Hyper-Text Markup Language) code in the file. HTML code describes how the page should look to the Web browser. If you have any recollection of the way that early word processors indicated that a string of text should be italicized or bolded, then you know how HTML works. A format code positioned in before the affected text indicates that the following text should be rendered in such-and-such a way and a finishing format code returns the style to the previous style. To bold the word *dog* in a sentence, you would code it in HTML as <B>dog</B>. The <B> tag starts the bold section and the </B> ends it. The HTML code may also indicate that there are additional objects required by the browser to properly render the page for viewing. For instance, the Web page may include an inline graphic (indicated by the <IMG SRC="myimage.gif"> tag). When the browser encounters this kind of HTML code, additional GET requests are generated asking the server for the indicated object.

ON THE WEB

http://www.w3.org   If you have no experience with HTML coding, you may want to check out Web sites that have good primers on HTML. For instance, this site contains a wealth of information on HTML.

Now that you understand how an individual Web page is served, understanding how a hypertext link works is simple. When you place the mouse pointer over a hypertext link and click, the browser issues a new GET request for the URL referenced in the HTML code.

Static Web Content

Our discussion so far has focused on how the various components of the World Wide Web work together to deliver Web pages to your computer screen. That's all well and good, but it doesn't say anything about what's in all these TCP/IP data packets flying over the network. And after all, that's what it's really about, isn't it? In its earliest form, HTML was designed to render text, and text only. As an HTML author, you could format text with headings of varying size. Words could be made bold or italicized for emphasis. This was state-of-the-art HTML with the HTML 1.0 standard. HTML was (and is), after all, a page description language. As with most technologies, however, the standards have developed over time (see fig. 1.4).

However, authors were anxious to add other types of Web content like graphic images to their Web pages. In the HTML 2.0 spec, information could be placed on a page basically in a vertical orientation with text blocks and graphics blocks following one another in order (see fig. 1.5).

Although the addition of graphics made the pages more like paper-based content, in the end you were still basically viewing a static page from a book on a computer screen. To many of us involved in the Internet at that time, it seemed like quite a waste of computing power. With more computing power on our desktops than it took to land Apollo 11 on the moon, the best we could do was to render a paper-like page of information on the computer screen!

FIG. 1.4
Transition of static
Web content.

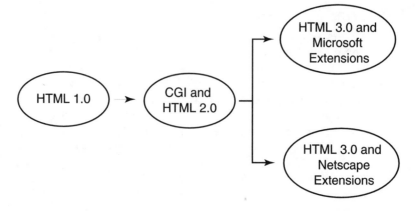

FIG 1.5
HTML 2.0 static
content model added
additional features.

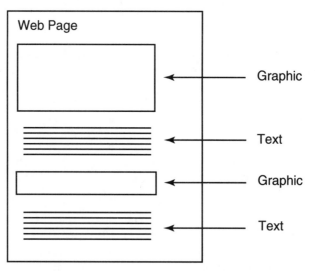

The rise of the Common Gateway Interface (CGI) application added a bit of dynamic quality to this static content model. Although the pages themselves still followed the HTML 2.0 static content model, the CGI could generate the page *on-the-fly* (that is based upon the conditional logic within the CGI program at execution time) at the time the user requested the Web page. But again, the real use of computing power was on the server side and the Web page content was still static. Once loaded into the browser, no changes, movement, or any other exciting events occurred.

Another technology applied to enrich the diversity of content available to Web authors, was the so-called *helper application*. Many browsers supported (and still support) the helper application. If you've listened to audio or viewed QuickTime video clips over the Web, you've probably used a helper application. The Web browser, Web developers reasoned, can't possibly know how to render all the content that a Web author might put in a Web page. When the Web browser downloads content that it doesn't know how to render, it asks the user to supply an application with which to view the content. So for instance, if a Web author made a QuickTime video clip part of a Web page, the video would not be rendered on the page, but would instead be shelled out to another application built to play QuickTime video.

But, of course, this model again ducks the issue of dynamic content in a Web page. The dynamic content, in the case of the Quick Time video just discussed, is shuttled off to another application for viewing. On the upside from a client/server perspective, the helper application system distributes additional computing responsibility to the client side of the equation. However, this model also creates two rather intractable problems:

- The user must know the appropriate application for viewing the content and properly configure the Web browser to launch it.
- The Web author must distribute the helper application in order to ensure that the content can be viewed.

Although most Web browsers make the installation of helper applications a relatively simple process, users seem to find it cumbersome to download and install new helper applications. This feeling, unfortunately, limits the propagation of helper applications through the market and creates a sort of Catch-22. From the perspective of the Web author, why develop content for helper applications with very limited user populations? From the perspective of the user, why go to the trouble of installing a helper application that is sparsely used by content providers? In the end, it basically results in very little usage of such applications. From the perspective of static versus dynamic content, helper applications simply provide Web authors with a static method to launch dynamic content in *other* applications. Not really very satisfying!

HTML 3.2 as of today is still a sort of evolving standard. Many browser developers have added their own specific extensions to the HTML language for page description. These additions have by and large made the description of pages more and more robust. Special features such as tables, frames, and other HTML code have made the diversity of content representation in Web pages easier and more flexible.

Of course, HTML 3.2 and browser specific HTML isn't sophisticated enough to be considered a dynamic content model on its own. Some dynamic features began appearing beginning with the Netscape Navigator 1.1 Web browser including client pull and server push.

Client pull gives Web authors a mechanism to supply a series of static HTML pages to the user automatically. To implement client pull, you must encode a special HTML tag (the <META> tag) in the HTML. The <META> tag causes the browser to pull another page from the server after a specified time has passed. So the Web author can program a tour of Web pages for the users or produce a simple text animation effect.

An excellent detailed discussion of both client pull and server push as well as instructions for implementing client pull are available at **http://home.netscape.com**. Although other browsers may support client pull, both Netscape Navigator and Microsoft Internet Explorer 3.0 certainly support this feature. Also, you can find an example implementation of client pull on the CD-ROM included with this book.

Unfortunately, transmitting a series of static pages automatically fails to distribute more computing responsibility to the client (the Web browser) and fails to animate any content within the Web page.

Server push is a bit more sophisticated than client pull and was the first truly dynamic element available to Web authors. The most common server push application implements a graphic animation. Conceptually, server push for graphic animation is quite simple to understand (see fig. 1.6).

FIG. 1.6
Server push is based on sending consecutive frames.

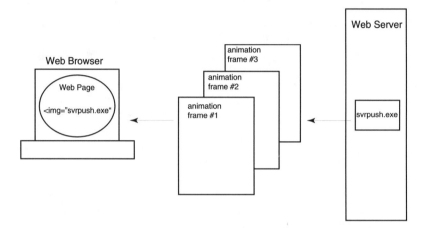

When the browser encounters an <IMG> tag, where the <IMG> object is a program, the browser instructs the server to execute that program. The program then loops through a list of static images transmitting each one in series. As long as the images are small (1K to 2K), a decent animation can be achieved.

Although a simple animation is a dynamic content element, server push still places the computing responsibility on the server. Also, server push is really limited to implementation of rudimentary animation.

Towards a Dynamic Content Model

Two basic problems plagued the static content model prior to the advent of Sun Microsystems' Java and Microsoft's ActiveX, which are as follows:

- The computing power of client machine executing the Web browser is woefully underused in the rendering of the content.
- The Web browser (or the user) had to know about and have available executable software capable of rendering downloaded content.

Sun Microsystems introduced the concept of *executable content*, or content that knows how to display itself (see fig. 1.7).

FIG. 1.7
Static versus dynamic
content model.

Static Model

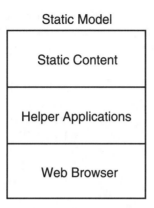

Dynamic Model

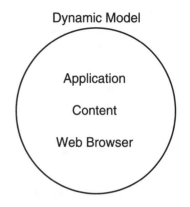

In the static content model, the Web browser, the content, and the content viewer are all separate objects. As shown in figure 1.7, each object is very separate with clear boundries. In the dynamic model, the content knows how to execute (that is, render) itself. The Web browser understands executable content in a generic sense. Thus, it knows how to render executable content objects. That's why figure 1.7 shows the dynamic content model as a single cohesive object.

The executable content concept addresses both of the deficiencies in the static model. Since the downloaded object knows how to render itself, the browser has no need to worry about helper applications and the like. Since the browser knows how to deal with executable objects such as Java applets (and ActiveX Controls as we'll cover in great deal throughout this book), the computing power available on the client side of the client/server equation is exercised more strenuously.

Hot Java, produced by Sun Microsystems, was the first browser to support the executable content model. However, Hot Java never really made much of a market penetration. The first market viable implementation of this model is found in Netscape Navigator 2.0. With Netscape Navigator 2.0, dynamic content is finally possible. This version supports:

- Java applets
- JavaScript
- Special plug-ins

As you'll see very clearly throughout this book, ActiveX and Microsoft Internet Explorer 3.0 support the dynamic content model in a robust fashion as well.

Let's look at each of these elements of the dynamic document and briefly mention the competing ActiveX item. You'll see that ActiveX offers similar capabilities and moves the technology further.

Java applets are downloadable, executable content. A Java applet contains both its content and instructions for rendering it within a Web page. Java applets can react to mouse and keyboard events, as well as interact with the browser (for instance, a Java applet can change the Web browsers status message bar). As this book explains, ActiveX also provides a similar paradigm for downloadable, executable content. These executable objects are ActiveX Controls, a continuation of the OLE 2.0 objects.

JavaScript allows the Web author to put programming logic directly into HTML code. The Web browser downloads the script and then acts as an interpreter to execute the JavaScript. This empowers Web authors to include text, list, and checkboxes and then process user input and execute conditional logic. ActiveX provides VBScript—a subset of Visual Basic, the popular Windows development language.

Plug-ins stem from Netscape's release of the Netscape plug-in API (Application Programming Interface). *Plug-ins* are basically helper applications integrated directly into the browser through an API. When the browser downloads such content, rather than spawning a helper application, the browser dynamically calls plug-in code to handle the rendering. In ActiveX, the rough equivalent is the DocObjects standard. A DocObject is an OLE object that has complete control over its host page.

The dynamic document model has applications well beyond the current implementation of Netscape Navigator 2.0. In many ways, Microsoft Internet Explorer 3.0 simply catches up with Netscape Navigator; however, ActiveX goes beyond catch-up. ActiveX controls can be placed in applications other than Web browsers. Your word processor, spreadsheet, and personal information manager might need access to Internet-based resources. With ActiveX controls, integrating Internet capabilities is straightforward.

Now that you've heard a bit about how ActiveX and the dynamic content model fit into the evolution of Internet-based application development, let's gets started building, using, and dealing with ActiveX Controls and Technologies. ●

CHAPTER 2

Overview of ActiveX

ActiveX is not a single technological thing. If you've
browsed Microsoft's Web site (**www.microsoft.com**),
you've probably gathered that ActiveX is a centerpiece of
Microsoft's overall Internet strategy. ActiveX helps application developers and Web content authors build dynamic
Internet tools, content, and sites. That's a pretty tall order.
To achieve this design goal, Microsoft needed to bring
together a number of different components. When you're
first introduced to a bunch of new items, it's often hard to
assimilate all the pieces of information into an overall
picture. (The old forest versus the trees problem). So this
chapter will take you through a quick tour of all the major
components of ActiveX, so that as you slice into the gory
detail you won't lose sight of the overall ActiveX design. ■

ActiveX Controls for the Internet

You'll use ActiveX Controls in many
of the places you're using Java
applets today.

ActiveX scripting services

The ActiveX scripting service empowers you to add scripting and
OLE automation capabilities to
programs.

ActiveX documents

ActiveX documents are based upon
a more general abstraction called
DocObjects—a set of extensions to
OLE documents.

The Internet Control Pack

Add Internet functionality to your
applications with these easy-to-use
ActiveX Controls.

ActiveX server framework

High performance server-side
application for the Web is made
possible with this framework.

ActiveX Controls for the Internet

As the content you consume from the Internet becomes more and more dynamic, the Web browser will be managing more and more of the computing tasks required to render that content. Much has been made of the executable content model for Web content. Sun Microsystem's Java takes early honors in the race for the development standard for executable content. Many Web sites employ simple multimedia widgets provided by Java, such as the Animator class.

ON THE WEB

You can find a wealth of information about Java and many of the freely available classes for Web page developers at **http://java.sun.com** or **http://www.gamelan.com**.

Netscape helped to push Java into prominence by releasing Navigator 2.0 with support for Java applets. Java provides Web developers with a highly sophisticated tool set for interacting with the user and the client machine. Microsoft, not to be outdone, announced support for Java in MSIE 3.0 and a new alternative called *ActiveX Controls*. ActiveX Controls are based upon the OLE 2.0 standard. ActiveX Controls are to Web pages what the VBX and OCX are to MS-Windows GUI development. You'll use ActiveX Controls in many of the places you're using Java applets today. However, ActiveX Controls have the following advantages over Java applets:

- They are built from tools you already know.
- They are easy to integrate with other applications.
- They are easy to employ in containers that are not Web pages.

Let's take a brief look at each of these advantages.

Built Using Tools You Already Know

Java requires that you learn an entire new language. Although Java and C++ have syntactic similarities, Java requires that you learn a whole new set of class hierarchies. (Of course, Java saves you from being engulfed in the search for "a pointer from hell" as in C++). When you consider all the methods and properties that you must learn to be proficient, its quite an undertaking. But, on the other hand, if you've been using C++ and have constructed an OCX, then you already know most of the basic concepts. Unfortunately, ActiveX Controls are not constructed using Microsoft Foundation Classes. Instead, Microsoft has made the ActiveX Template Library (ATL) available to help developers build ActiveX controls.

Easy to Integrate with Other Applications

Because ActiveX Controls are based upon the OLE 2.0 specification, the potential for ActiveX Controls to interact with other applications like word processors, spreadsheets, and presentation opens many possibilities. Although stand-alone applications can be constructed using Java, Java does not really offer the same potential interaction with other existing applications yet.

Easy to Employ in Containers

As mentioned previously, Java can be used to produce other stand-alone applications. However, Java applets are intended to execute in a Web browser and not as controls in other applications. The Internet ActiveX Control Pack demonstrates the value of ActiveX in other development environments like Visual C++, Delphi, Visual Basic, and MS-Access. Microsoft's use of the OLE 2.0 specification as the basis for ActiveX Controls and their use in these other environments provides additional interoperability characteristics.

Of course, there are a couple of problems with the use of ActiveX Controls. You'll want to consider the following concerns:

- They are not currently supported in Netscape.
- They are not currently supported on UNIX platforms.

Why are these disadvantages important? Let's take a moment and discuss each problem briefly.

Netscape Support   If Netscape continues to dominate the browser market and ActiveX is slow to take off, there is little advantage for Netscape in supporting ActiveX. Netscape provides support for Java and sees Microsoft as a significant competitive threat. However, Microsoft provides a *plug-in* (actually built by a third party) to allow support for ActiveX. (You can download it from **www.microsoft.com**.) Plug-ins add functionality to Web browsers. So it is unlikely that this potential disadvantage will significantly affect the long run viability of ActiveX.

UNIX Support   Many computers connected to the Internet are UNIX-based machines. Unfortunately, Microsoft has made no significant effort to deploy Microsoft technology to the UNIX platform. The Internet has thrived on the concept of open platform support. That is, most major Internet applications work on a diverse set of platforms. In fact, much of the Internet's recent surge in popularity is due to the platform independent nature of Web pages. With so many Internet users relying on UNIX machines, failure to support ActiveX on UNIX might seriously hamper market acceptance. However, Microsoft has indicated that ActiveX will be supported in the UNIX environment.

ActiveX Scripting Services

Netscape added another highly useful feature to Navigator called JavaScript. JavaScript provides a simple mechanism for placing conditional logic and user interface elements in Web pages without CGI applications. Basically, the Web browser provides an interpreter platform for this script. ActiveX provides a similar scripting service for MSIE 3.0. But the ActiveX scripting service is a more general service than that offered by Netscape. The ActiveX scripting service empowers you to add scripting and OLE automation capabilities to programs. ActiveX scripting provides a platform for developing script engines. The script language, syntax, and execution model can vary based upon the design of the script language developer. There are two types of ActiveX scripting components:

- ActiveX scripting hosts
- ActiveX scripting engines

Part
I

Ch
2

ActiveX Scripting Hosts

An ActiveX scripting host provides a platform on which to run the ActiveX scripting engine. The principle ActiveX scripting host is MSIE 3.0. However, under ActiveX there are a number of potential script hosts, such as the following:

- Other Web browsers
- Internet authoring tools
- Web servers (server-based scripting)

ActiveX Scripting Engines

An ActiveX scripting engine is basically the language to be executed on the ActiveX scripting host. The first ActiveX scripting engine is VBScript, a subset of the popular Visual Basic 4.0 development environment. However, ActiveX provides any number of potential script engine environments, such as the following:

- Perl
- Lisp
- Delphi
- Scheme

ActiveX Documents

An existing application that doesn't need to be embedded in a Web page can be converted to an ActiveX document. Documents that conform to the ActiveX standard can be opened within other ActiveX document containers including the following:

- Microsoft Internet Explorer 3.0
- Microsoft Office Binder
- Forthcoming new Windows shell

ActiveX documents are based upon a more general abstraction called *DocObjects*. The DocObjects technology is a set of extensions to OLE documents, the compound document technology of OLE. As with OLE documents, the DocObjects standard requires a container to provide the display space for a DocObject. This technology allows the browser to present documents from Office and Office-compatible applications. Such functionality might allow any kind of document to be displayed within the Web browser.

Recall the OLE convention that an embedded object is displayed within the page of its owner document. Embedded objects do not, however, control the page on which they appear. These types of objects are usually quite small and hold very little persistent data. A spreadsheet with a few columns and rows, for instance, might be included in a Word document.

ActiveX documents, on the other hand, provide a fully functional document space. ActiveX documents also control the page in which they appear (called a DocObject container). This means that ActiveX documents can be considerably more feature rich than the related embedded object.

One of the reasons for the rise of the Internet is the way that the Web has created an environment where every document is viewable in a single application. The ActiveX document standard aims to take those features another step beyond. ActiveX documents make the technology to use the Web as a vehicle for distribution of application specific documents. Microsoft's Internet Explorer 3.0 is an excellent example of an ActiveX document hosting engine.

Part

I

Ch

2

Internet ActiveX Control Pack

The Internet ActiveX Control Pack (ICP) is not really ActiveX per se. ICP is, instead, an application of ActiveX. But don't let that stop you. With ICP, it's easy to integrate ActiveX Controls into your Visual Basic programs. The ICP contains controls for most of the major Internet services you'll want to integrate into your own applications.

The TCP Control

The Transmission Control Protocol (TCP) is the first of two principle methods for transmitting data over the Internet today. TCP is a connection-oriented protocol most often used for transmitting Internet Protocol (IP) packets over a network. Connection-oriented protocols like TCP are responsible for ensuring that a series of data packets sent over a network all arrive at the destination and are properly sequenced. That's why you'll frequently see the moniker "TCP/ IP." The ActiveX TCP control allows you to easily handle TCP data packets in your applications without knowing much about the details of the TCP protocol.

The UDP Control

The User Datagram Protocol (UDP) is the second of two principle methods for transmitting data over the Internet today. UDP is a connectionless protocol regularly used for transmitting Internet Protocol (IP) packets over a network. Unlike TCP and other connection oriented protocols, UDP doesn't care about the sequence of data packets. A UDP packet must stand on its own. The UDP control allows you to handle UDP data packets in your applications without knowing much about the details of the UDP protocol.

The FTP Client Control

The File Transfer Protocol (FTP) is probably the second most popular application used on the Internet today. FTP allows Internet users to upload and download files across the network. FTP also provides a mechanism to obtain filename, directory name, attributes, and file size information. As with most Internet based applications, FTP employs the client/server paradigm. The

FTP server responds to requests for files from an FTP client. You'll use the FTP client control when your applications need to transfer text and binary files from FTP servers somewhere on the network.

The HTTP Client Control

The HyperText Transfer Protocol (HTTP) is used by absolutely the most popular application on the Internet. HTTP governs the interaction between an HTTP server and the Web browser. The HTTP client control allows you to directly retrieve HTTP documents. You'll use the HTTP control to create applications like HTML browsers.

The HTML Client Control

Programming Web content requires Hypertext Markup Language (HTML) programming. Typically, the job of a Web browser parses and renders the HTML. HTML describes the placement and size of text and graphics. You'll use the HTML control to parse and layout HTML data, as well as provide a scrollable view of the selected HTML page. Unfortunately, the HTML client control only supports HTML 2.0 and not the evolving HTML 3.0 standard. The HTML control lets you implement an HTML viewer, with or without automatic network retrieval of HTML documents, into any application.

The SMTP Control

Many users find e-mail to be a convenient and easy way to exchange personal and corporate information. Electronic mail finds its way over the Internet using the Simple Mail Transfer Protocol (SMTP). The SMTP client control sends Internet mail messages to SMTP servers. The SMTP control supports all SMTP commands used in sending out a mail message. So integrating e-mail directly into new and existing applications is easy.

The POP Client Control

E-mail is typically stored on the SMTP server and then distributed to the actual recipient via the Post Office Protocol (POP). The POP control provides access to Internet mail servers using the POP3 protocol. If your applications need to retrieve and delete messages from Internet mail servers, the POP client control makes it easy.

The NNTP Control

UseNet newsgroups are distributed over the Internet via the Network News Transmission Protocol (NNTP). The NNTP client control enables interaction with newsgroups on the Net. With this control, you'll connect to a newsserver, retrieve a list of available newsgroups and their descriptions, and view news messages. Newsgroups contain a wealth of information on an extremely diverse set of topics, so you may have many applications that require scanning of newsgroup posts.

ActiveX Server Framework

The ActiveX Server Framework provides an alternative to the Common Gateway Interface method of executing applications on a Web server and interacting with the Web browser dynamically. There are two major types of applications that can be developed using the ActiveX Server Framework:

- ISAPI applications
- ISAPI filters

Part

I

Ch

2

ISAPI Applications

Web servers spawn Common Gateway Interface applications in separate processes with a separate environment. The Internet Server Application Programming Interface (ISAPI) specification provides an alternative to CGI programs with potentially higher performance type capabilities for the Microsoft Internet Information Server (IIS). ISAPI allows Web developers to build applications that execute in the same process space as the Web server (see fig. 2.1).

FIG. 2.1
CGI and ISAPI have different approaches to use of process space.

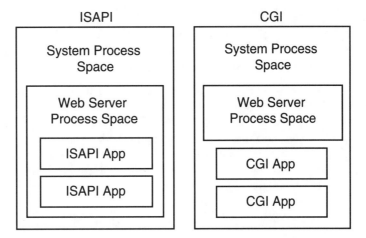

Applications written using ISAPI should be faster simply because the operating system does not have to duplicate the environment and spawn a new process as is required by CGI.

ISAPI applications are actually Dynamic Link Libraries (DLLs). Note that operating in the server's process space carries higher risk while providing somewhat higher performance. Since the ISAPI application is loaded in the same process as the HTTP server, an access violation by the ISAPI application may crash the HTTP server.

ISAPI Filters

The Internet Survey Application Programming Interface (ISAPI) also provides a mechanism for modifying the behavior of the server in specific ways. You'll employ ISAPI filters in cases where the default behavior of the server is inappropriate for the application. ISAPI filters can modify the behavior of the following server functions:

- Authentication
- Compression
- Encryption
- Logging
- Traffic Analysis

Authentication   If you've been surfing the Web, you've probably come across Web sites with pages that require a user name and password. Web site managers may want to control access to Web pages for any number of reasons. For instance, you might want to sell subscriptions to valuable content on your Web site. By default, most Web servers provide a basic authentication scheme. Usually this is a simple user name and password verification step. With ISAPI, you can replace this basic authentication with a customized authentication process. Perhaps, your environment requires that all user names and passwords for all systems be verified with a centralized database (so-called Single Sign On procedures). ISAPI filters provide a mechanism to accomplish this goal.

Compression   Sufficient bandwidth is perhaps the greatest inhibitor to complex content on the Internet. With an ISAPI filter, you can provide custom compression filters to improve throughput in high-end custom applications of Web technology.

Encryption   Many believe that commerce, the buying and selling of goods and services, will largely take place over the Internet. Because commerce requires the exchange of information (such as credit card numbers) that creates a tasty target for hackers, encryption is a key enabling technology. Encryption may be important in other applications as well. For instance, a company may want to transmit sensitive data to customers or suppliers. Encryption protects the data while it is in transit from source to destination. You can implement encryption to protect your data using an ISAPI filter.

Logging   When a Web server services a request for a Web page, the server makes an entry in the access log file. The access log file indicates which Web page, CGI, or ISAPI application was accessed. If the user has authenticated via the Web servers built-in authentication, the access log also contains the user name in access record. Date, time, and some other information is also recorded in the log as well. One of the ways Web site operators make money is through advertising sales. Advertisers buy ad space based upon how many people will see their ad. So reporting information about how and by whom Web pages are accessed is extremely critical. You'll customize logging functionality using ISAPI filters.

Traffic Analysis   You may want to handle requests for a specific URL differently. For instance, you might want to catch all **http://www.yourhost.com/../../etc/passwd** requests and handle them in a certain way. You might want to examine other details of the transactions between Web browsers and your server. You'll use ISAPI filters to engage in traffic analysis. ●

OCX and ActiveX Controls

The Component Object Model

ActiveX is based upon the Component Object Model (COM), so a quick review is in order.

Types of COM objects

COM objects come in three flavors: In Process servers, Local servers, Remote servers.

ActiveX and the COM standard

ActiveX represents a consolidation of the OLE and OCX implementations under a new name.

Microsoft has combined and enhanced its OLE and OCX technologies and renamed the consolidated standard *ActiveX*. ActiveX refines the OLE specification for OLE controls, which makes them smaller and more efficient. New OLE interfaces are also defined enhancing control over data and property management. Using the the new ActiveX Control class, generated controls are lightweight and Internet-aware. ■

The 3.2 Common Object Model

The Component Object Model (COM) is a client/server object based model designed to allow software components and applications to interact with each other in a uniform standard way.

The COM standard is partly a specification and partly an implementation. The specification defines mechanisms for object creation and communication between objects. This part of the specification is paper-based and is not dependent on any particular language or operating system. Any language can be used as long as you adhere to the standard.

The implementation part is the COM library, which provides a number of core services to support the binary specification of COM.

A Simple View of How COM Works

When a client COM object wants to use the services of a server COM object, it uses one of the core services in the COM library. The COM library is responsible for creating the server COM object and establishing the initial connection between the client and server. The connection is made when the server returns a pointer to the client. The pointer points to an Interface in the server object. From this point forward, the COM library plays no further part in the process. The two objects are free to communicate with each other directly.

Objects communicate through Interfaces. *Interfaces* are small sets of related functions that provide some sort of service. An object may have more than one interface. When a client object has a pointer to a server object Interface, the client may invoke any function available through the Interface.

When an object is finished using the services provided by another object, the client informs the server that it is finished and terminates communication.

Please note that software objects may be client objects, server objects, or both.

What is an Interface?

COM Interfaces are discrete sets of logically or semantically related functions. Interfaces are used to supply a service from a server object to a client object. Client objects never see the internal representation of the server object. An Interface can be thought of as a type of contract between two software components. The contract states that the server supplies the client with one type of service and nothing more.

In a complex system, human readable name clashes are a fact of life. In order to avoid these clashes, Interfaces are given a unique name. It is called a Globally Unique Identifier (GUID). This is a 128-bit number that is almost guaranteed to be unique. (According to the official COM specification, 10 million GUIDs could be generated every second for the next 3,500 years or so and every single one would be unique!) GUIDs are also used in other parts of COM and OLE to assign unique names. Interfaces may also be given human readable names but these are locally scoped to a single machine.

Server objects that supply more than one service implement an Interface for each service they supply. A client may only invoke functions in Interfaces on the server objects for which they have a pointer. They may obtain pointers to other Interfaces through the IUnknown interface. This is a fundamental Interface that all COM objects must support. This Interface has a function called QueryInterface. Since all Interfaces are derived from IUnknown, this function is present in every Interface. This function knows about every Interface in the server object and can give a client a pointer to any of the Interfaces that it requests access. A client may not know about every interface in the server. The server may have other Interfaces that a client does not know about. This in no way compromises a client's ability to use a server. It uses the interfaces that it knows.

When a client is finished using a server, it informs the server that it is finished. This allows server objects to release themselves from memory when they are no longer servicing any clients.

Advantages of Interfaces

Interfaces allow objects to evolve independently over time. The definition and functionality of an Interface is never changed. If the functionality of an Interface changes or new functionality is added to the object, then a new Interface is added. This allows a server object to continue to be used by clients who only know about the old Interfaces. New clients who know about the new Interfaces can use them as well as the old Interfaces.

Interfaces allow objects to be replaced by better objects from a different vendor as long as the Interface definitions do not change.

Interfaces are language independent. Any language that can create structures of pointers, and either explicitly or implicitly call a function through a pointer, can implement COM interfaces—languages such as C, C++, Smalltalk, and Pascal.

Types of COM Objects

There are three different types of COM server objects:

- **In Process servers**—These server objects can be loaded into the client's process space. Under the Microsoft Windows operating systems, these objects are implemented in Dynamic Link Libraries (DLLs).
- **Local servers**—These server objects run in a separate process on the same machine. This type of server is usually another application.
- **Remote servers**—These server objects run on a remote machine connected by a network. These objects always run in a different process space. Remote servers may be implemented as either Dynamic Link Libraries or applications.

COM is designed such that regardless of where a server object is running, a client object always communicates with it in the same way. There is one single programming model for all types of objects. A client object accesses the services of the server object through a pointer to an Interface on the object. If the server is running In Process, then the pointer accesses the

Part

I

Ch

3

Interface directly. If the server is a Local or a Remote server, then the pointer accesses a proxy server running in the same process as the client. This proxy is supplied by COM. Its purpose is to generate a call to the appropriate server, either Local or Remote.

At the other end, a stub object supplied by COM receives the call and turns it into a call on the Interface. Both client and server therefore always communicate with some piece of In Process code.

Foundation COM Components

Although COM is fundamentally concerned with object creation and communication, it provides the following other system level objects based on the fundamentals.

- **Persistent Storage Objects**—COM defines a standard set of Interfaces that allow other objects to save their state to a persistent storage device. The implementation of these interfaces provide structured files. Information within such a file can be arranged in a hierarchical fashion, much like MS-DOS directories and files. It is often considered a file system within a file. Other benefits it offers are transactioning and incremental access. Applications may also browse the contents of a structured file to enumerate the named elements within it.

- **Persistent Intelligent Names (Monikers)**—COM defines a standard set of Interfaces for moniker usage. The implementation of monikers build a lot of intelligence into a name. An instantiation of a particular object may be given a name such that a client can reconnect to the exact same instance of that object with the exact same state at a later time by merely specifying the name. Operations of some sorts may also be given a name that would allow clients to repeatedly perform the operation by using the name only.

- **Uniform Data Transfer**—COM defines standard interfaces through which a server and a client can exchange information. A client may also use these interfaces to register its desire to have the server inform it when the data it received changes. The COM standard also defines data structures, which can be used to describe the data and the medium through which the data passes between server and client (see fig. 3.1).

FIG. 3.1
COM is built in progressively higher layers of technology.

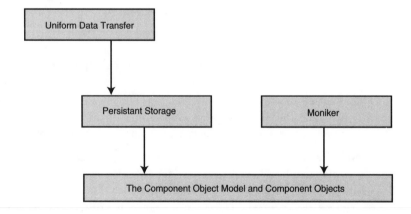

The object management services and the foundation COM components form the bedrock of information management. Microsoft's OLE 2.0 technology is built on this bedrock.

Examining OLE and ActiveX Controls

OCX controls are the standard solution for Windows component software. They are implemented using OLE 2.0 technology and are designed for use on the desktop environment. Most OCX controls today are built using the Control Development Kit, which is supplied as an integrated part of Microsoft Visual C++ version 4.x. The controls built using this Kit are excellent for use in the desktop environment. Some of these controls are even able to make the leap to the Internet environment without any modification. However, most will need to be modified to operate more efficiently and cooperatively.

Controls developed with Visual C++ are built using the standard OLE 2.0 interfaces, some of which were mandatory. This means they contain a lot of unnecessary code. They are also dependent on the *Microsoft Foundation Classes* (*MFC*) libraries, which are several megabytes in size. These controls are therefore relatively big in size, which may limit their useability in the slow Internet environment. Also, in order to use these controls on the Internet, the user must first have the MFC libraries on their machine. A one time download of these libraries for all controls to share may not be too much of a penalty, but MFC is being revised and released approximately every three months. This means users of these controls must download these new libraries every three months or their controls may not work.

Management of data and properties is another potential problem. OCX controls on the desktop operate synchronously. Function calls made to the OLE libraries or a control container do not return until they have completed. While this is not a problem on the desktop, where data and properties are stored locally in files and can be retrieved quickly, it causes problems in a slow environment like the Internet, where large amounts of data have to be retrieved from a remote site and loaded into the control. A 24-bit bitmap file for instance, can be several megabytes in size and take many minutes to download. It would be unacceptable for the user's browser software to *freeze* during this process.

ActiveX

Microsoft has consolidated all its OLE and OCX technologies under the heading of *ActiveX*. ActiveX defines a new specification for OLE controls, which allows them to be much smaller and more efficient. New OLE interfaces are also specified which addresses the problem of data and property management. Controls that are built using the new ActiveX lightweight control class are smaller than their Visual C++ control wizard generated counterparts, and they can use the new interfaces to function efficiently and cooperatively with control containers in the Internet environment.

The *OLE Control and Control Container Guidelines V2.0* defines a control as a COM software component that is self-registering and implements the IUnknown interface. In order to support self-registration, the control must export the DLLRegisterServer and DLLUnRegisterServer function calls. All the OLE interfaces that were previously mandatory are now optional. Controls are free to implement as many or as few of the standard interfaces as they require, which leads to the first question about ActiveX controls. Previously, a control container could depend on functionality being present in the control because of the mandatory OLE interfaces. If a control only implements the IUnknown interface, how does a control container, such as a browser or authoring tool, know or find out what a controls functionality is? The answer is component categories.

Examining Component Categories

Component categories describe different prescribed areas of functionality. Each component category is identified by a Globally Unique Identifier and each defines a set of standards that a control must meet in order to be a part of that category. Component categories are stored as entries in the system registry with GUIDs and human readable keys.

Previously, when a control was registered on a client machine it also registered the keyword Control under its CLSID. This keyword advertised the control's suitability for insertion into container applications like Access and Visual Basic. The Control keyword is now obsolete, but it remains for the benefit of older applications that do not understand component categories.

Component categories are a natural extension of this process. They allow a control to describe its functionality in far more detail than plain OLE interface signatures. When a control self-registers in the system registry, it adds entries under its CLSID for the GUID for a control, the GUID for each category that it supports, and the GUID of each category that it requires support for from a container in order to function properly. Additionally, it registers its own CLSID under each category registry entry (see fig. 3.2).

Until now, when an application wanted to find out if a particular control supported a piece of functionality, the application had to instantiate the control and use QueryInterface. If a valid pointer to a new interface was returned, then the application knew that the control supported the desired functionality. This is a very expensive and cumbersome operation.

Using categories and new OLE interfaces in the OLE libraries that allow categories to be registered and unregistered, enumerated and queried, means that an application does not have to instantiate a control anymore. It can get information about controls from the system registry through these new interfaces in one of two ways. If a control's CLSID is known to the application, then the application can retrieve the category GUIDs under the control's registry entry to find out the functionality of the control. If a specific area of functionality is required, then the application can go to the registry entry for the category and retrieve a list of the controls on the machine that have registered support for that functionality. It can then go to each control's registry entry and determine if it can host the control. The list can then be presented to the user of the application via an application or system user interface, and the user can choose which control to use.

FIG. 3.2
Component categories
are registered.

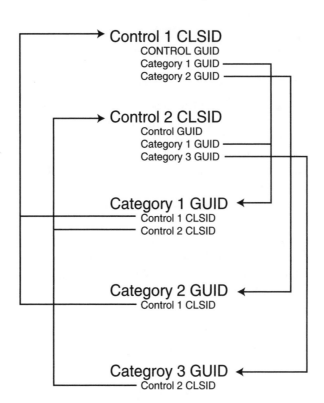

Management of Data and Properties

The major difference between controls designed for use on the desktop and controls which are Internet-aware is the management of data and properties. A control may have any or all of the types of data listed in the following table which need to be stored so that they can be easily retrieved by a control container when it recreates the control. These types do not imply any form of structure or storage location. A control's properties and BLOB data collectively make up its state.

Data Type	Size	Purpose
Class Identifier (CLSID)	16 bytes	The CLSID of the control class that can read the data that follows.
Properties	Around 10K–30K	Standard and custom property values.
Binary Large Objects (BLOB)	Arbitrary size	Any number of large binary files. These files may be in any format (for example, bitmaps, multimedia files, etc.).

Part

I

Ch

3

If a control has no persistent state, then none of the above are present in an HTML document. The control container CLSID retrieves the CLSID of the control class directly from the attribute of the HTML <OBJECT> tag or indirectly from the CODE attribute. The control can then be instantiated and no further initialization is required.

When the user of an application which is hosting a control gives the command to save, the control container calls QueryInterface on the control for a persistent storage interface and the control serializes its state through it. Similarly, when a control is recreated, it retrieves its state through a persistent storage interface. Where the application stores the control's state is up to the user of the application that is hosting the control. The control is not concerned. It may be embedded within the HTML document, or in a separate file that is linked to the HTML document. This linking and embedding mechanism is familiar territory to anyone with knowledge of OLE compound documents.

Although the control is not concerned with the actual storage of its state, it is concerned with the interfaces through which its state is saved and retrieved. One of the goals Microsoft had when creating the ActiveX specification was to introduce as little new technology as possible. However, the existing persistence interfaces used in the current OLE compound document architecture are potentially unsuitable for Internet-aware controls.

In OLE compound documents, an object and its native data can be stored in two ways (see fig. 3.3). They can be embedded in the document or linked to the document. In the embedding case, the object's CLSID, its native data, and a presentation cache are stored within the document. In the linking case, a moniker and a presentation cache are stored within the document. The moniker points to a file that contains the object's CLSID and native data.

FIG. 3.3
Data can be stored in embedded and linked documents.

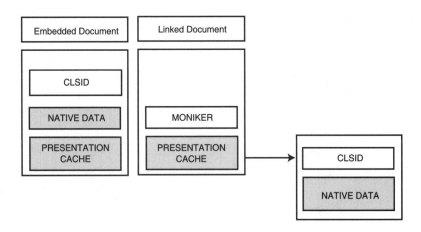

The problems with this architecture are as follows:

- The compound document usually contains a presentation cache. This can lead to document sizes that are too large for effective use on the Internet.
- Embedded objects can only use the IPersistStorage interface for saving and loading data. This interface is a heavy duty interface and is not well-suited to small, simple

controls. Implementing this interface leads to code that is not required and is simply extra baggage for small simple controls.

■ When a compound document recreates an object, the object retrieves its native data and properties synchronously. That is, when an object makes a call to a persistence interface to retrieve data, execution control does not return to the object until the data has been completely retrieved. This is not a problem on the desktop, as the data is stored locally in files on a high speed disk subsystem. The length of time for which the user interface is frozen while retrieval takes place, therefore, is usually very small. In a relatively slow environment like the Internet, synchronous retrieval of large amounts of data from a remote site freezes the user interface for an unacceptably long time.

■ If an OLE compound document wants to use linking to save an object's native data and properties, then it must implement the `IPersistFile` interface for moniker binding. File monikers however, are designed to work with Universal Naming Convention (UNC) file and path names. They do not work with the Uniform Resource Locator (URL) file and path names that are used on the Internet.

■ Any references to external data that are contained within the embedded or linked object's native data are known only to the object that created the data. This prohibits the control container from participating in the retrieval of the external data. Asynchronous retrieval of this data may not be possible.

Part

I

Ch

3

Persistent Linking and Embedding

The problem of the presentation cache was eliminated for the embedding scenario in the first release of the OLE control specification in 1994. Controls could implement a new lightweight interface called `IPersistStreamInit`, which can be used in preference to `IPersistStorage`. `IPersistStreamInit` allows all properties and BLOBS to be channeled into one stream and stored by the application in the document. This eliminated the cache because the data could simply and quickly be reloaded into the control when the document was loaded and the control was instantiated and initialized. In the linking case, because the objects data and properties were stored locally in files and could be retrieved quickly, the presentation cache was also eliminated.

Because of the shortcomings of the existing persistence mechanisms, Microsoft developed new persistence mechanisms and monikers that extend the concept of linking and embedding beyond the OLE Compound Document architecture (see fig. 3.4). These new mechanisms also allow for asynchronous retrieval of properties and BLOBs from remote sites, and are as follows:

■ **Persistent Embedding**—The control's CLSID, properties, and BLOBs are stored within the HTML document itself. This is only useful where the aggregate size of this information is small. It is not suitable for large amounts of data because the time taken to download the page and make it active would be unacceptable.

■ **Persistent Linking**—A single URL moniker is stored in the HTML document. This moniker points to a file on a remote site that contains the CLSID, properties, and BLOBs for the control.

FIG. 3.4
The new extensions employ the concept of persistant linking and embedding.

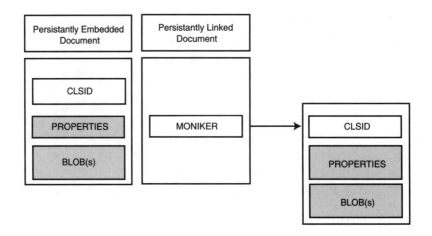

The specification of embedding and linking in OLE compound documents entails adherence to certain user interface standards. Specifically, linked objects may not be in-place activated. Persistent linking and embedding are not concerned with user interface and the standards are not relevant. Their sole function is for storage management of properties and BLOBs. Controls that are in-place activated, therefore, can still work with persistently linked data.

The persistent interface mechanisms that can now be used by a control are summarized in the following table:

Mechanism	Use	Comments
IPersistStorage	Embedding/linking	Standard persistence mechanism used in OLE compound documents. The container supplies an IStorage pointer to a storage object. The control may create any data structure within that object for its state.
IPersistStreamInit	Embedding/linking	This is a lightweight alternative to IPersistStorage. All of the control's state can be serialized into one stream.
IPersistMemory	Embedding/linking	The container defines a fixed size block of memory into which a control saves or retrieves its state. The control must not try to access memory outside the block.
IPersistPropertyBag	Embedding	The container and control exchange property/value pairs in Variant structures.

| IPersistFile | linking | The container gives the control a UNC filename and is told to save or retrieve its state from that file. |
| IPersistMoniker | linking | The control is given a moniker. When the control reads or writes its state, it may choose any storage mechanism (IStorage, IStream, ILockBytes, etc.) it wants. If the storage mechanism chosen by the control is asynchronous then IPersistMoniker must support asynchronous transfer. |

For each mechanism that a control implements, the control container must provide the appropriate support.

A control container that wants to support embedding must provide the appropriate support for the persistence interfaces exposed by the control, as in the following table:

Control Persistence Interface	Container Supplied Support
IPersistStreamInit	IStream
IPersistStorage	IStorage
IPersistMemory	Memory (*void)
IPersistPropertyBag	IPropertyBag

A control container that wants to implement linking must use a moniker that can supply support for the persistence interfaces exposed by the control. At the time of this writing, the only available moniker is the URL moniker.

If a control implements the IPersistMemory or the IPersistFile mechanism, it should also implement one other interface as both of these require that the data be present locally. These mechanisms do not work well with asynchronous downloads of properties and BLOBs.

Controls are free to implement as many of these new persistence mechanisms as the developer of the control sees fit. For maximum flexibility, therefore, a control container should implement support for as many of these interfaces as possible. This ensures that it can work with a wide range of controls that may not implement all of the new persistence mechanisms.

These new persistence mechanisms define the protocol through which the container and the control exchange information. What happens when an application decides to save a control's state (perhaps in response to a user request), depends on the application's (users) preferences for storage. It can either be embedded in the HTML document or in a separate file and linked to the document.

When embedding is used, the control container chooses which persistence interface to use. The sequence in which a container looks for persistence interfaces is generally up to the designer of the container. However, IPersistMemory and IPersistStreamInit may be given precedence over `IPersistProperyBag` and `IPersistStorage`, as they generally produce the smallest amount of data. It is perfectly acceptable for a container to have a control save its state in one location, and then copy it to another location. All that is required is that the container is able to retrieve the saved state, and give it back to the control via the same interface. For example, a container could ask a control to save its state in a memory block. The container may then save the contents of that memory block in a storage location of its choosing. When the control is initialized, the container must retrieve the saved state and give it back to the control via a memory block.

When linking is used, the container is not concerned with any of the persistence interfaces. The container must store and interact with a URL moniker. The moniker takes care of all the interface querying. URL monikers query for persistence interfaces in the following order:

- `IPersistMoniker`
- `IPersistStreamInit`
- `IPersistStorage`
- `IPersistMemory`
- `IPersistFile`

In both linking and embedding, the container is responsible for the asynchronous transfer of data from the remote site. For more information on this, see the "Compound Files on the Internet" document supplied as part of the Sweeper SDK. All the persistence interfaces, with the exception of `IPersistMoniker`, are synchronous in operation. When a control receives a call to the `Load` member of one of its persistence interfaces, it expects all of the data to be available.

Data paths serve two purposes. They allow a control to store its BLOBs separately from its properties, and they solve the problem of embedded links. Controls may have links to BLOBs buried in their native data that only they know. This prohibits the container from participating in the retrieval of these BLOBs. One solution to this is data path properties. Data path properties are properties that hold text string values. These string values are simply URL filenames. Data path properties can be used with either persistent embedding (see fig. 3.5) or persistent linking (see fig. 3.6).

In a control's type library, data path properties must be marked as `[bindable]` and `[requestedit]`. This allows container applications to update these properties through its own user interface. These properties may also be updated through the control's property sheet. Properties are also tagged with a special custom attribute which identifies them as data path properties. The custom attribute is called `GUID_PathProperty`. It has its own GUID. Additionally, a control's `coclass` entry in its type library is also tagged with a special attribute that signifies that it has data path properties. This attribute is called `GUID_HasPathProperties`, and it too has its own GUID.

FIG. 3.5
Data paths in a
persitently embedded
document.

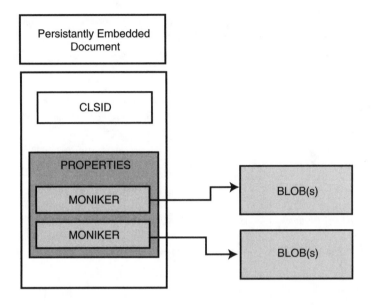

Persistantly Embedded
Document

CLSID

PROPERTIES

MONIKER

MONIKER

BLOB(s)

BLOB(s)

FIG. 3.6
Data paths in a
persitently linked
document.

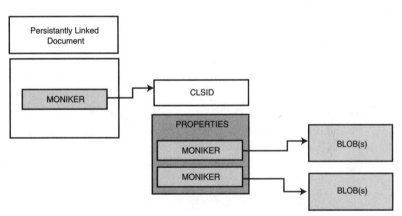

Persistantly Linked
Document

MONIKER

CLSID

PROPERTIES

MONIKER

MONIKER

BLOB(s)

BLOB(s)

N O T E Applications, such as authoring tools and Web site management tools, can query controls
for data path properties and use them to perform link management or other tasks. ▪

When a control wants to retrieve the file named by a data path property, it gives the URL to the
container and asks it to create a moniker for the URL. The moniker is created in the implementation of the IBindHost interface. This interface is supplied as a service by the container site's
IServiceObject implementation. In order for the control to call members of IBindHost, the
control must provide a way for the container to pass a pointer that identifies the
IServiceObject interface. A control could implement the IOleObject interface in order to
achieve this. This interface has a function called SetClientSite that allows a container to pass

the pointer to the control. However, the IOleObject interface is a large interface. All its functionality may not be required by a small control. A smaller interface called IObjectWithSite can be implemented. It has just two member functions, one of which, SetSite, allows the container to pass the required pointer.

N O T E Any control that uses data path properties must support a siting mechanism—either IOleObject or IOleObjectWithSite. This is a requirement of the specification. ■

In order to get the IBindHost interface, two steps are required. First, the control calls QueryInterface on the site pointer for the IServiceProvider interface. Then the control calls QueryService on the IServiceProvider interface for the IBindHost interface.

In order to get a moniker for the file and data path property names, the control calls the ParseDisplayName function of the IBindHost interface. The data path may be either an absolute path name, or a path name relative to the location of the document. Either way, a moniker is returned, which the control can use to retrieve data.

When downloading data, the control should be as cooperative as possible with the container and other controls by supporting asynchronous retrieval of data. This allows the user interface to remain active while data trickles down in the background.

Before initiating a retrieval operation, a control should check to see if the moniker that it is supplied with is an asynchronous one. It does this by calling QueryInterface on the moniker for the IMonikerAsynch interface. If this interface is not present, the moniker is synchronous and the control has to bind directly to the storage identified by the moniker by creating a bind context and calling the BindToStorage member of the moniker.

If the moniker is asynchronous, the control should get its bind context from the container through the GetBindCtx member of IBindHost. By obtaining it this way, the container has a chance to register itself as an interested party in the download process. It can monitor the download and display some sort of progress indicator for the user's convenience, or perhaps allow the user to cancel the download.

Once a control has the bind context, it registers its own FORMATETC enumerator and a pointer to its IBindStatusCallBack interface in the bind context. The control initiates an asynchronous download in the Load member of a persistence interface. In this function, another asynchronous stream should be obtained so that the moniker and the bind context can be released. This allows the Load function to return immediately, and execution control can return to the container. When data arrives, the OnDataAvailable member of the IBindStatusCallBack interface is called. The control should obtain the data exclusively through this function.

For detailed information on how the control, the container, and the moniker interact in asynchronous downloads, see the "Asynchronous Monikers" specification in the Sweeper SDK.

Data transfer may be aborted by a call to the OnStopBinding member of the IBindStatusCallBack interface. If a control receives such a call, there are two possibilities. The first possibility occurs if the control has received all its data. Then the call is merely a notification that the transfer is complete. The second possibility occurs when the data transfer has been aborted for some reason.

A control may abort the data transfer by calling the Abort member of the IBinding interface. The control receives a pointer to this interface through the IStartBinding member of the IBindStatusCallBack interface.

Since the container has control and data is trickling down in the background, you may wonder how a container knows when a control is ready to begin full interaction. One way to tell is to return a new code, E_PENDING, from member functions of the control when the control is not yet ready to fully interact. When this code is not returned, the control may be ready to interact. This, however, does not allow for progressive changes in a control's ability to interact with the application and/or the user. Microsoft solved this problem by defining a new standard property, ReadyState, and a new standard event, OnReadyStateChanged. When the control's ready state changes, the new standard event is fired with the value of the ReadyState property to notify the container. The ReadyState property may progressively have the following values:

Uninitialized	The control is waiting to be initialized through the Load member of a persistence interface.
Loading	The control is synchronously retrieving its properties. Some may not yet be available.
Loaded/Can Render	The control has retrieved its properties and is able to draw something through the Draw member of the IViewObject2 interface.
Interactive	The control may interact with the user in a limited way. It has not yet received all of its data from the asynchronous download.
Complete	The control is completely ready.

The control does not have to support all of the above states. It only has to support as many as it needs.

When a control is requested to save its state by a call to the Save member of a persistence interface, it saves all of its properties, including data path properties as strings, through the interface, and then saves all the BLOBs referred to by any data path properties. It does this by obtaining a moniker for each data path through the container's IBindHost as described above and synchronously saving the BLOB. When the Save function returns, a control is assumed to have saved all of its state.

Instantiation of a Control

The instantiation and initialization sequence for a control is as follows. The assumption is made that the control is already on the client machine and properly registered.

The application obtains the CLSID of the control from the CLSID attribute of the HTML <OBJECT> tag and instantiates the control.

The DATA attribute contains either the property data encoded in MIME or a URL that names a file on a remote site that contains the property data.

If the DATA attribute contains the property data, the container obtains a persistence interface on the control and calls the Load member with a stream containing the property data.

If the DATA attribute contains a URL, the container makes a URL moniker and calls the IBindToObject member of the IMoniker interface in order to retrieve the property data from a remote site. Inside this function the URL moniker attempts to get an IPersistMoniker interface on the control. If it succeeds, it passes a pointer to itself to the Load member of this interface. The control then has complete control over retrieval of its properties from the remote site.

N O T E   Since properties are usually very small amounts of data, measured in hundreds of bytes or so, asynchronous retrieval may not be the best method. Synchronous retrieval may be a better option as it may allow the control to become interactive sooner. ■

If it cannot get the IPersistMoniker interface, it gets another persistence interface. It then retrieves the property data, wraps it up in an IStream object if necessary, and calls the Load member function of the interface with a pointer to the object. The control then retrieves its property data from the IStream object.

Inside the Load member of the persistence interface, the control also initiates any asynchronous download of BLOBS. It asks the container to make URL monikers so that the container may also bind to them and participate in the download process. The control binds to each moniker and registers its IOnBindStatusCallback interface in order to receive data. Control is then returned to the container.

As BLOBs trickle down in the background, the control changes the value of the ReadyState variable and notifies the container of any change in its state through the OnReadyStateChange event. The ReadyState variable is passed as a parameter of the event.

Summary of Requirements for Internet-Aware Controls

If a control has no data path properties, then a control need only implement as many of the persistence interfaces as the developer sees fit. The more interfaces a control implements, the more flexibility it has for initialization by control containers and URL monikers.

Controls that have data path properties and BLOBs must meet the following requirements:

- They must support either IOleObject or IObjectWithSite as a siting mechanism.
- They must mark data path properties with the [bindable] and [requestedit] attributes as well as the custom GUID_PathProperty attribute.
- They must mark its coclass entry in its type information with the GUID_HasPathProperties custom attribute.
- They must follow the rules for moniker creation and persistence using the container's IBindHost as necessary.

- They must bind with an asynchronous moniker using a container provided bind context from `IBindHost` and receive its data through the `OnDataAvailable` member of the `IBindStatusCallback` interface.
- They must coordinate data retrieval and begin interaction as soon as possible.

Additionally, controls should supply a `ReadyState` variable and an `OnReadyStateChange` event if they are required. They should also support `IPersistPropertyBag` for supporting HTML `PARAM` attributes. ●

Part

I

Ch

3

THOMAS COMPUTER CONSULTANTS, INC.
33333 W. TWELVE MILE RD., SUITE 101
FARMINGTON HILLS, MICHIGAN 48334
(810) 489-0707

CHAPTER 4

Introduction to the ActiveX Control Pad

The ActiveX Control Pad provides an integration environment for combining three major elements of the basic World Wide Web dynamic document interface. You'll combine your basic HTML, ActiveX Controls, as well as client-side scripts into a single development tool with the ActiveX Control Pad. In terms of editing HTML, the ActiveX Control Pad is really no better than a simple text editor. However, managing your ActiveX Controls and scripts is visual and easy when you use the ActiveX Control Pad. ■

Creating an HTML layout

An HTML layout provides WYSIWYG design space for placing several controls. HTML layouts can be used, for example, in common elements that are repeated in many Web pages such as navigation elements like toolbars.

Inserting an object

ActiveX objects can be inserted into your HTML documents using the ActiveX Control Pad. Editing parameters are similar to editing properties in Visual Basic.

Inserting an HTML layout

HTML layouts can be inserted into your HTML documents using the ActiveX Control Pad, as well. Select and add controls using the Control toolbox and properties.

The Script Wizard Interface

Adding scripts to your HTML Web pages is simple using the ActiveX Control Pad. Use the List View and the Code View to manage VB scripts in your Web pages.

Customizing the ActiveX Control Pad Development Environment

The ActiveX Control Pad Development Environment has some limited ability for customization.

Using the ActiveX Control Pad

While the ActiveX Control Pad provides no general support for WYSIWG HTML editing, inserting ActiveX Controls and adding client-side scripting like VBScript is straightforward.

You'll recognize many of the elements of the user interface from other applications you use, like Lotus 1-2-3 or Microsoft Word. Most of the common items are there, including the File toolbar for saving, creating, and opening new HTML files. However, there are also a couple of elements that you probably haven't seen before. The first of these two new items is found on the toolbar (the second button from the right) that uses a scroll as its icon. Pressing this button brings up the Script Wizard. The second item is in the document window. Take a look at the document window in figure 4.1. Notice the gray vertical bar along the left side of the screen.

FIG. 4.1
Objects and scripts can be opened by clicking the icons in the Control Pad margin bar.

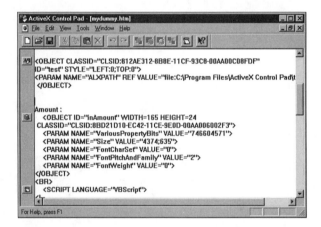

Since you'll be inserting objects and scripts into the HTML documents in this window, the margin bar makes keeping track of where objects and scripts are inserted in the document fast and easy. The scroll icon indicates the start of a script. Pressing the scroll button in the margin bar opens the Script Wizard (which you'll use in a moment), and loads the appropriate script. ActiveX objects are indicated in the margin bar by a small cube icon. This iconography indicates the start of an <OBJECT> declaration in the HTML. Pressing the ActiveX object button in the gray margin bar brings up a window containing the object, and a window containing its property sheet. The Control Pad uses a special icon for insertions of HTML layouts. HTML layouts are indicated in the margin bar by a small icon containing the letter A, a circle, and a square. Pressing this button brings up the HTML Layout Editor and its associated toolbar.

Creating an HTML Layout

The ActiveX Control Pad is not an HTML editing environment per se. There are no built-in tools to make the general HTML coding easier. However, ActiveX includes a control called the HTML Layout control, which is used for building forms, laying out toolbars, and for making reusable elements in your Web pages. The ActiveX Control Pad provides a Visual Basic like interface for creating HTML layouts. To create an HTML layout, follow these steps:

1. Start the ActiveX Control Pad.
2. Select File, New HTML Layout from the menu bar. This brings up two windows—the Layout window and the Toolbox window. Your screen should resemble figure 4.2.

FIG. 4.2
Create an HTML layout.

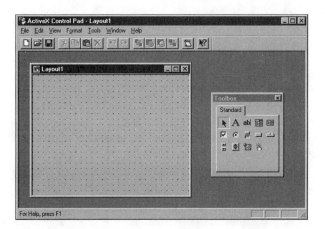

3. Try adding a command button to the layout. From the toolbox, select the command button tool. Then place your cursor over the Layout window and it changes to cross hairs. Press the left mouse button, and draw in the control. When you're finished, the screen should resemble figure 4.3.

FIG. 4.3
Add a command button.

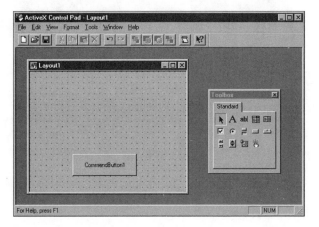

4. To edit the properties of this control, select View, Properties. Select the Caption property, and place your cursor in the Apply text box. Now type a suitable caption like **Press Me**. Your screen should resemble figure 4.4.

Part

I

Ch

4

FIG. 4.4

Change the caption property.

5. Open the property sheet again, select the ID property, and place your cursor in the Apply text box. Type a name like **cmdPressMe**.

6. Add a text box to your layout. Select the text control tool from the toolbox, then place your cursor over the Layout window. The cursor changes to cross hairs. Press the left mouse button, and draw in the control. Your screen should look like figure 4.5.

FIG. 4.5

Add a text control.

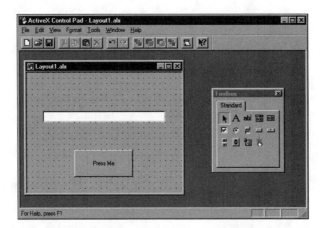

7. Select View, Properties, and change the ID and Text properties. Select the ID property, and place your cursor in the Apply text box. Set the ID to something like **cmdPressMe**. Select the Text property, and add some initialization text. When you've finished, your screen will look like figure 4.6.

8. Save your layout to a file. The file extension for an HTML layout is .alx. If you open an .alx file with a text editor, you'll find that the code is itself HTML.

FIG. 4.6
The complete
HTML layout.

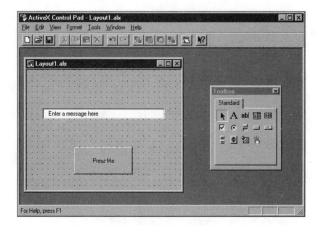

Using the ActiveX Control Pad Script Wizard

The ActiveX Control Pad provides a graphical user interface for adding VBScript to HTML
pages and HTML layouts. In this section, you'll add two simple VB scripts to your previous
HTML layout using the Script Wizard. To add VBScripts using the Script Wizard, take the
following steps:

1. Start the ActiveX Control Pad, if it's not already running.

2. Open the HTML Layout you created previously.

3. Start the Script Wizard. You can do this in two ways: Press the Script Wizard toolbar
   button (the one with the scroll icon), or select Tools, Script Wizard from the menu bar.
   Your screen will look something like figure 4.7.

Part

I

Ch

4

FIG. 4.7
Start the Script Wizard.

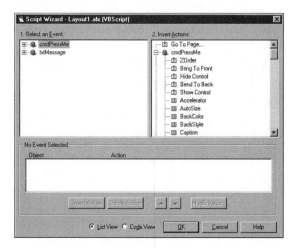

Notice that the Script Wizard has two different views: List View and Code View. The List View is a graphical tool for making scripts. The Code View provides a method for entering custom scripts by typing in VBScript syntax.

4. Add a simple script using the List View. Adding a script element in the List View is a three step process: Select an event to respond to, select an action to take, and (if necessary) provide a value or parameter. Let's take it one step at a time. From the Event list (the list box in the upper left third of the screen), expand the txtMessage item and select the KeyDown event.

5. Next, expand the txtMessage item on the Action list (the list box in the upper right third of the screen). Select the BackColor property and double-click. The color selection window comes forward (see fig. 4.8).

FIG. 4.8

Set the BackColor property.

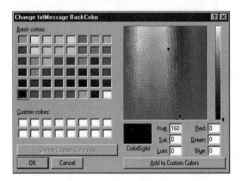

Go ahead and select the color that you want to change the txtMessage box to when a key is pressed and press OK. You'll see both the object and the action listed in the script List window.

6. Change the Script Wizard to the Code View by selecting the Code View radio button. From the Event list, expand the cmdPressMe object, and select the Click event. Your screen will look something like figure 4.9.

7. Add a simple VBScript in the code window. For now, enter the following text into the code window: **MsgBox txtMessage.Text** (see fig. 4.10).

8. Finally, collapse all of the items in the Action list. You'll notice that there is now a Procedures object. Expand the Procedures object. You should see an entry for the two events for which you've now added scripts (see fig. 4.11).

9. Save the HTML layout to a file.

FIG. 4.9

Add a script in the
Code View.

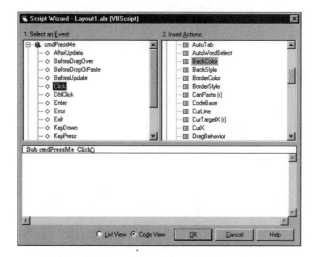

FIG. 4.10

Enter the script.

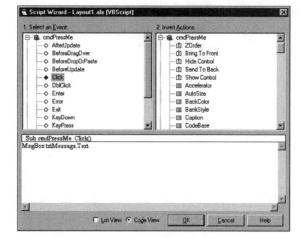

Part

I

Ch

4

FIG. 4.11

Check the Procedures object.

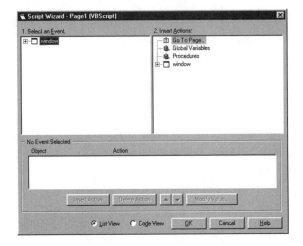

Using the Script Wizard Interface

Now that you've had a quick test drive through the Script Wizard, there are a couple of features that require some additional explanation. This section takes the Script Wizard and breaks it down into its components to give you an in-depth look at coding scripts using the Script Wizard. Specifically, you'll work through the following processes:

- **Navigating the Event window**—ActiveX Control Pad uses a number of conventions for identifying events that are fired by the controls on your Web pages. Much of your user interface programming revolves around responding to these events.

- **Navigating the Action window**—The Action window makes it simple to identify the responses your script makes to various events.

- **Using the List View script editor**—The List View editor provides a friendly interface for editing your scripts. Inserting, deleting, and modifying script actions can be accomplished from here.

- **Using the Code View script editor**—More complicated actions will need to be handled by using the Code View. The Code View basically requires that you type VBScript syntax.

Navigating the Event Window

Many of the objects that you'll use on your Web pages trigger various events. To make your Web page interactive with the user, select events and assign actions that execute in response to the selected event. VBScript makes events available to the browser window itself. When you start a new HTML document, you can respond to events that occur to the browser window. Figure 4.12 shows the events available to you even when the HTML document is empty.

FIG. 4.12

The Script Wizard when the HTML document is empty.

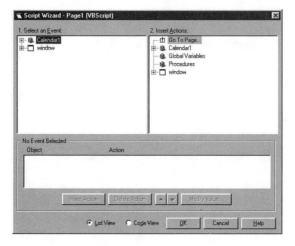

When you add an ActiveX control to your HTML document, the Script Wizard adds an object entry to the Event window. In figure 4.13, the Event window is shown after a `Calendar` control was added to the document.

FIG. 4.13

Add an additional object in the event window.

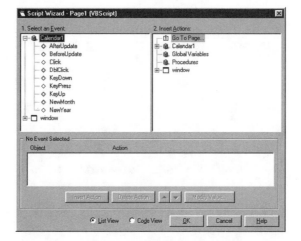

Part

I

Ch

4

The `Calendar` control uses a small blue cube as its icon. The document window uses a small replica of a window as its icon. To select an event for creating a response procedure, expand the entry for the `Window` object in the Event window. The `Window` object triggers two events, the `OnLoad` and `OnUnload`. Figure 4.14 shows a selection of the `OnLoad` event.

FIG. 4.14

Display the `Window` object's events.

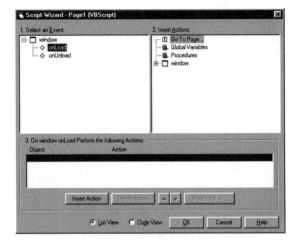

Each object that fires events appears in the Event window. Of course, each object may have any number of different events associated with actions on the object. For instance, the `Calendar` control fires several events. To add an action for any of these events, expand the `Calendar1` object entry in the Event window, and select the desired event (see fig. 4.15).

FIG. 4.15

Showing an object's events.

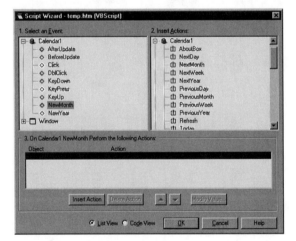

Navigating the Action Window

Once you've selected an object and an event, the next step is to select an action to be executed. The Action window provides an interface for selecting and entering the following actions:

- Invoking methods exposed by ActiveX objects
- Setting properties of ActiveX objects

- Entering and setting global variables
- Invoking procedures

The following sections take each of these items in turn.

Invoking the Methods of ActiveX Objects   Many ActiveX objects expose methods. The Action window methods are represented by a small exclamation point icon. For instance, if you placed a `Calendar` control in a Web page and wanted to invoke one of the methods supported by `Calendar` in response to some event, you would take the following action. After selecting an event in the Event window, expand the `Calendar` object's entry in the Action window.

Setting the Properties of ActiveX Objects   ActiveX objects also contain properties. In the Action window, properties are indicated by a small property sheet icon. The process of setting a property for an ActiveX object in the Script Wizard varies depending on the nature of the property itself. However, the process always begins when you double-click the property you want to change. If you wanted to set the `Year` property of the `Calendar` control, figure 4.16 shows the dialog box that the ActiveX Control Pad supplies in response to the double click.

FIG. 4.16
Set a property.

Depending on the property, the dialog box may differ. Setting the `TitleFont` property in the Calendar control, for instance, brings forward the windows standard Fonts dialog box—any property that requires a color brings forward the standard windows Color dialog box.

Entering and Setting Global Variables   Many applications require global variables for storing information. Of course, global variables must first be added to the Web page before you can set them to a value. To create a global variable, place the cursor over the Action window and press the right mouse button. Select New Global Variable, and you'll be presented with the dialog box in figure 4.17.

FIG. 4.17
Add a global variable.

Once you've entered a name for your global variable, press OK. When you're done, expand the `Global Variables` object in the Action window and you'll see the global variable you just entered (see fig. 4.18).

FIG. 4.18

Expand the `Global Variables` object in the Action window.

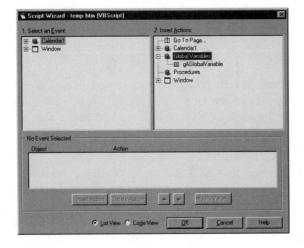

Now your global variable can be set and checked just like the property of an ActiveX control. If you want to set `gAGlobalVariable` to ten when the page is loaded, select the `Window`'s `OnLoad` event, double-click `gAGlobalVariable`, and enter **10** into the text box (see fig. 4.19).

FIG. 4.19

Set a global variable.

Editing Scripts in the List View

Once you press OK as shown in figure 4.19, the action is entered into the List View's Action list (see fig. 4.20).

The List View displays each of the statements from the script for the event you're handling. The List View provides the following several command buttons for editing the script:

- Insert action
- Delete action
- Move up action
- Move down action
- Modify value

FIG. 4.20
The List View editor.

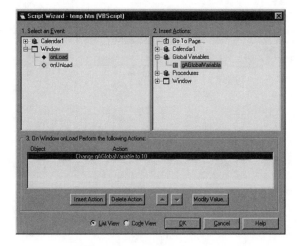

If you want to select the next day on the `Calendar` control before setting `gAGlobalVariable` to ten, select the `NextDay` action and then press the Insert Action button. When you've pressed the Insert Action button, a new command appears above the command setting `gAGlobalVariable` (see fig. 4.21).

FIG. 4.21
Insert an action.

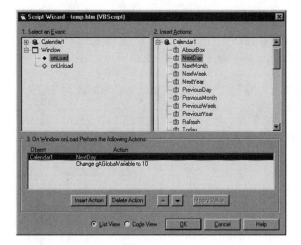

Part

I

Ch

4

Perhaps the actions you've entered are in the wrong order in the List View. To change the order of actions, use the Up and Down arrow buttons. Figure 4.22 shows the List View after pressing the Up arrow key. Of course, pressing the Delete button would remove the action just added to the script.

FIG. 4.22

Move an action up.

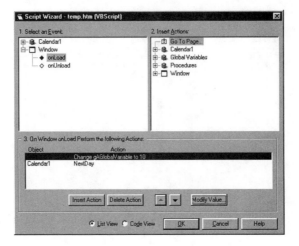

Pressing the down arrow returns the script to the order shown figure 4.21.

Editing Scripts in the Code View

The List View is good for making simple scripts quickly and easily. However, many times the application requires more sophisticated programming. The Code View provides developers with a rudimentary editor for including VBScripts that you hand code. To take a look at the Code View, select the Code View radio button. Next, press the right mouse and select New Procedure from the menu as shown in figure 4.23.

FIG. 4.23

Try the Code View.

Typically, you change the name of the procedure to a useful name, and then code the logic for the procedure. Figure 4.24 shows a coded procedure.

FIG. 4.24

A coded procedure in Code View.

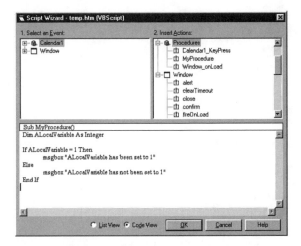

Notice that MyProcedure is now included under the procedure item in the Action window. If you're familiar with Visual Basic or VBScript, you'll notice that MyProcedure has no End Sub because ActiveX Control Pad inserts the End Sub for you.

If you switch back to the List View, or if you open a procedure developed in the Code View in the List View, the ActiveX Control Pad only shows a message as shown in figure 4.25.

FIG. 4.25

Code View procedures cannot be viewed in the List View.

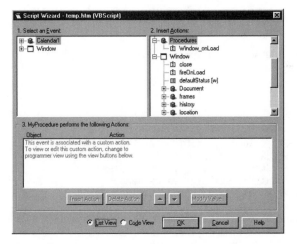

When you close the Script Wizard, the ActiveX Control Pad adds the VBScript to your HTML document. Depending on the procedures you've created, you may have several VBScript tag pairs within the HTML document. Listing 4.1 shows the HTML document you've been playing with throughout this chapter.

Part

I

Ch

4

On the CD

Listing 4.1 *TEMP.HTM* **VB Scripts Inserted by the ActiveX Control Pad**

```
<HTML>
<HEAD>
    <SCRIPT LANGUAGE="VBScript">
<!--
dim gAGlobalVariable

-->
    </SCRIPT>
    <SCRIPT LANGUAGE="VBScript">
<!--
Sub MyProcedure()
  Dim ALocalVariable As Integer

  If ALocalVariable = 1 Then
                msgbox "ALocalVariable has been set to 1"
  Else
                msgbox "ALocalVariable has not been set to 1"
  End If

end sub
Sub Window_onLoad()
call Calendar1.NextDay()
gAGlobalVariable = 10
end sub
-->
    </SCRIPT>
<TITLE>New Page</TITLE>
</HEAD>
<BODY>
    <SCRIPT LANGUAGE="VBScript">
<!--
Sub Calendar1_KeyPress(ByVal KeyAscii)
call MyProcedure()
end sub
-->
    </SCRIPT>
    <OBJECT ID="Calendar1" WIDTH=372 HEIGHT=279
     CLASSID="CLSID:8E27C92B-1264-101C-8A2F-040224009C02">
        <PARAM NAME="_Version" VALUE="458752">
        <PARAM NAME="_ExtentX" VALUE="9843">
        <PARAM NAME="_ExtentY" VALUE="7382">
        <PARAM NAME="_StockProps" VALUE="1">
        <PARAM NAME="BackColor" VALUE="12632256">
        <PARAM NAME="Year" VALUE="1996">
        <PARAM NAME="Month" VALUE="6">
        <PARAM NAME="Day" VALUE="30">
    </OBJECT>
</BODY>
</HTML>
```

This listing was copied directly from the ActiveX Control Pad, so the formatting of the code leaves a little to be desired. Notice how the procedures MyProcedure and Window_OnLoad are not separated by a blank line. Most programmers prefer that procedures are separated by white space to make them easily readable. However, since the Script Wizard makes building and editing scripts easier and more graphical, this is a minor complaint.

Inserting an HTML Layout

An HTML layout can be inserted in a Web page quite easily. HTML layouts are excellent for elements that are repeated in numerous Web pages on your Web site. You can simply build the HTML layout once, and then include it in any appropriate Web page. To include an HTML layout, take the following steps:

1. Start the ActiveX Control Pad if it's not already running.

2. Start a new HTML document by adding an H1 heading with text like **My HTML Layout**. Also, add a <BR> tag to make a break between the heading and the HTML layout. When you're finished, the screen should resemble figure 4.26.

FIG. 4.26
Add the H1 tag and heading text.

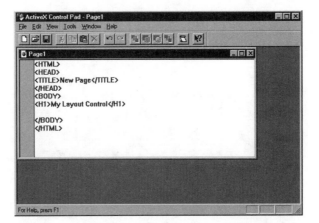

3. Insert the HTML layout that you created in the previous section. To do this, select Edit, Insert HTML Layout from the main menu. Then select the HTML layout you just created and press Open. When you're finished, your screen will look something like figure 4.27.

   The gray margin bar now shows an HTML layout button. Pressing this button launches the Layout editor as described previously.

4. Save your HTML page to a file.

FIG. 4.27

Add an HTML layout.

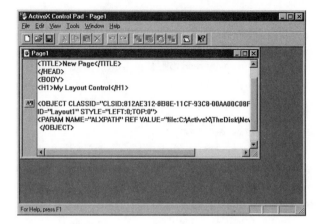

Now that you've completed the HTML document, you can test your work using Microsoft Internet Explorer 3.0. These next steps take you through testing out your HTML document.

1. Start Microsoft Internet Explorer 3.0.

2. Open your HTML document by choosing File, Open, or by typing the fully qualified path to the document.

   If you've done everything correctly, the HTML document will look something like figure 4.28.

FIG. 4.28

Test the HTML layout in Microsoft Internet Explorer 3.0.

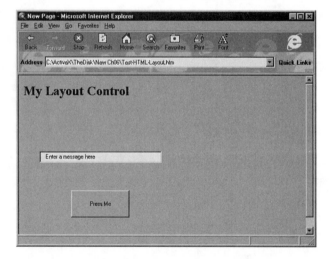

3. Now, enter some text in the text box. When you type, the color of the text changes to the color selected (see fig. 4.29).

FIG. 4.29
This dialog box tells you
that your action was
successful.

Inserting an Object

An HTML layout is an object, so inserting additional objects in a Web page is quite easy. HTML layouts are excellent for elements that are repeated in numerous Web pages on your Web site. However, the ActiveX Control Pad makes inserting any type of object easy. To include an object, follow these steps:

1. Start the ActiveX Control Pad if it's not already running.
2. Select File, New HTML, and start a new HTML file.
3. Add an H1 heading with some text like **My Calendar**. Also, add a <BR> tag to make a break between the heading and the HTML layout.
4. Add an ActiveX object. Select Edit, Insert ActiveX Control from the menu bar. Select the Calendar control from the list. When you're finished, the screen should resemble figure 4.30.

Part

I

Ch

4

FIG. 4.30
Add an object to
a Web page.

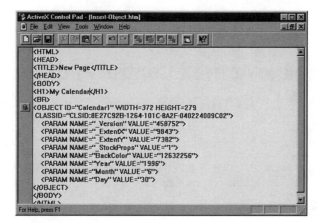

5. Save your HTML page to a file.

Now that you've completed the HTML document, you can test your work using Microsoft Internet Explorer 3.0.

The next steps take you through testing out your HTML document:

1. Start Microsoft Internet Explorer 3.0.

2. Open your HTML document by choosing File, Open, or by typing the fully qualified path to the document.

   If you've done everything correctly, the HTML document will look something like figure 4.31.

FIG. 4.31

Testing the page.

Customizing the ActiveX Control Pad Development Environment

The ActiveX Control Pad provides limited ability to customize the development environment. You can customize the behavior of the HTML Layout Editor and the Script Wizard.

The HTML Layout Editor provides a grid of dots that makes it easy to align controls within the layout. The grid has the following configuration options:

- Vertical grid line spacing
- Horizontal grid line spacing
- Grid on/off
- Snap to grid

Figure 4.32 shows the dialog box for configuring these items—the HTML Layout Options dialog box. To obtain this dialog box, select Tools, Options, HTML Layout Options.

FIG. 4.32

The ActiveX Control Pad permits HTML layout editor configuration.

The Script Wizard also allows limited customization of the Script Wizard environment. You can set the following options by selecting Tools, Options, Script Wizard from the toolbar:

- Default script pane view
- Script pane font
- Default script language

Figure 4.33 shows the dialog box for configuring these items.

FIG. 4.33

The ActiveX Control Pad permits configuration of the Script Wizard.

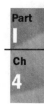

Part

I

Ch

4

Including ActiveX Controls in Your Web Pages

Building ActiveX Controls is a pretty technical exercise. Using C++ and ActiveX Template Libraries requires a thorough understanding of the OLE and COM object specifications. However, you don't need to build ActiveX Controls in order to produce dynamic Web pages. In fact, Microsoft is quite hopeful that a large third-party market in ActiveX Controls will develop, much as the VBX and OCX market has developed. Using ActiveX Controls in a Web page is really a straightforward exercise, once you've learned a few basics. ■

Use the `<OBJECT>` HTML tag

Although the ActiveX Control Pad helps to hide some of the details of the `<OBJECT>` tag from you, it's good to understand the details of this important part of HTML.

Learn about the `<PARAM>` HTML tag

Passing parameters to an ActiveX control helps you the tap the power of dynamic content.

Build a dynamic Web page that uses the Microsoft ActiveX Controls

Microsoft provides a variety of ActiveX Controls that make for exciting Web pages, such as the Timer and Label controls that are used in an example to demonstrate the power of ActiveX.

Introducing the *<OBJECT>* HTML Tag

HTML 2.0 provided a very simple content model for insertion of multimedia into HTML documents: the <IMG> tag. Unfortunately, this tag does not treat multimedia as a more general sort of item. With ActiveX and Java and other types of robust multimedia applications, Web page authors require a more general mechanism for including these applications into Web pages. There have been a few attempts at other types of multimedia tags such as the following:

- DYNSRC, a Microsoft attribute for video and audio
- <EMBED>, Netscape's tag for compound document embedding
- <APP> and <APPLET>, Sun Microsystems' tags for including Java into Web HTML documents

These varying alternatives all take a swipe at defining a more general nomenclature for describing new multimedia content. Serving in its role of developing standards for the Web, the World Wide Web Consortium (W3C) convened a group of experts to define a new tag, <OBJECT>, which encompasses the <IMG> tag and provides a general solution for handling diverse multimedia content. In addition, <OBJECT> allows you to specify various parameters for initializing the object when it is placed on a Web page.

The <OBJECT> tag allows you to specify object parameters in a number of ways including the following:

- Another file referenced via URL
- Inline data
- Named properties

ActiveX Controls typically use named properties to initialize. Note that there are also standard properties, such as HEIGHT and WIDTH, that may be specified for all objects.

This tag can also point to the code that is to be executed in the object's space. This makes it easy for Web authors to include and change referenced objects. The code can also be referenced in the following ways:

- Explicit reference
- Class name
- Media type

ActiveX, as you'll see, uses the class name option to be referenced.

A Simple *<OBJECT>* Tag Example

Before we dive into a detailed discussion of each of the parameters, let's take a brief look at how the <OBJECT> tag is used. In its simplest form, the <OBJECT> tag would look something like Listing 5.1.

On the CD

Listing 5.1 *5-1LSTNG.HTM* Object Tag Example #1

```
<! ---------------------------------------------------
<! --
<! --     Description:    Simple OBJECT tag Example #1
<! --
<! --     Author:         Brian Farrar
<! --
<! --   Date:           5/11/96
<! ---------------------------------------------------

<HTML>

<TITLE>Simple OBJECT Tag Example #1
</TITLE>

<BODY>

<H1>Simple Object Tag Example #1</H1>

<P>
If your browser supports display of avi movies inline you'll see a movie here,
otherwise you'll see a simple graphic.
<OBJECT
     DATA=SomeFile.avi
     TYPE="application/avi">

     <IMG SRC=SomeGif.gif ALT="ActiveX">
</OBJECT>

</BODY>

</HTML>
```

Part
I

Ch
5

If the Web browser you use supports in-line playing of AVI video format, the movie called SomeFile.avi would be played. Otherwise, the Web browser will substitute the graphic SomeGif.gif. Thus, the <OBJECT> tag allows you to include specific content that is not supported by all browsers, without getting involved in content negotiation.

N O T E Various Web browsers support different features. For instance, Netscape Navigator 2.0 and Microsoft Internet Explorer 3.0 both support frames. However, most other browsers do not. In order to use more advanced features like frames without excluding those who use browsers that don't support an advanced feature, Web authors sometimes engage in *content negotiation*. Content negotiation usually employs a CGI application to examine the USER_AGENT field passed through the CGI (which indicates the type of browser) and selects a page optimized for the requesting browser. ■

The TYPE attribute makes it easy for Web browsers to determine if the indicated <OBJECT> is supported and, if it is not supported, does not download the object thereby avoiding unnecessary bandwidth use. Making TYPE available also allows the Web browser to avoid guessing at the application format based on the extension.

The *<OBJECT>* Tag in Detail

The <OBJECT> tag has a number of attributes that can be specified. Table 5.1 explains how you'll be using these attributes working with ActiveX Controls.

Table 5.1 *<OBJECT>* **Tag Attributes**

Attribute	Description
ALIGN	Determines placement of the object relative to other items on the page
BORDER	Suggests the width of the border to be placed around the display
CLASSID	Identifies an implementation of the object to be rendered on the page
CODE	Some objects (like Java applets) need this as reference to other code
DATA	Points to any data required by the object referred to by CLASSID
DECLARE	Indicates whether the object referred to in CLASSID is to be declared or instantiated
HEIGHT	Suggests the height that the Web browser should provide for display of the object
HSPACE	Area to be preserved as white space to the left and right of the border and display space of the <OBJECT>
ID	A document-wide identifier used to refer to the <OBJECT>
ISMAP	When the object is clicked, this attribute causes the mouse coordinates to be sent to the server
NAME	Used to indicate if the <OBJECT>'s value should be included in a FORM
STANDBY	Identifies the text to be displayed while the object is being loaded
TYPE	Refers to Internet Media Type (RFC 1590) of the item referred to in the CLASSID field
USEMAP	Points to a client-side image map
VSPACE	Area to be preserved as white space above and below the border and display space of the <OBJECT>
WIDTH	Suggests the width that the Web browser should provide for display of the object

Use the summary table as a quick reference for the <OBJECT>'s tag attributes. Each of these attributes bears a bit of explanation.

The *ALIGN* Attribute   You'll use the ALIGN attribute to determine the placement of your ActiveX control in the Web page. ActiveX objects can be placed as part of the current text line or as a distinct element aligned left, right, or center. You'll set the ALIGN attribute to one of the values found on Tables 5.2 and 5.3, depending on the appearance you want to achieve.

Table 5.2   Values for the *ALIGN* Attribute Relative to the Current Text Line

Value	Meaning
TEXTTOP	The top of the object aligned with the top of the current font
MIDDLE	The middle of the object aligned vertically with the baseline
TEXTMIDDLE	The middle of the object vertically aligned with a position halfway between the baseline and the height of the lowercase letter *x*
BASELINE	The object's bottom aligned with the baseline of the text line on which it appears

Table 5.3   Values for the *ALIGN* attribute as a Free-Floating Object

Value	Meaning
LEFT	The object will be placed on the left margin below the previous text or object in the page.
CENTER	The object will be placed midway between the left and right margins.
RIGHT	The object will be placed on the right margin below the previous text or object in the page.

The ALIGN tag is currently fully implemented in MSIE 3.0.

The *BORDER* Attribute   If the object is part of a hypertext link, the BORDER attribute suggests the width to be used as a border around the object's visible area. For instance, if you didn't want the object to have a border as a hypertext link, you would set BORDER=0. The BORDER attribute is currently fully implemented in MSIE 3.0.

The *CLASSID* and *CODE* Attributes   The CLASSID attribute is used to refer to the ActiveX control to be placed within the object's borders. There are several different ways to indicate the object to be executed here. ActiveX uses the CLASSID: URL scheme to specify the ActiveX class identifier.

ON THE WEB

http://www.w3.org/pub/WWW/Addressing/clsid-scheme   For further information on the CLASSID: URL scheme, check out this Web site.

The CLASSID for any ActiveX control can also be obtained from the registry in Windows 95. To do this, follow these steps:

1. Press the Start button.
2. Select Run.

continues

Part

I

Ch

5

continued

3. Type **regedit.**

4. Press OK.

5. Select the HKEY_CLASSES_ROOT registry key.

6. Scroll down to an ActiveX control name like `ieChart.ieChartCtl`.

7. Double-click the control's registry key.

8. Select the CLSID registry key.

9. From the data window, copy the CLASSID string and use it in your HTML as necessary.

If the CLASSID attribute is missing, ActiveX data streams will include a class identifier that can be used by the ActiveX loader to find the appropriate control. The CODE attribute can be used to provide an URL from which the control can be obtained.

The *DATA* Attribute   The DATA attribute contains an URL that points to data required by the object—for instance, a GIF file for an image. MSIE 3.0 currently supports the DATA attribute.

The *DECLARE* Attribute   You'll use the DECLARE attribute to tell the browser whether to instantiate the object or not. If the DECLARE attribute indicates that the object should not be instantiated until something references it, then the object is not loaded. At this writing, the DECLARE attribute has not been implemented in MSIE 3.0. However, Microsoft indicates that DECLARE will be supported.

The *HEIGHT* Attribute   The HEIGHT attribute suggests the height in pixels to be made available to the ActiveX control when rendered by the browser (see fig. 5.1). The Web browser may (or may not) use this value to scale an object to the requested height. The HEIGHT attribute is currently supported in MSIE 3.0.

The *HSPACE* Attribute   The HSPACE attribute suggests the amount of space, in pixels, that should be kept as white space on the left and right as a buffer between the ActiveX control and surrounding page elements (refer to fig. 5.1). The Web browser may (or may not) use this value to allocate white space. The HSPACE attribute is currently supported in MSIE 3.0.

The *ID* Attribute   The ID attribute defines a document-wide identifier. This can be used for naming positions within documents. In order to communicate between objects within the Web browser, the ID attribute may be set. The ID attribute is currently supported in MSIE 3.0.

The *ISMAP* Attribute   The ISMAP attribute indicates that the Web server provides an image map. The object must appear within an anchor tag indicating a hypertext link in order for ISMAP to make sense. ISMAP requires that mouse clicks be sent to the server in the same manner as the <IMG> element. There is still disagreement among the W3C committee members working on the <OBJECT> tag definition, so the ISMAP attribute is not currently supported in MSIE 3.0. However, Microsoft has indicated that ISMAP will be supported if it remains a part of the <OB-JECT> tag specification.

The *NAME* Attribute   Use the NAME attribute to indicate whether an object wrapped in a <FORM> tag will be submitted with the form. If you specify NAME, the Web browser submits the VALUE property of the object to the host. If you don't specify NAME, the ActiveX control is assumed to be decorative and not functional in form. The NAME attribute is currently supported in MSIE 3.0.

FIG. 5.1
How placement attributes affect the <OBJECT> tag.

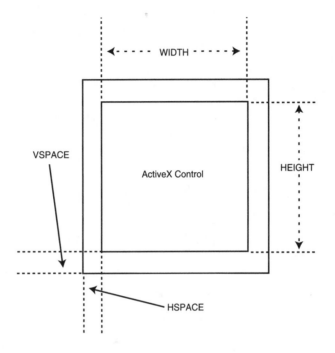

The *STANDBY* Attribute   A short string of text can be displayed while the browser loads the ActiveX control. Use the STANDBY attribute to specify this text. The STANDBY attribute is not currently supported in MSIE 3.0; however, Microsoft will likely implement this attribute.

The *TYPE* Attribute   The TYPE attribute is used to specify the the Internet Media Type for the ActiveX control identified by CLASSID before actually retrieving it.

ON THE WEB

ftp://ds.internic.net/rfc/rfc1590.txt   You can learn more about Internet Media Types by referring to RFC 1590, which you can find at this FTP site.

Currently, the TYPE attribute is supported in a limited fashion in MSIE 3.0. Microsoft has indicated that TYPE will be implemented for all relevant MIME types.

The *USEMAP* Attribute   The USEMAP attribute is included for use with static images. The value in USEMAP specifies a uniform resource locator for a client-side image map. The USEMAP attribute is currently not supported in MSIE 3.0, but Microsoft has indicated that MSIE 3.0 will support USEMAP in the future.

The *VSPACE* Attribute   The VSPACE attribute suggests the amount of space, in pixels, to keep as white space on the top and bottom as a buffer between the ActiveX control and surrounding

Part

I

Ch

5

page elements (refer to fig. 5.1). The Web browser may (or may not) use this value to allocate the requested white space. The VSPACE attribute is currently supported in MSIE 3.0.

The *WIDTH* Attribute   The WIDTH attribute suggests the width, in pixels, to make available to the ActiveX control when it is rendered by the browser (refer to fig. 5.1). The Web browser may (or may not) use this value to scale an object to the requested width. The WIDTH attribute is currently supported in MSIE 3.0.

The *<PARAM>* Tag in Detail

You may want to pass parameter values to your ActiveX control. The <PARAM> tag provides a mechanism to supply a list of named property values. Note that the <PARAM> tag has no closing </PARAM> tag. (Just to keep it simple for you!) Table 5.4 lists the attributes of the <PARAM> tag.

Table 5.4   Attributes of the *<PARAM>* Tag

Attribute	Description
NAME	Defines the name of the property. Your ActiveX control can treat the name as case-sensitive, if desired.
VALUE	Specifies the value of the property identified in NAME.
VALUETYPE	Can be one of REF, OBJECT, or DATA.
TYPE	Refers to Internet Media Type (RFC 1590) of the item referred to in the VALUE field when VALUETYPE = REF.

There is no need to go through all of these attributes. Except for the VALUETYPE attributes, they are mostly self-explanatory. The VALUETYPE attributes are explained briefly in Table 5.5.

Table 5.5   Values for *VALUETYPE* Attribute

Value	Meaning
REF	Indicates that the value found in the VALUE attribute is an URL.
OBJECT	Indicates that the value found in the VALUE attribute is the URL of another OBJECT element.
DATA	Indicates that the value found in the VALUE attribute is intended to be passed to the OBJECT as a string. This is the default VALUETYPE.

Using Some of the Microsoft ActiveX Controls

Microsoft provides a few demonstration ActiveX Controls that turn out to be quite useful for Web developers. In this section, you'll use three of these controls in step-by-step examples. The four controls that you'll be using are the following:

- The New control
- The Label control
- The Chart control
- The Timer control

In each of the following sections, you'll work an example and then review important properties.

Using the New Control

If you're maintaining a Web site, you know that to keep your audience you must add new content on a regular basis. Whether you run a simple personal page or a corporate Web site with thousands of pages and links, you always want to draw attention to the new stuff. The problem with specially marking new content is that you have to unmark it after it isn't new anymore. Maintenance headache. The New control solves this problem for you.

Working an Example   All of the examples in this chapter assume that you have a simple HTML template file. Having a template saves you the time of retyping comment headers and the basic tags that are found in all HTML documents. Your template might look something like Listing 5.2.

On the CD

Listing 5.2   *HTMLSTUB.HTM*   HTML Document Template

```
<! ------------------------------------------------------
<! --
<! --      Description:
<! --
<! --      Author:            Brian Farrar
<! --
<! --   Date:
<! ------------------------------------------------------

<HTML>

<TITLE>
</TITLE>

<BODY BGCOLOR=#FFFFFF>

<H1></H1>

<P>

<OBJECT

</OBJECT>

</BODY>

</HTML>
```

Part
I

Ch
5

To use the New control in HTML document, follow these steps:

1. Start the ActiveX Control Pad, and open your HTML template file.

2. Update the comment header, TITLE value, and major heading to reflect the example your working on.

3. Save the file to a convenient working directory as NEWCTL.HTM. It should now look similar to Listing 5.3.

On the CD

Listing 5.3 *NEWCTL.HTM* Customizing the HTML Template

```
<! -------------------------------------------------
<! --
<! --  Description:      Using the New Control
<! --
<! --  Author:          Brian Farrar
<! --
<! --   Date:           5/12/96
<! -------------------------------------------------
<HTML>
<TITLE>
New Item ActiveX Control Example
</TITLE>

<BODY BGCOLOR=#FFFFFF>

<H1>What's New on Our Web Site</H1>

<P>

</BODY>

</HTML>
```

4. Add the masthead graphic NEW.GIF, provided on the CD.

5. Place a horizontal rule—the <HR> tag—below the <H1> enclosed title.

6. Place an <H3> heading that indicates a date when the following items will no longer be considered new. Be sure to pick a date that is past today's date. So, if today is 9/25/96, pick something like 10/12/96.

7. Select Edit, Insert ActiveX Control from the menu. Choose newbCtl Object from the pick list of ActiveX Controls and press OK. Or you can specify the <OBJECT> by entering the code directly into the document. Make sure to set the attributes as shown in Listing 5.4. Note that the CLASSID field should be filled in for you by the ActiveX Control Pad. Be sure that the date <PARAM>'s value is set to the date indicated in the <H3> heading of step 6.

On the CD

Listing 5.4   *2NEWCTL.HTM*   First Instance of *<OBJECT>* in *NEWCTL.HTM*

```
<OBJECT
            ID="NewLabel"
CLASSID="CLSID:642B65C0-7374-11CF-A3A9-00A0C9034920"
      WIDTH=20
      HEIGHT=10
      HSPACE=10
>
      <PARAM NAME="date" value="6/1/96">
</OBJECT>
```

8. Add some text that indicates that there is new information available on the Web site somewhere. Do this by typing text after the </OBJECT> tag.

9. Repeat steps 7 and 8 several times.

10. Place another <HR> horizontal rule below your last <OBJECT> from step 9.

11. Place an <H3> heading that indicates a date when the following items will no longer be considered new. Be sure to pick a date that is earlier than today's date. So, if today is 9/25/96, pick something like 9/11/96.

12. Copy and paste the <OBJECT> tag information after a breaking line (<BR>). Specify the <OBJECT> attributes something like that shown in Listing 5.5. Be sure that the date <PARAM>'s value is set to the date indicated in your <H3> heading from step 11.

On the CD

Listing 5.5   *3NEWCTL.HTM*   Expired New Control *<OBJECT>* Listing

```
<OBJECT
            ID=NewLabel
CLASSID="CLSID:642B65C0-7374-11CF-A3A9-00A0C9034920"
      WIDTH=20
      HEIGHT=10
      HSPACE=10
>
      <PARAM NAME="date" value="5/1/96">
</OBJECT>
```

Part
I

Ch
5

13. Add some text that indicates that there is new information available on the Web site somewhere. Do this by typing some text after the </OBJECT> tag.

14. Repeat steps 12 and 13 several times.

15. Save your work as NEWCTL.HTM.

Now that the HTML document is complete, you can test your work using Microsoft Internet Explorer 3.0. To test your HTML document, follow these steps:

1. Start Microsoft Internet Explorer 3.0.

2. Place the text cursor in the document text box and type **NEWCTL.HTM**. Be sure to include the fully qualified path to your document. Press Enter.

3. If you've done everything correctly, the New graphic will appear next to the top items and not next to the bottom items (see fig. 5.2).

FIG. 5.2
First test of
NEWCTL.HTM.

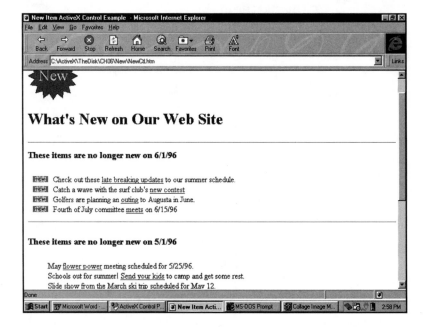

4. Open a DOS window, type the DOS date command, and press Enter.

5. Set the date to a time before the date you selected in step 11. The date selected in the example here was 5/1/96, so I entered 4/15/96 at the DOS date prompt.

6. Now press the reload button on MSIE 3.0. The results should look something like figure 5.3. If you've done everything right, the New graphic will appear next to all the items on your page.

7. Open a DOS window again, type the DOS date command, and press Enter.

8. Set the date to a time after the date you selected in step 6. The date selected in the example here was 6/1/96, so I entered 6/15/96 at the DOS date prompt.

9. Now press the reload button on MSIE 3.0. If you've done everything right, the New graphic will not appear at all.

If you've managed a Web site, you can see the tremendous benefit for an ActiveX control like the New control.

Important Properties   There are two critical properties to be set for the New ActiveX control—the DATE parameter and the IMAGE parameter (see Table 5.6).

FIG. 5.3
Second test of
NEWCTL.HTM.

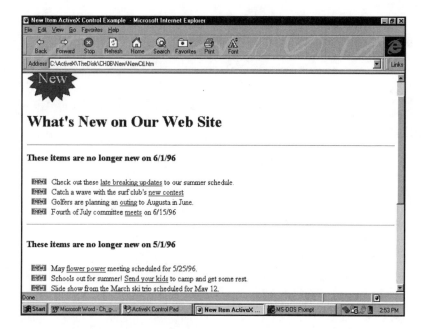

Table 5.6   Important New Control Properties

Property	Description
DATE	This property sets the date on which the New sticker should expire. This allows a document to decide for itself whether the content is new.
IMAGE	This property allows you to select an image other than the default image. Provide an URL to an appropriate image.

Part

I

Ch

5

Using the Label Control

HTML makes it easy for you to deal with most of the standard types of text information. As long as the orientation of the text is left to right, HTML provides all the tools necessary. But sometimes, your page may need something a little bit more daring. This is where the Label control steps in.

Working an Example   To use the Label control in an HTML document, follow these steps:

1. Start the ActiveX Control Pad, and open your HTML template file.

2. Update the comment header, TITLE value, and <H1> major heading to reflect the example you're working on.

3. Save the file to a convenient working directory as LABEL.HTM.

4. Add an <HR> tag below the <H1> title you entered.

5. Select Edit, Insert ActiveX Control from the menu. Choose `sprLabelCtl Object` from the list of ActiveX Controls and press OK. Or simply enter the `<OBJECT>` data for the Label control as shown in Listing 5.6. This sets up a label that rises at a 30-degree angle using the Impact TrueType font.

Listing 5.6   *LABEL.HTM*   *<OBJECT>* Tag For Inserting Label ActiveX Control

```
<OBJECT
        CLASSID="clsid:99B42120-6EC7-11CF-A6C7-00AA00A47DD2"
                ID=label
                WIDTH=200
                HEIGHT=100
                VSPACE=0
                ALIGN=left
>
        <PARAM NAME="angle" value="30">
        <PARAM NAME="alignment" value="3">
        <PARAM NAME="BackStyle" value="0">
        <PARAM NAME="caption" value="Announce">
        <PARAM NAME="FontName" value="Impact">
        <PARAM NAME="FontSize" value="40">
        <PARAM NAME="frcolor" value="255">
</OBJECT>
```

CAUTION

Note that the order parameters that appear in the code depend upon whether you typed the code or used the ActiveX Control Pad's Edit menu and property sheet. The examples in this chapter were typed.

6. Add some text to appear to the right of the `<OBJECT>`. Make sure you put in enough text to ensure that the following text and Label control appear below the `<OBJECT>` entered in step 5.

7. Enter the `<OBJECT>` data for the Label control as shown in Listing 5.7. This sets up a string of text that will be rendered upside down using the Brush Script MT TrueType font.

Listing 5.7   *2LABEL.HTM*   Second Label Control in *LABEL.HTM*

```
<OBJECT
        CLASSID="clsid:99B42120-6EC7-11CF-A6C7-00AA00A47DD2"
                ID=label
                WIDTH=300
                HEIGHT=100
                VSPACE=0
                ALIGN="center"
>
        <PARAM NAME="angle" value="180">
        <PARAM NAME="alignment" value="2">
```

```
      <PARAM NAME="BackStyle" value="0">
      <PARAM NAME="caption" value="Surprise">
      <PARAM NAME="FontName" value="Brush Script MT">
      <PARAM NAME="FontSize" value="110">
      <PARAM NAME="frcolor" value="16776960">
</OBJECT>
```

8. Add some text to appear below the <OBJECT> you just created.

9. Save your work as LABEL.HTM.

Now that you've completed the HTML document, you can test your work using Microsoft Internet Explorer 3.0. To test your HTML document, follow these steps:

1. Start Microsoft Internet Explorer 3.0.

2. Place the text cursor in the document text box and type **LABEL.HTM**. Be sure to include the fully qualified path to your document. Press Enter.

3. If you've done everything correctly, the HTML document will look something like figure 5.4.

FIG. 5.4
Check your Label control example results.

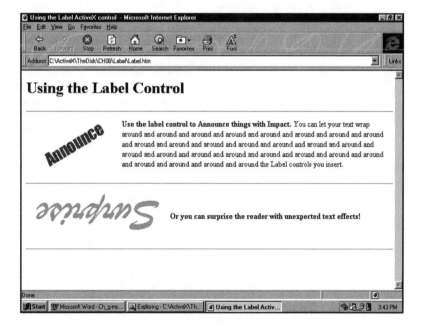

Part

I

Ch

5

Important Properties   Let's take a look at the properties that can be set for the Label control. Table 5.7 provides a quick look at all the properties. It is followed by a brief discussion of a few critical items.

Table 5.7 Properties for the Label ActiveX Control

Property	Description
Caption	Indicates the text to be displayed within the Label control. The appearance of this text will be affected by other properties.
Angle	Indicates the angle of the base line for the text. This item is specified in degrees counter-clockwise from horizontal.
Alignment	Indicates the alignment of the control within the rectangular area specified for the control.
BackStyle	Indicates how to display the area of the control not covered by the caption text.
FontName	Indicates the TrueType font used to draw the Caption text.
FontSize	Indicates the size of the font used to draw the Caption text.
FontItalic	Indicates that the Caption text should be italicized.
FontBold	Indicates that the Caption text should be bolded.
FontUnderline	Indicates that the Caption text should be underlined.
FontStrikeout	Indicates that the Caption text should be marked with strikethrough.
FrColor	Indicates the RGB triplet for the color.

The following sections examine a few details related to some of these properties.

The Angle Property   The Angle property indicates the angle of the baseline along which the text will be drawn. The value used to express this angle is in degrees. Degrees are counted in a counter-clockwise fashion from horizontal. That is, to turn a bit of text upside down, the Angle property is set to 180.

The Alignment Property   You'll use the Alignment property to situate the caption text within the ActiveX control's rectangular space on the page. Table 5.8 summarizes the effect of various Alignment settings.

Table 5.8 Values for the *Alignment* Property

Value	Description
0	Causes the control to be aligned along the left edge of the control's frame.
1	Causes the control to be aligned along the right edge of the control's frame.
2	Causes the control to be centered within the control's frame.
3	Causes the control to be aligned along the top of the control's frame.

Value	Description
4	Causes the control to be aligned along the bottom of the control's frame.

The `BackStyle` *Property* You'll use the `BackStyle` property to set the background treatment for area within the control's frame not covered by the `Caption` text. Table 5.9 summarizes the effect of various `BackStyle` settings.

Table 5.9   Values for the *BackStyle* Property

Value	Description
0	Transparent—the area within the control's frame not covered by the `Caption` text is set to the page's background color.
1	Opaque—the area within the control's frame not covered by `Caption` text is set to a default color (usually gray).

Important Methods and Events The Label control also implements one method (the `About` method) and one event (`Mouse Click`). Events will be discussed in the next example.

Using the Timer Control

The Timer control provides you with the ability to enact changes to a control based on the expiration of an arbitrary timer. Unlike the other ActiveX Controls you've worked with so far, the Timer is an invisible control. That is, you won't see it on your Web pages. Instead, you'll use the Timer to trigger changes in another control or item on the page. Timer controls are a bit tricky at first but, once you've worked an example, you'll see all kinds of uses for them. Also unlike the controls you've used so far, you'll need to add a bit of VBScript to your Web page to make the Timer control work. Don't worry though; you'll only need a snippet of VBScript to make it work.

Part

I

Ch

5

Working an Example To use the Timer control in an HTML document, follow these steps:

1. Start the ActiveX Control Pad and open your HTML template file.
2. Update the comment header, `TITLE` value, and `<H1>` major heading to reflect the example you're working on.
3. Save the file to a convenient working directory as `TIMER.HTM`.
4. Add an `<HR>` tag below the `<H1>` title you entered.
5. Select Edit, Insert ActiveX Control from the menu. Choose `sprLabelCtl Object` from the list of ActiveX Controls and press OK. Or simply type the `<OBJECT>` data for a Label control as shown in Listing 5.8. This sets up a Label with no angle using the Monotype Corsiva TrueType font. Select an initial `FontSize` as well.

Listing 5.8 *TIMER.HTM* **Label Control for Use with Timer Control**

```
<OBJECT
        CLASSID="clsid:99B42120-6EC7-11CF-A6C7-00AA00A47DD2"
        ID=Spinner
        WIDTH=350
        HEIGHT=350
        ALIGN=center
        HSPACE=30
        VSPACE=50
>
        <PARAM NAME="angle" value="0">
        <PARAM NAME="alignment" value="2">
        <PARAM NAME="BackStyle" value="0">
        <PARAM NAME="caption" value="Spin a web">
        <PARAM NAME="FontName" value="Monotype Corsiva">
        <PARAM NAME="FontSize" value="30">
</OBJECT>
```

6. Now place the <OBJECT> data for the Timer control as shown in Listing 5.9. Start with an initial TimeOut setting of 100. (You may want to play with this later.)

Listing 5.9 *2TIMER.HTM* **Timer Control**

```
<OBJECT
        CLASSID="59CCB4A0-727D-11CF-AC36-00AA00A47DD2"
        ID=SpinTimer
        ALIGN=middle
>
        <PARAM NAME="TimeOut" value="100">
        <PARAM NAME="enable" value="1">
</OBJECT>
```

7. When a Timer control is enabled, it throws a time event at every TimeOut interval. In order to harness the Timer control and make dynamic changes to your Web page, you must implement a response function. The response function is invoked when the event is thrown. (You'll learn more about VBScript in Chapter 6, "Using VBScript.")

Enter the code from Listing 5.10 into your TIMER.HTM document. To accomplish this, select Tools, Script Wizard. The Script Wizard dialog box appears. Select the SpinTimer object's Time event. Place the Script Wizard into Code View by selecting the Code View radio button and enter the code as shown in Listing 5.10. Your screen should look like figure 5.5.

FIG. 5.5

Enter the code in Code View from the Script Wizard.

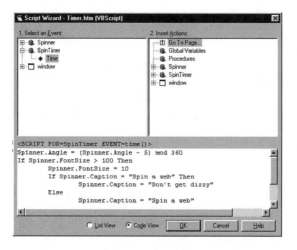

On the CD

Listing 5.10 3TIMER.HTM VBScript to Implement Timer Response Function

```
<SCRIPT LANGUAGE="VBScript" FOR="SpinTimer" EVENT="time">

        Spinner.Angle = (Spinner.Angle - 5) mod 360
        If Spinner.FontSize > 100 Then
              Spinner.FontSize = 10
              If Spinner.Caption = "Spin a web" Then
                    Spinner.Caption = "Don't get dizzy"
              Else
                    Spinner.Caption = "Spin a web"
              End If
        Else
              Spinner.FontSize = Spinner.FontSize + 5
        End If

</SCRIPT>
```

Part

I

Ch

5

8. Save your work as TIMER.HTM.

Take a minute and study what this function does. First, the Angle property of the Spinner Label control is decreased by five. Then the modulus of the result and 360 is taken. (This ensures that the result is always less than 360 degrees.) As the Angle property is being changed, the FontSize property is increased until it exceeds 100. When the FontSize exceeds 100, the Caption property is toggled between two different strings.

Now that you've completed the HTML document, you can test your work using Microsoft Internet Explorer 3.0. These next steps take you through testing your HTML document:

1. Start Microsoft Internet Explorer 3.0.

2. Place the text cursor in the document text box and type **TIMER.HTM**. Be sure to include the fully qualified path to your document. Press Enter.

3. If you've done everything correctly, the HTML document well look something like figure 5.6.

FIG. 5.6

Timer control example results.

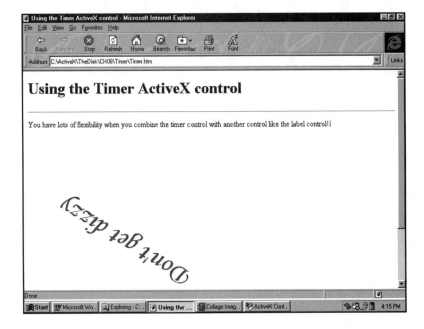

Important Properties   Let's take a look at the properties that can be set for the Timer control. Table 5.10 describes the properties and a brief discussion of a few critical items follows.

Table 5.10	Timer Control Properties
Property	**Description**
Enable	This property indicates whether the timer has been enabled or not.
TimeOut	Use this property to set the time, in milliseconds, when the timer is triggered.

The Enable Property   A Timer control can be enabled or disabled. When the timer is disabled, no Time event is triggered. When the timer is enabled, the Time event is triggered and response functions can take any desired action (see Table 5.11).

Table 5.11	Enable Property Settings
Status	**Meaning**
1	Timer is enabled
0	Timer is disabled

The TimeOut *Property*   The Timer control generates a Time event on a regular interval. You'll set the interval by changing the value of TimeOut. TimeOut assumes that the number you provide is in milliseconds. Passing a negative value has the same effect as setting Enable to zero.

Important Methods and Events   The Timer control also implements one method (the About method) and one event (the Time event). Note that the proper form for an event response function is ID_EVENT. In our example, the timer had ID=SpinTimer and the control throws the time event so the response function has the name SpinTimer_time.

To experiment with response function naming, go back to the LABEL.HTM file created previously and implement a response function for the Mouse Click event. A simple way to do this is to use the MsgBox function, which takes a text string as a parameter. ●

Using VBScript

One of the most exciting features of ActiveX, is lightweight scripting availability in any number of languages. Application developers adopted Visual Basic with open arms because it was easy to generate Windows applications fast without concern for many of the details of Windows programming. Microsoft hopes that providing VBScript under the ActiveX scripting services platform will drive Web development in a similar manner. As you'll see in the next few chapters, VBScript enables you to put sophisticated conditional logic and event processing into a Web page without compiling anything. And, if you already know Visual Basic, VBScript will be a snap. If you've never even seen Visual Basic before, don't worry, because VBScript is much like any other programming language and you'll pick it up quickly. ■

The `<SCRIPT>` tag

Scripts are included in your Web pages wrapped by a `<SCRIPT>` and `</SCRIPT>` tag pair. The ActiveX Control Pad will insert this HTML for you. However, you should know the details.

Another look at `SpinTimer`

In the `Timer.HTM` example from Chapter 6, you built a simple `Timer` event response function without really knowing VBScript. The VBScript details are reviewed here.

Build a VBScript application

As always, the best way to learn VBScript is to use it in an example.

Using the *<SCRIPT>* Tag

The general industry term for ActiveX scripting services is *client-side scripting*. HTML 2.0 provided no mechanism for implementation of client-side scripting. This means that all conditional logic, forms processing, and data editing on form fields requires a Common Gateway Interface (CGI) application. In a bandwidth limited environment like the Internet, the CGI model doesn't always make sense. For instance, a simple form to calculate your income tax or to calculate a mortgage payment does not require interaction with any data other than the input fields on the form. When these types of applications are implemented via CGI, you end up wasting two trips over the Internet. The first trip wasted is the transmission of the form fields from the browser to the server for processing by the CGI application. The second wasted trip occurs when the CGI application calculates the results and returns a page to the user for review.

Client-side scripting solves this problem. Serving in its role of developing standards for the Web, the World Wide Web Consortium (W3C) convened a group of experts to define a new tag, <SCRIPT>, to specify the implementation of client-side scripting. Because Netscape's JavaScript was already in wide distribution when the process began, W3C relied heavily on the JavaScript implementation.

The <SCRIPT> tag allows Web developers to execute client-side script processing within the Web browser. More specifically, a client-side script can be supplied to the browser in two ways:

- Directly in an HTML page
- As a separate file

Even more impressive than processing input fields and computing implied values, ActiveX objects can generate events, and scripts can handle those events in a sophisticated way (as you briefly saw in Chapter 5).

This last point deserves a bit more discussion. Application development environments such as Visual Basic provide a mechanism for binding events that occur on user interface objects like fields, buttons, and list boxes to procedures for handling those events. In the Timer control example in Chapter 5, you used (without really knowing it) this binding property to catch a Timer event and takes some action. The <SCRIPT> tag provides you with this mechanism for binding events and procedures together.

HTML Intrinsic Events

Binding events to procedures sounds great, but exactly what types of events are we really talking about? The <SCRIPT> specification proposes a set of so called "intrinisic events." Conceptually, an intrinsic event is generated by an object that is associated with an HTML element. All HTML elements should implement this list of intrinsic events. Presumably, that means that the event is intrinsic to the object. Nomenclature aside, the events themselves are pretty straightforward as shown in Table 6.1.

Table 6.1   HTML Intrinsic Events

Event	Description
Change	This is sent by an object when it is changed, for instance, when the text element in an object changes.
OnClick	Mouse clicks cause an object to send this event.
DblClick	A double mouse click causes an object to send this event.
GotFocus	When a text entry box gets the keyboard cursor, this event is generated.
Hide	Objects send this event when they are hidden by another window or the HTML page has been pushed to the history list.
KeyDown	This event is generated when a user presses a key.
KeyPress	This event indicates that a user has pressed and released a key.
KeyUp	This event occurs when the user releases a key.
Load	This is sent by an object when it is loaded by the browser. This is intended for initialization processes.
LostFocus	When a text box loses the keyboard cursor, this event is generated.
MouseDown	When the mouse is placed over an object and the mouse button is depressed, this event occurs.
MouseMove	When the mouse is moved across an object, this event is generated.
MouseUp	After a MouseDown is released, this event is generated.
Show	Objects send this event when they are shown. (This is the opposite of Hide).
Submit	When a form is submitted this event is generated.
Unload	Sent by an object when it is destroyed by the browser. Use this to implement object shut down procedures.

A Quick Look at the *<SCRIPT>* Tag

An ActiveX script can be included in a Web page either as an embedded script coded directly into your HTML page or as a separate file. But before we dive into the details of the <SCRIPT> tag, let's take another look at the script we included in the Timer example from Chapter 5 (see Listing 6.1).

On the CD

Listing 6.1   *TIMER.HTM*   Timer Example from Chapter 5

```
<SCRIPT LANGUAGE="VBScript" FOR="SpinTimer" EVENT="time">
      Spinner.Angle = (Spinner.Angle - 5) mod 360
      If Spinner.FontSize > 100 Then
            Spinner.FontSize = 10
            If Spinner.Caption = "Spin a web" Then
                  Spinner.Caption = "Don't get dizzy"
            Else
                  Spinner.Caption = "Spin a web"
            End If
      Else
            Spinner.FontSize = Spinner.FontSize + 5
      End If
</SCRIPT>
```

Ignore the program logic and focus on the elements of the <SCRIPT> tag. The first line opens the tag and declares that the script is coded in VBScript. The <FOR> tag says that the SpinTimer object uses this script when the time EVENT fires. Recall from Chapter 5 that SpinTimer is an instance of the Timer ActiveX control used to trigger the movement of the spinning text. The Timer object throws an event called time for which this script is the response function.

The *<SCRIPT>* Tag in Detail

The <SCRIPT> tag has a number of attributes that can be specified. Let's briefly go through each attribute and explain how you'll be using these attributes working with ActiveX scripts (see Table 6.2).

Table 6.2   Attributes of the *<SCRIPT>* Tag

Attribute	Description
EVENT	The intrinsic or object specific event that this script handles.
FOR	Used for binding an object to an event.
IN	Specifies the form or object ID for which this procedure is in scope.
LANGUAGE	Defines the scripting language that the script is written in.
TYPE	Refers to Internet Media Type (RFC 1590) of the script.
SCRIPTENGINE	The URL of the script interpreter to be used to process the SRC.
SRC	The URL of the script source code to be processed by the SCRIPTENGINE.
TYPE	Refers to Internet Media Type (RFC 1590) of the script.

Remember that your HTML documents can contain any number of <SCRIPT> tag blocks. Several of these attributes bear a bit of explanation.

The *SRC* Attribute   A script doesn't have to be embedded directly in your HTML document. You can provide the appropriate URL for your script file using the SRC attribute. For example, you could have saved the body of the script from Listing 6.1 in a file called MYSCRIPT.VBS and coded the HTML document as shown in Listing 6.2.

Listing 6.2   Script Tag Using the *SRC* Attribute

```
<SCRIPT LANGUAGE="VBScript" SRC="myscript.vbs">

   Other script syntax _

</SCRIPT>
```

Note that the logic contained in MYSCRIPT.VBS will be executed before any embedded script syntax in the body of the <SCRIPT> tag.

The *SCRIPTENGINE* Attribute   The script interpreter need not be built directly into the Web browser; the W3C <SCRIPT> tag specification provides a mechanism for inserting the script interpreter directly in an HTML document. The SCRIPTENGINE attribute contains the URL of an interpreter to execute a script. The usage of this attribute is shown in Listing 6.3.

Listing 6.3   Use of the *SCRIPTENGINE* Attribute

```
<OBJECT
 ID="MyScriptEngine"
 CLASSID="clsid:642B65C0-7374-11CF-A3A9-00A0C9034920"
 CODE="http://my.web.com/my/dir/MyScriptEngine"
>
</OBJECT>
<SCRIPT LANGUAGE="MyLanguage"  SCRIPTENGINE="#MyScriptEngine">
  Script code goes here
</SCRIPT>
```

Note that SCRIPTENGINE, LANGUAGE, and TYPE can all be used to specify the interpretive environment for a script. At least one of these attributes must be present. If more than one of these attributes is supplied, then there is a potential conflict. Web browsers will resolve these conflicts using the following order of precedence: SCRIPTENGINE supersedes TYPE, which supersedes LANGUAGE.

Part

I

Ch

6

Extending *TIMER.HTM* Using VBScript

The TIMER.HTM example from Chapter 5 requires that the text that spins be entered directly into the <OBJECT> tag. In addition, the text can spin in only one direction. In the Internet space, Web developers want to give users the power to customize the rendering of Web content to individual tastes. So in this section, you'll change the Timer example to allow the user to select the spinning text and the direction of the spin. In the process, you'll be exposed to the following:

- Processing text box events
- Processing radio button events
- Processing command button events

Laying Out the Form

Since you'll have quite a few objects lying around on this screen, let's start by taking a look at the basic layout of the objects on the page (see fig. 6.1).

FIG. 6.1

Layout of the timer extension form.

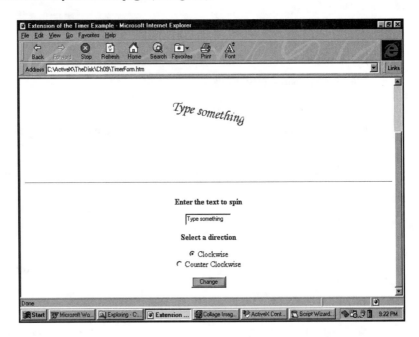

Centered at the top of the page, you'll place an ActiveX Label control. In the VBScript application, this OBJECT will be referred to as "Spinner." The Spinner will interact with the Timer ActiveX control as in the example in Chapter 5. But the Spinner will also interact with each of the following screen objects:

- Textbox (called TextToSpin)
- Radio button (called DirectionRadioBtn)
- Command button (called ChangeBtn)

 T I P   All of the examples in this chapter assume that you have a simple HTML template file (the same template from Chapter 5 if you used it).

To build this more robust version of the Timer example, follow these steps:

1. Start the ActiveX Control Pad, and open your HTML template file from Chapter 5.

2. Update the comment header and `TITLE` value.

3. Save the file to a convenient working directory as `TIMERFORM.HTM`.

   These next steps take you through the process of building the form. The complete listing of `TIMERFORM.HTM` is on the CD so you'll want to check your work against it.

4. After the `<BODY BGCOLOR=#FFFFFF>` tag, add the Label control centered at the top of the page. You can add the control by selecting Edit, Insert ActiveX Control from the Control Pad menu, or you can enter the `<OBJECT>` code directly in the document. Be sure to add some comments to your document to make it easier to read. Your code should look something like Listing 6.4.

Listing 6.4 *TIMERFORM.HTM* Label ActiveX Control Insertion

```
<BODY BGCOLOR=#FFFFFF>
<CENTER>
     <H2>Timer Example Extension</H2>
     <BR>
<OBJECT ID="Spinner" WIDTH=150 HEIGHT=150 ALIGN=center
          HSPACE=30
          VSPACE=50
   CLASSID="CLSID:99B42120-6EC7-11CF-A6C7-00AA00A47DD2">
        <PARAM NAME="angle" VALUE="0">
        <PARAM NAME="alignment" VALUE="2">
        <PARAM NAME="BackStyle" VALUE="0">
        <PARAM NAME="caption" VALUE="Spin a web">
        <PARAM NAME="FontName" VALUE="Monotype Corsiva">
        <PARAM NAME="FontSize" VALUE="30">
     </OBJECT>
```

Note that we have not closed the `<BODY>` tag with a `</BODY>`. You'll take care of that in a moment.

5. Recall from Chapter 5 that the Timer control was used to trigger the repainting of the text within the Label control. The `TIMERFORM.HTM` extension requires this Timer ActiveX control as well. So enter it now. Your code should look something like Listing 6.5.

Listing 6.5 *2TIMERFORM.HTM* Adding the Timer Control

```
<OBJECT ID="SpinTimer" ALIGN=middle
     CLASSID="CLSID:59CCB4A0-727D-11CF-AC36-00AA00A47DD2">
        <PARAM NAME="TimeOut" VALUE="100">
        <PARAM NAME="enable" VALUE="1">
     </OBJECT>
</CENTER>
        <HR>
```

Part

I

Ch

6

6. After the <HR> tag, you'll start the form and include the textbox for entry of the TextToSpin value. The NAME attribute of INPUT is the proper reference to this object from within your script. Your code should look something like Listing 6.6.

Listing 6.6   *3TIMERFORM.HTM*   Start of *FORM* and Code for the *Textbox* Object

```
<! ------------------------------------------------------->
<! -- Form collects parameters for Spinner Label Control >
<! ------------------------------------------------------->
        <FORM NAME="ControlForm">
        <CENTER>
                <B>Enter the text to spin</B><P>
                        <INPUT VALUE="Spin the web" SIZE=15 NAME="TextToSpin"
MAXLENGTH="15">
                        <P>
```

Note that we have not closed the CENTER and FORM tags with a </CENTER> and a </FORM>.

7. Next you'll need to add the radio button set. Your code should look something like Listing 6.7. Don't worry about what the onClick does. We'll get to that in a moment.

Listing 6.7   *4TIMERFORM.HTM*   Code for the Radio Button Object

```
<B>Select a direction</B><P>
        <INPUT TYPE=RADIO VALUE="Clockwise" ONCLICK="GoClockwise"
        CHECKED ID="Clockwise" NAME="DirectionRadioBtn" =True> Clockwise
        <BR>
        <INPUT TYPE=RADIO VALUE="Counter" ONCLICK="GoCounterClockwise"
        ID="Counter" NAME="DirectionRadioBtn"> Counter Clockwise
        <P>
```

Remember that to link radio buttons together (to implement mutually exclusive selection), you use the same NAME. The NAME attribute is also the proper reference to this object from within your script. Don't forget to offer some descriptive text for each of the options.

8. Finally you'll need to include a command button. You'll also want to close out your FORM and CENTER tags from above as well. Your code should look something like Listing 6.8.

Listing 6.8 5   *TIMERFORM.HTM*   Code for Including the Command Button Object

```
<INPUT TYPE=Button VALUE="Change" ONCLICK="DoChangeBtn" NAME="ChangeBtn">
        </CENTER>
        </FORM>
</BODY>
</HTML>
```

In three of these control items, you've used an attribute called OnClick. This is an intrinsic event common to all controls as discussed previously. The onClick event is used to execute a procedure when the object is clicked. So let's examine each example for a moment:

- **DirectionRadioBtn**—When the user selects the Clockwise option, the browser executes the GoClockwise procedure. When the user selects the Counter Clockwise option, the browser executes the GoCounterClockwise procedure.

- **ChangeBtn**—When the user clicks the change button, the browser executes the DoChangeBtn procedure.

Coding the Script

In building the form, you created a requirement for four functions. Table 6.3 summarizes the functions you'll need to build.

Table 6.3 Procedures Required for the *TIMERFORM.HTM* Example

Procedure	Description
DoChangeBtn	This procedure sets the values of ChangeInAngle and Spinner.Caption.
GoClockwise	The user may select a direction for the text to spin. This procedure sets ChangeInAngle to turn clockwise.
GoCounterClockwise	The user may select a direction for the text to spin. This procedure sets ChangeInAngle to turn counterclockwise.
SpinTimer_Time	This procedure responds to the Time event thrown by SpinTimer.

These functions require some additional variables that are contained with brief explanation in Table 6.4.

Table 6.4 Other Variables Required for *TIMERFORM.HTM*

Variable	Description
ChangeInAngle	The Label control spins by changing the Spinner.Angle field. The amount to change this angle controls the speed and direction of the spinning text.
NextAngle	The change in direction must be triggered by pressing the command button. This variable stores the next ChangeInAngle value.

Part

I

Ch

6

To start the script portion of TIMERFORM.HTM, follow these steps:

1. First, you'll insert a script immediately following the <TITLE> tag set before the start of the <BODY>. To do this, place your cursor after the </TITLE> tag and select Tools, Script Wizard. Place your cursor over the Global Variables entry in the Insert Actions box.

Press the right mouse button and select New Global Variable from the list (see fig. 6.2). The first global variable to declare is ChangeInAngle.

FIG. 6.2

Declare the required global variables.

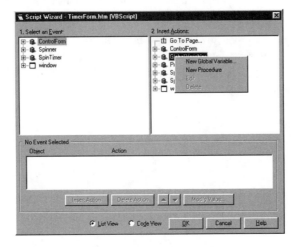

2. Repeat this step for NextAngle. Your code should look something like Listing 6.9. Note that you'll also need to initialize both variables as shown in Listing 6.9.

On the CD

Listing 6.9 *6TIMERFORM.HTM* Start of *<SCRIPT>* and Initialization

```
<TITLE>Extension of the Timer Example</TITLE>

<SCRIPT LANGUAGE="VBScript">
    '-------------------------------------------------
    '-- Declare and intialize script-wide variables
    '-------------------------------------------------
    Dim ChangeInAngle
    Dim NextAngle

    ChangeInAngle = 5
    NextAngle = -5
```

3. Next, you'll code the DoChangeBtn procedure that is executed when the command button is pressed. Remember that DoChangeBtn's job is to set the Caption and Angle values in Spinner. To add DoChangeBtn, select the Procedures item in the Script Wizard's Action List. Press the right mouse button and select New Procedure. For this procedure, you'll need to select the Code View in order to enter the required VBScript code shown in Listing 6.10.

Listing 6.10   *7TIMERFORM.HTM*   Coding the *DoChangeBtn* Procedures

```
'------------------------------------------------
'-- Handle change button presses
'------------------------------------------------
sub DoChangeBtn
     Spinner.Caption = ControlForm.TextToSpin.Value
     ChangeInAngle = NextAngle
end sub
```

Look carefully at the reference to the text within your textbox object. To set Spinner.Caption to the appropriate value, the code references ControlForm.TextToSpin.Value. Table 6.5 breaks the construction of this reference down for you.

Table 6.5   How Textbox Objects are Accessed in VBScript

Reference	Explanation
ControlForm	The NAME of the FORM where the textbox appears.
TextToSpin	The NAME of the textbox INPUT object.
Value	The attribute of the textbox INPUT object to be referenced. In this case, the reference is to the VALUE attribute.

4. Next code the GoClockwise and GoCounterClockwise procedures that are triggered by clicks on the radio button object DirectionRadioBtn. These functions are responsible for setting the NextAngle variable. Use the Script Wizard to add new procedures as described in the previous step. Your code should look something like Listing 6.11.

Listing 6.11   *GoClockwise* and *GoCounterClockwise* Procedures

```
'------------------------------------------------
'-- Set the direction to Clockwise
'------------------------------------------------
sub GoClockwise
 NextAngle = -5
end sub


'------------------------------------------------
'-- Set the direction to Counter Clockwise
'------------------------------------------------
sub GoCounterClockwise
 NextAngle = 5
end sub
```

Part
I

Ch
6

5. Finally, you'll code the response procedure for the Timer ActiveX control `Time` event. This function is quite similar to the script you used in the Chapter 5 example. Your code should look something like Listing 6.12. (And don't forget to close out the `<SCRIPT>` tag.)

On the CD

Listing 6.12 *9TIMERFORM.HTM* The *SpinTimer_Time* Procedure

```
'------------------------------------------------
'-- Handle timer event
'------------------------------------------------
sub SpinTimer_Time
  Spinner.Angle = (Spinner.Angle + ChangeInAngle) mod 360
 If Spinner.FontSize > 100 Then
   Spinner.FontSize = 10
 Else
   Spinner.FontSize = Spinner.FontSize + 5
 EndIf
end sub
</SCRIPT>
```

Instead of using the `FOR` and `EVENT` attributes of the `<SCRIPT>` tag, this example requires an alternative reference for binding an `EVENT` and its response procedure. This function employs the alternative `ID_EVENT` form for an event response function. In this example, the timer has an `ID=SpinTimer` and throws the `EVENT` time; the response function has the name `SpinTimer_Time`.

6. After adding these procedures, you'll need to associate them with the appropriate events. This is done in the ActiveX Control Pad by using the Select an Event window. Start with the `ChangeBtn onClick` event. Select this item from the Select an Event window. Then double-click the `DoChangeBtn` procedure from the the Insert Actions window. When you're finished, the screen should look like figure 6.3.

FIG. 6.3

Link events to actions with the Script Wizard.

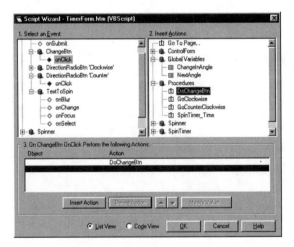

Go ahead and link the events associated with other elements of the interface using this procedure. Table 6.6 lists the associations you must link.

Table 6.6   Events and Actions

Event	Action
ChangeBtn.OnClick	DoChangeBtn
DirectionRadioBtn.OnClick "Clockwise"	GoClockwise
DirectionRadioBtn.OnClick "Counter"	GoCounterClockwise
SpinTimer.Time	SpinTimer_Time

7. Save your work as TIMERFORM.HTM.

Now that you've completed the HTML document, you can test your work using Microsoft Internet Explorer 3.0. These next steps take you through testing out your HTML document:

1. Start Microsoft Internet Explorer 3.0.

2. Place the text cursor in the document text box and type TIMERFORM.HTM. Be sure to include the fully qualified path to your document. Press Enter.

3. If you've done everything correctly, the HTML document will look similar to figure 6.1.

Part

I

Ch

6

ActiveX Scripting Services

Web browsers such as Netscape have recently begun providing scripting languages. This empowers Web developers to include conditional logic and basic forms processing directly into the Web page. Microsoft's Internet Explorer 3.0 provides a subset of Visual Basic called *VBScript*. However, ActiveX Scripting provides much more than just a scripting language for Web browsers. ActiveX is a platform for developing any number of scripting languages for whatever purpose Web developers require. Using ActiveX script services, a scripting language can be implemented on any number of platforms. ■

VBScript data types

VBScript data types are all subtypes based on the `Variant` data type.

VBScript variables and constants

Variables and constants are required for any serious programming. VBScript supplies all the support you need.

VBScript operators

VBScript supports logical, arithmetic, and comparison operators.

VBScript flow of control

VBScript provides a number of the traditional constructs for controlling program flow.

VBScript procedures

Build your own procedures to call from HTML pages using VBScript.

VBScript runtime functions

VBScript provides an excellent set of runtime functions.

ActiveX Scripting

ActiveX Scripting is constructed from two basic major components:

- **ActiveX Scripting Hosts**—The applications on which a script is run.
- **ActiveX Scripting Engines**—The language the script is written in.

ActiveX Scripting can be hosted on any number of applications. The best example of an ActiveX Scripting host is MSIE 3.0. MSIE 3.0 supports VBScript. In addition, ActiveX Scripting provides an environment to support scripting on Web servers, Internet authoring tools, or other applications, in any number of scripting languages. So, look forward to some new languages in addition to VBScript and JavaScript.

Relationship to VBA and VB 4.0, and VBScript Language Overview

Microsoft has positioned Visual Basic for Applications (VBA) as the scripting tool for use in applications like Word and Excel. Visual Basic 4.0 provides a complete development kit for the Windows environment. VBA and VBScript are both subsets of the richer VB4 development platform. Don't worry though, you'll see that VBScript is a robust tool that's easy to use.

Before you start using VBScript, take note of the following section. The following sections provide an introduction to the lexical structure and syntax of VBScript. If you've developed software in Visual Basic before, you'll be off and running in no time.

VBScript Data Types

VBScript handles many different types of data; however, all of these data types (called *subtypes* in Microsoft-speak) are based upon the base type Variant (see Table 7.1). The Variant type provides an intelligent container for data because it's smart enough to behave properly whether it contains an integer or a string.

Table 7.1   VBScript Data Types

Subtype	Description
Boolean	Valid values for this type of data are True and False.
Byte	Used for integers in the range 0 to 255.
Date	Used to store data to be represented as dates. The date must be between January 1, 100 to December 31, 9999.
Double	Used for floating point numbers in the range of $-1.79769313486232E308$ to $-4.94065645841247E-324$ for negative values and $4.94065645841247E-324$ to $1.79769313486232E308$ for positive values.

Subtype	Description
Empty	When the data is uninitialized, it contains a value of zero for number variables or an empty string for string type variables.
Error	Stores the error number.
Integer	Used for integers in the range –32,768 to 32,767.
Long	Used for integers in the range –2,147,483,648 to 2,147,483,647.
Object	Contains OLE automation objects.
Single	Stores floating point numbers in the range of –3.402823E38 to –1.401298E-45 for negative values and 1.401298E-45 to 3.402823E38 for positive values using this type.
String	Stores variable length character data in variables of this type.

There are numerous functions available to convert one data type to another. Table 7.2 summarizes some of the more important functions.

Table 7.2 Data Type Conversion Functions

Function	Description
CBool	Converts any expression to a Boolean subtype.
CByte	Converts any expression to a Byte subtype.
CDate	Converts any date expression to a Date subtype.
CStr	Converts any expression to a String subtype.
Str	Converts any numeric expression to a String subtype.
Val	Converts any string expression containing numbers to a number.

Most of these are self-explanatory, but let's take a moment and look at the CStr function in more detail. You'll use the CStr function all the time because HTML is constructed from text, so many of your outputs will have to be CStr'ed before display time.

Table 7.3 explains how CStr converts various types of data.

Table 7.3 CStr Conversion Rules

Expression	Conversion
Boolean	A String variable containing either True or False
Date	A String containing the date in the system's short format

continues

Part

I

Ch

7

Table 7.3 Continued

Expression	Conversion
Empty	An empty String
Error	A String containing Error: and the error number
Other numeric	A String containing the number

VBScript Variables and Constants

In general, variables refer to a place in memory used to store a particular value. To access the data stored in memory, your program refers to the data's variable name. All variables in VBScript are Variant type (including all the subtypes mentioned previously). The following sections guide you through the important facts concerning variables in VBScript including:

- Rules for naming variables
- Variable declaration
- Assignment
- Variable scope

Rules for Naming Variables   Names of functions and variables all must conform to the same rules in VBScript. The following criteria are required to construct a valid name for variables and functions:

- Maximum length for any name is 255 characters.
- All names must begin with an alphabetic character.
- Names may not contain embedded periods.
- Names must be unique within their scope.

Variable and Constant Declaration   There are two ways to declare a variable within VBScript:

- Implicit declaration
- Explicit declaration

Implicit declaration means that you can instantiate a new variable simply by using within a code block. This is not, however, the recommended method. You could get unpredictable results simply by misspelling a variable name within the script (creating a second variable and thoroughly confusing things). Instead, the recommended approach is to use explicit declaration. *Explicit declaration* requires that all variables be declared before use. Under this method, variables are declared using the Dim statement.

TIP Its good practice to have Option Explicit set directly after your opening <SCRIPT>. This is a good time to declare all of your variables with the Dim statement as well. This practice ensures that you use the preferred explicit declaration method and that all your variables are declared.

The best way to get familiar with the Dim statement is to look at a couple of quick examples.

Listing 7.1 Declaring a Single Variable

```
<SCRIPT LANGUAGE="VBScript">

      Option Explicit

 Dim i

 </SCRIPT>
```

Listing 7.1 shows the declaration of a single item i. Of course, you can declare multiple variables on a single line by using the comma separator as shown in Listing 7.2.

Listing 7.2 Declaring Multiple Variables

```
<SCRIPT LANGUAGE="VBScript">

       Option Explicit

 Dim i, j, k, l

 </SCRIPT>
```

You can also use an array to store a list of data. There are two types of arrays you'll want to use: dynamic arrays and static arrays. Static arrays are declared as shown in Listing 7.3.

Listing 7.3 Declaring a Static Array

```
<SCRIPT LANGUAGE="VBScript">

       Option Explicit

 Dim A(5)

 </SCRIPT>
```

Part

I

Ch

7

Note that VBScript array indices start from zero. Of course, you can have multidimensional arrays as well (see Listing 7.4).

Listing 7.4 Declaring a Static Multidimensional Array

```
<SCRIPT LANGUAGE="VBScript">

    Option Explicit

Dim A(6,5)

</SCRIPT>
```

The array A in Listing 7.4 contains six rows and five columns of data. An array may contain up to 60 dimensions.

Dynamic arrays are declared in a somewhat similar fashion (using ReDim) and then are sized as appropriate at runtime. Listing 7.5 shows the proper declaration and ReDim of a dynamic array.

Listing 7.5 Declaring a Dynamic Array and a Constant

```
<SCRIPT LANGUAGE="VBScript">

    Option Explicit

Dim A()
Dim iItemCount
Dim GLOBAL_MAX

    GLOBAL_MAX = 6
...
...
iItemCount = FromSomeWhere()

if (iItemCount < GLOBAL_MAX) Then
        Redim A(iItemCount)
Else
 Redim A(GLOBAL_MAX)
EndIf

</SCRIPT>
```

Declaring a constant in VBScript is no different than declaring a variable. So, if your applications require constants, you may want to adopt a naming standard for declaring constants versus variables. Most VBScript developers will probably declare all constants with names that are all capital. For example, look at the declaration and usage of GLOBAL_MAX in Listing 7.5.

Assignment   Once a variable is declared, it is usually initialized to some value with an assignment statement. Assignment for variables in VBScript is accomplished using the equal sign (=). Listing 7.6 shows a simple assignment statement in VBScript.

Listing 7.6 Simple Assignment Statement

```
<SCRIPT LANGUAGE="VBScript">

      Option Explicit

 Dim A
 ...
 ...
 A = 5
 ...
</SCRIPT>
```

Initializing arrays is quite straightforward, as well. See Listing 7.7 for example syntax.

Listing 7.7 Initializing an Array

```
<SCRIPT LANGUAGE="VBScript">

      Option Explicit

 Dim A(5)
 ...
 ...
 A(0) = 52
 A(1) = 47
 A(2) = 22
 A(3) = 512
 A(4) = 524
 A(5) = 2

</SCRIPT>
```

Variable Scope   All programming languages apply the concept of scope to variables and procedures. *Scope* refers to the visibility of variables. If a variable is within a procedure's scope, it can be read or changed. In VBScript, a variable declared within a procedure is visible only within that procedure. These types of variables are often referred to as local variables or procedure-level variables.

A variable may also be declared within a script outside of any single procedure. This variable is visible to all the procedures within the <SCRIPT> and </SCRIPT> pair. These types of variables are often referred to as *script-level variables*.

A few examples will illustrate how scope rules work within VBScript. The first example demonstrates that two procedures can have a variable of the same name referencing different values (see Listing 7.8).

Part

I

Ch

7

Listing 7.8   Example of Local Variable Names

```
<SCRIPT LANGUAGE="VBScript">

     Option Explicit

 sub DoSomeThing

          Dim Thing

          Thing = 5
          If Thing = 5 Then
           msgbox "The Thing = 5"
          Else
           msgbox "The Thing does not = 5"
  EndIf
 end sub

 sub DoAnotherThing

          Dim Thing, AnotherThing

          Thing = 8
          If Thing = 5 Then
           msgbox "The Thing = 5"
          Else
           msgbox "The Thing does not = 5"
  EndIf
 end sub

</SCRIPT>
```

In this case, Thing is equal to 5 while the DoSomeThing procedure is executing, but equal to 8 when DoAnotherThing is executing. In fact, the two Things point at completely different areas of memory. The procedure DoSomeThing, however, has no visibility to the AnotherThing variable declared in DoAnotherThing.

The persistence or lifetime of a variable is also an important part of scope. Note that when the procedure DoSomeThing is executing, the variable Thing is set to 5. However, when the procedure ends, the variable Thing dies. So, when DoSomeThing is entered again, Thing is not equal to five until the assignment statement (Thing = 5) is executed.

The second example, shown in Listing 7.9, demonstrates the scope of script-level variables.

Listing 7.9   Example of Script-Level Variables

```
<SCRIPT LANGUAGE="VBScript">

          Option Explicit

          Dim Thing
```

```
            Thing = 5

    sub DoSomeThing

            If Thing = 5 Then
             msgbox "The Thing = 5"
            Else
             msgbox "The Thing does not = 5"
     EndIf
    end sub

    sub DoAnotherThing

            If Thing = 5 Then
             msgbox "The Thing = 5"
            Else
             msgbox "The Thing does not = 5"
     EndIf
    end sub

    </SCRIPT>
```

In this case, Thing is set equal to 5 script-wide. The procedures DoSomeThing and AnotherThing both see the same Thing with the same value. The lifetime of a script-wide variable is (shockingly enough) the same as the life of the script. While the script is being executed, Thing is visible to all procedures within the script.

VBScript Operators

All programming languages employ a set of operators to represent the manipulation of data within the application. There are three types of operators of concern:

- Arithemetic operators
- Logical operators
- Comparison operators

Arithmetic Operators Table 7.4 summarizes the arithmetic operators available for use in VBScript applications.

Table 7.4 VBScript Arithmetic Operators

Operator	Description
^	Exponentiation
-	Unary negation
*	Multiplication

continues

Part

I

Ch

7

Table 7.4 Continued

Operator	Description
/	Division
\	Integer division
Mod	Generates the remainder from division
+	Addition
-	Subtraction
&	String concatenation

The order of precedence for these operators is the same as their order in Table 7.4. Exponentiations are evaluated before unary negation. For expressions that contain more than one multiplication/division operation, the expression is evaluated from left to right. This same process is followed for addition/subtraction operations. Note that string concatenation is not really an arithmetic operation, but in terms of precedence it is reflected accurately.

Logical Operators   Table 7.5 summarizes the logical operations that can be accomplished with VBScript.

Table 7.5 Logical Operators

Operator	Description
Not	Logical negation
And	Logical combination
Or	Logical or
Xor	Logical exclusive or
Eqv	Logical equivalence
Imp	Logical implication

Comparison Operators   Table 7.6 summarizes the comparison operations that can be accomplished with VBScript.

Table 7.6 Comparison Operators

Operator	Description
=	Equality
<>	Inequality
<	Less than

Operator	Description
>	Greater than
<=	Less than or equal to
>=	Greater than or equal to
ls	Evaluates to true when two variables point at the same object.

Flow of Control in VBScript

Control structures, or *conditional logic*, are the cornerstone of any programming language. VBScript offers a complete complement of control structures for use in your applications. This section briefly touches on each of the following:

- If...Then...Else
- Do...Loop
- While...Wend
- For...Next

If...Then...Else   This construct is the seminal control structure for programming languages. Flow of control is passed based upon the evaluation of Boolean expression. Listing 7.10 demonstrates the use of this control structure in a VBScript application.

Listing 7.10   *If...Then...Else* Example

```
<SCRIPT LANGUAGE="VBScript">

     Option Explicit

     Dim bDataEntered
     Dim iCheckData

     iCheckData = 1

 bDataEntered = CheckDataStatus(iCheckData)
 If bDataEntered Then
  msgbox "The data has been entered."
 Else
  msgbox "The data has not been entered"
 EndIf

</SCRIPT>
```

Part

I

Ch

7

In this example, assume that CheckDataStatus returns either True or False, indicating if some data has been entered by the user. If the CheckDataStatus returns True, then the message box presented to the user indicates that the data has been entered. Otherwise, the message box indicates that the data has not been entered.

Do...Loop   The Do...Loop control structure is used to execute a block code while a condition is True, or until a condition is True. Use this syntax when the number of times you need to execute a set of statements is indeterminate. Listing 7.11 demonstrates the use of Do...Loop with the While comparison operation.

Listing 7.11   *Do...Loop* Using *While* Evaluate Before

```
<SCRIPT LANGUAGE="VBScript">

     Option Explicit

     sub Counter(NumberToCountTo)

      Dim iCurrentCount

          iCurrentCount = 0


      Do While iCurrentCount <= NumberToCountTo
       iCurrentCount = iCurrentCount + 1
      Loop
   end sub

 </SCRIPT>
```

Note that the While expression evaluation can also occur at the end of the loop as shown in Listing 7.12.

Listing 7.12   *Do...Loop* Using *While* Evaluate After

```
<SCRIPT LANGUAGE="VBScript">

     Option Explicit

     sub Counter(NumberToCountTo)

      Dim iCurrentCount

          iCurrentCount = 0


     Do
       iCurrentCount = iCurrentCount + 1
     Loop While iCurrentCount <= NumberToCountTo
   end sub

 </SCRIPT>
```

You can also use Do to repeat a block of code until some condition becomes true. Consider the following example in Listing 7.13.

Listing 7.13 Do...Loop Using *Until*

```
<SCRIPT LANGUAGE="VBScript">

      Option Explicit

      sub Counter(NumberToCountTo)

            Dim iCurrentCount

            iCurrentCount = 0


        Do Until iCurrentCount = NumberToCountTo
         iCurrentCount = iCurrentCount + 1
        Loop
   end sub

</SCRIPT>
```

Note that Until can be evaluated after Loop, as well as a part of the Do shown in Listing 7.13.

The Do loop also provides a mechanism to exit the loop based on some other condition. Say, for example, that you wanted the Counter function above to always count to NumberToCountTo unless NumberToCountTo is higher than 50. A way to implement this is shown in Listing 7.14.

Listing 7.14 Using *Exit Do*

```
<SCRIPT LANGUAGE="VBScript">

      Option Explicit

      Dim MAX_TO_COUNT

      MAX_TO_COUNT = 50

      sub Counter(iNumberToCountTo)

       Dim iCurrentCount

            iCurrentCount = 0


        Do Until iCurrentCount = iNumberToCountTo
         If iCurrentCount > MAX_TO_COUNT Then
          Exit Do
         EndIf
         iCurrentCount = iCurrentCount + 1
        Loop
   end sub

</SCRIPT>
```

Part

I

Ch

7

While...Wend   Microsoft included the `While...Wend` statement for programmers making the transition from older versions of VB. The `While...Wend` control structure is not as flexible as the `Do...Loop`. So, most new applications should use `Do...Loop`. However, you can use `While...Wend` to execute a block of code while some condition is `true`. The following example in Listing 7.15 reworks the example in Listing 7.11.

Listing 7.15   Using the *While...Wend* Statement

```
<SCRIPT LANGUAGE="VBScript">

    Option Explicit

    sub Counter(NumberToCountTo)

    Dim iCurrentCount

        iCurrentCount = 0

    While iCurrentCount <= NumberToCountTo
      iCurrentCount = iCurrentCount + 1
    Wend
  end sub

</SCRIPT>
```

For...Next   When you need to execute a series of statements for a fixed number of times, the `For...Next` loop is your best choice (see Listing 7.16).

Listing 7.16   Using the *For...Next* Loop

```
<SCRIPT LANGUAGE="VBScript">

    Option Explicit

    sub CountTo10()

    Dim iCounter

    For iCounter = 1 To 10
      DoSomething
    Next
  end sub

</SCRIPT>
```

The `Next` statement triggers an increment of size `Step` in `iCounter`. Say you wanted to execute the same logic as in Listing 7.16, only incrementing by two rather than one. You'll use `Step` to make this happen (see Listing 7.17).

Listing 7.17   Using *For...Next* with *Step*

```
<SCRIPT LANGUAGE="VBScript">

     Option Explicit

     sub CountTo10()

      Dim iCounter

      For iCounter = 2 To 20 Step 2
       DoSomething
      Next
 end sub

</SCRIPT>
```

Now Next increments iCounter by two on each iteration.

The For loop also provides a mechanism to exit the loop based on some other condition. Say, for example, that you wanted CountTo10 to execute DoSomething all ten times unless a monitoring function called SomeError returns True. One way to implement this is shown in Listing 7.18.

Listing 7.18   Exiting a *For...Next* Loop

```
<SCRIPT LANGUAGE="VBScript">

     Option Explicit

     sub CountTo10()

      Dim iCounter

      For iCounter = 1 To 10

                  DoSomething

                  If SomeError Then
                   msgbox "Some error occurred"
                   Exit For
                  EndIf
       Next
 end sub

</SCRIPT>
```

Part

I

Ch

7

VBScript Procedures

VBScript provides the following two different types of procedures for organizing blocks of code:

- Sub
- Function

You've already seen the Sub procedure in a previous example with no accompanying explanation. Now, let's define things a bit more clearly. A Sub procedure is appropriate when the block of code you're executing does not need to return a value. For example, Listing 7.18 shows that the function CountTo10 executes the DoSomething procedure ten times. If SomeError occurs, then the procedure is halted. CountTo10 does not have any responsibility for returning information to the calling procedure.

You'll use Function procedures in cases where a value needs to be returned. Listing 7.19 demonstrates the proper way to declare and implement a Function.

Listing 7.19   Declaring and Implementing a *Function*

```
<SCRIPT LANGUAGE="VBScript">

     Option Explicit

     Function CentimetersToInches(Centimeters)

       CentimetersToInches = Centimeters * 2.54

  End Function

 </SCRIPT>
```

Note that all functions return a value of type Variant (as with all values within VBScript).

Once Function and Sub procedures are declared and implemented, other procedures must call them. You'll call a Sub procedure in one of two ways. Listing 7.20 demonstrates both of these methods.

Listing 7.20   How to Call a *Sub* Procedure

```
<SCRIPT LANGUAGE="VBScript">

 DoSomethingWith This, That, TheOtherThing

 Call DoSomethingWith(This, That, TheOtherThing)

 </SCRIPT>
```

The Sub procedure DoSomethingWith, takes three parameters. In the first example, each of the three parameters are placed after the Sub call and are separated by commas. The second example uses the Call statement. Parameters passed to a Sub called with the Call statement must be comma separated and enclosed within parentheses.

You'll call a Function procedure in one of two ways, as well. Because Function and Sub procedures play different roles, the syntax for using them is slightly different (see Listing 7.21).

Listing 7.21 How to Call a *Function* Procedure

```
<SCRIPT LANGUAGE="VBScript">

 fInches = CentimetersToInches(fCentimeters)

     msgbox = fCentimeters & "cm converts to" & = CentimetersToInches(fCentimeters)
        & " in"

</SCRIPT>
```

The first usage in Listing 7.21 sets fInches equal to the result of executing the CentimetersToInches Function. The second usage demonstrates that the Function procedures can be placed anywhere that the results returned by that Function can be placed.

VBScript Runtime

To get an idea of some of the runtime procedures available for writing your scripts, this next section reviews some of the important available functions. Of course, this section makes no attempt to catalog and document the entire VBScript runtime library. The best source for documentation on VBScript functions and procedures is the VB 4.0 help file. You can also find a pretty good downloadable documentation set on Microsoft's Web site at **http://www.microsoft.com/vbscript/default.htm**. Instead, this section briefly summarizes the tools available to your VBScript applications.

Working with Date and Time   VBScript provides a number of tools for working the date and time data in your scripts. Table 7.7 briefly summarizes a few of the most often used functions.

Table 7.7 Date and Time Functions for VBScript

Function	Description
Date	Gets the current system date
Time	Gets the current system time
Day	Provides a date and returns a number between one and 31, giving the day of the month

Part

I

Ch

7

continues

Table 7.7 Continued

Function	Description
Month	Provides a date and returns a number between one and 12, giving the month of the year
Year	Provides a date and returns the year
Hour	Provides a date and returns a number between one and 23, indicating the hour
Minute	Provides a date and returns a number between one and 59, indicating the minute
Second	Provides a date and returns a number between one and 59, indicating the second

Working with Math   VBScript also provides a diverse set of mathematical functions for manipulating numbers in your scripts. Table 7.8 briefly summarizes a few of the most often used functions.

Table 7.8 VBScript Math Functions

Function	Description
Atn	Provides a number and returns the arctangent of that number
Cos	Provides a number and returns the cosine of that number
Sin	Provides a number and returns the sine of that number
Tan	Provides a number and returns the tangent of that number
Exp	Provides a number and returns e raised to the power of that number
Log	Provides a number and returns the natural logarithm of that number
Sqr	Provides a number and returns the square root of that number

Working with Strings   VBScript gives developers an excellent group of functions for handling strings within your scripts. Table 7.9 briefly summarizes a few of the most often used functions.

Table 7.9 String Functions in VBScript

Function	Description
Asc	Returns the ASCII character code of the first letter of the supplied string
Chr	Returns the character of the supplied ASCII code

Function	Description
Instr	Returns the position of the first supplied string in the second supplied string
Len	Returns the number of characters in the supplied string
Lcase	Returns the supplied string as an all lowercase string
Ucase	Returns the supplied string as an all uppercase string
Left	Returns a specified number of characters from the left of a supplied string
Right	Returns a specified number of characters from the right of a supplied string
Trim	Returns the supplied string stripped of leading and trailing spaces
LTrim	Returns the supplied string stripped of leading spaces
Rtrim	Returns the supplied string stripped of trailing spaces

Working with the User Interface   VBScript provides only two functions that allow you to generate stand-alone windows from your Web page. Table 7.10 briefly summarizes these two functions.

Table 7.10   User Interface Functions in VBScript

Function	Description
InputBox	Displays a dialog box to obtain input from the user
MsgBox	Displays a dialog box with a message and an OK button

Working with *Variant* Subtypes   Recall that VBScript has only one base type of data called Variant. Of course, the Variant holds data in a number of forms called *subtypes*. You'll use functions from Table 7.11 to find out the proper subtype for an object.

Table 7.11   VBScript Functions for Working with *Variant*

Function	Description
IsArray	Returns true when the supplied variable contains an array
IsDate	Returns true when the supplied variable contains a date
IsEmpty	Returns true if the supplied variable is uninitialized or set explicitly to Empty (zero for numbers, the empty string (()) for strings)

Part

I

Ch

7

continues

Table 7.11 Continued

Function	Description
IsError	Returns true when the supplied variable contains a valid Error number
IsNull	Returns true when the supplied variable contains no valid data
IsNumeric	Returns true when the supplied variable can be evaluated as a number
IsObject	Returns true when the supplied variable points to an OLE automation object
VarType	Returns a string containing the subtype of the specified variable

CHAPTER 8

Using VBScript—A Customer Survey

You can use VBScript to implement forms that collect information from users. In this chapter, you'll follow a central example that shows how to implement such a form smoothly and easily. ∎

Use VBScript for client-side scripting

Adding program functionality to your Web pages can be done with sophistication by using VBScript.

Comparing VBScript with JavaScript

If you've already been using JavaScript with Netscape, a quick comparison to JavaScript will ease your introduction to VBScript.

Building VBScript procedures

Breaking functions up into procedures is an important part of using VBScript.

Responding to events fired by <FORM> elements

User interface elements on the <FORM> can trigger events and execute procedures.

Building the Application

This chapter is based upon a single, extensive example. You'll construct a Web page to collect customer survey information. Using VBScript, you'll build the form and write the survey results to a simple message dialog box.

N O T E   After you've mastered the SMTP control in Chapter 19, you might want to come back to this application and add the capability for the user to e-mail results from the form. ■

In this example, you'll work with a number of different form elements, including:

■ Radio buttons

■ Checkboxes

■ Text fields

■ Command buttons

To process the customer survey information, you'll build six functions:

■ `setSex()`—This function sets the text to be printed in the customer survey output based on the customer's gender.

■ `setMagazineText()`—This function sets the text to be printed in the customer survey output based on what magazines the customer reads.

■ `setIncome()`—This function sets the text to be printed in the customer survey output based on the customer's income.

■ `setPayAmount()`—This function sets the text to be printed in the customer survey output based on the amount a customer would pay for a hypothetical new service.

■ `setRating()`—This function sets the text to be printed in the customer survey output based on the customer's rating of service received to-date.

■ `makeMessage()`—This function uses text set by the other functions to produce the properly formatted survey output for presentation in a dialog box.

The next two sections show you a JavaScript implementation of the example, and then a VBScript implementation. The review of JavaScript will be cursory. The ActiveX sections will guide you step-by-step through the process of building the example.

Using JavaScript

Many Web developers are making the transition from using JavaScript to using VBScript. To help you get started quickly with VBScript, the following section briefly describes the construction of the customer survey example in JavaScript.

Begin by looking at Listing 8.1, which shows the script portion of the implementation for the customer survey application in JavaScript.

Listing 8.1 *JAVA-CUSTOMER-SURVEY.HTM* **JavaScript Version of the Customer Survey**

```
<HTML>
<HEAD><TITLE>Customer Survey Example</TITLE>
<SCRIPT LANGUAGE="JavaScript">

        var incomeText;
        var sexText;
        var magazineText = "";
        var payAmountText;
        var ratingText;


        function setSex(sex) {

              if ( sex.value == "Male" ) {
                    sexText = "You're a girl !";
              }
              else {
                    sexText = "You're a boy !";

              }

        }

        function setMagazineText(magazine) {

              var form = magazine.form;

              if ( magazine.checked ) {
                    magazineText = magazineText + magazine.value
              }
              else {
                    magazineText = ""
                    form.timeMagazine.checked = false;
                    form.usNews.checked = false;
                    form.newsWeek.checked = false;
                    form.atlanticMonthly.checked = false;
                    form.tvGuide.checked = false;
              }
        }

        function setIncome(incomeBracket) {

              if ( incomeBracket.value == "incomeBracket1" ) {
                    incomeText = "Modest Income"
              }

              if ( incomeBracket.value == "incomeBracket2" ) {
                    incomeText = "Middle Income"
              }

              if ( incomeBracket.value == "incomeBracket3" ) {
```

continues

Listing 8.1   Continued

```
                        incomeText = "High Income"
            }

    }

    function setRating(rating) {
        ratingText = rating.value;
    }

    function setPayAmount(amount) {

        if ( amount.value < 15 ) {
            payAmountText = "Tight wad";
        }
        if ( amount.value >= 15 && amount.value < 25 ) {
            payAmountText = "Bargain hunter";
        }
        if ( amount.value >= 25 ) {
            payAmountText = "Sucker";
        }

    }

    function makeMessage() {

        var messageText;
        if ( ratingText == "excellent" ) {

            messageText = "So you gave us an excellent rating. We find that a"
                        + payAmountText
                        + " seems to respond well to our service.  So we
                                won't tell your mother that "
                        + sexText
                        + " And with a"
                        + incomeText
                        + " you can continue on as a  "
                        + magazineText + "aficionado!!"
                alert(messageText);
        }

        if ( ratingText == "good" ) {
            messageText = "So you gave us a good rating. We find that a "
                        + payAmountText
                        + " like you probably would. Your mother tells us that "
                        + sexText
                        + " With a "
                        + incomeText
                        + " that often acts like a "
                        + magazineText + "genius!!"
                alert(messageText);
        }

        if ( ratingText == "fair" ) {
```

```
                    messageText = "So you gave us a fair rating. Of course a "
                              + payAmountText
                              + " like you probably would. But does your mother
                                    know that "
                              + sexText
                              + " People like you with a "
                              + incomeText
                              + " are known to be "
                              + magazineText + "IDIOTS!!!!"
                        alert(messageText);
            }

            if ( ratingText == "poor" ) {
                messageText = "So you gave us a poor rating. Of course a "
                              + payAmountText
                              + " like you probably would. But does your mother
                                    know that "
                              + sexText
                              + " People like you with a "
                              + incomeText
                              + " are known to be "
                              + magazineText + "IDIOTS!!!!"
                        alert(messageText);

            }
        }

</SCRIPT>
</HEAD>
```

Listing 8.2 shows the construction of the form with JavaScript.

On the CD

Listing 8.2 *2JAVA-CUSTOMER-SURVEY.HTM* *<FORM>* Implementation for the JavaScript Version of the Customer Survey

```
<BODY BGCOLOR=#FFFFFF>
<H1>Customer Survey</H1>
<HR>

<FORM NAME="customerSurvey">
<PRE>
Please indicate the income bracket that your family falls into, counting the
income of all working family members.

    <INPUT TYPE=radio NAME=incomeBracket VALUE="incomeBracket1"
onClick=setIncome(this)> $0 - $49,999
    <INPUT TYPE=radio NAME=incomeBracket VALUE="incomeBracket2"
onClick=setIncome(this)> $50,000 - $99,999
    <INPUT TYPE=radio NAME=incomeBracket VALUE="incomeBracket3"
onClick=setIncome(this)> $100,000 - $200,000

Please indicate your sex.
```

continues

Listing 8.2   Continued

```
        <INPUT TYPE=radio NAME=sex VALUE="Male" onClick=setSex(this)> Male
        <INPUT TYPE=radio NAME=sex VALUE="Female" onClick=setSex(this)> Female

Indicate which of the following publications that you subscribe to.

        <INPUT TYPE=checkbox NAME=timeMagazine VALUE="Time Magazine reading, "
onClick=setMagazineText(this)> Time Magazine
        <INPUT TYPE=checkbox NAME=usNews VALUE="US News scanning, "
onClick=setMagazineText(this)> US News and World Report
        <INPUT TYPE=checkbox NAME=newsWeek VALUE="Newsweek buying, "
onClick=setMagazineText(this)> Newsweek
        <INPUT TYPE=checkbox NAME=atlanticMonthly VALUE="Atlantic Monthly
            browsing, "
onClick=setMagazineText(this)> Atlantic Monthly
        <INPUT TYPE=checkbox NAME=tvGuide VALUE="TV Guide opening, "
onClick=setMagazineText(this)> TV Guide

How much would you be willing to pay for our EnhancedPlus service?

        <INPUT TYPE=text NAME=serviceCost onChange=setPayAmount(this)>

Please rate the service you've received from our company.

        <INPUT TYPE=radio NAME=rateUs VALUE="excellent" onClick=setRating(this)>
            Excellent
        <INPUT TYPE=radio NAME=rateUs VALUE="good" onClick=setRating(this)> Good
        <INPUT TYPE=radio NAME=rateUs VALUE="fair" onClick=setRating(this)> Fair
        <INPUT TYPE=radio NAME=rateUs VALUE="poor" onClick=setRating(this)> Poor


</PRE>
<BR>
<BR>
<INPUT TYPE="button" VALUE="Tell Us"    onClick=makeMessage()>
<INPUT TYPE="reset"  VALUE="Reset">

</FORM>

</CENTER>

</BODY>
</HTML>
```

When you code this application in VBScript, you'll notice a couple of differences from the JavaScript version. The first difference is that, in JavaScript, the keyword this refers to the current control as an object. Take a look at the rateUs radio button set in Listing 8.2. Each radio button calls setRating in response to the onClick event. The value of the rateUs radio button set is then accessed by referring to rating.value within the setRating() function. As you'll see in a moment, the VBScript implementation of this example passes the value of the radio button set as a separate variable.

The second difference is a variation on the first one. The `setMagazineText()` function needs to reference the other magazine checkbox objects. One way to reference those values in JavaScript is to pass the current control as `this` and then access the `this.form` attribute within the called function. The function `setMagazineText()` is a good example of this technique. As you'll see in a moment, the VBScript implementation uses a global reference to access the same data.

Using VBScript

In this section, you'll build a customer survey form using VBScript. Most of the real functionality on the Internet is implemented through forms. To really make your forms come to life, you need to use a variety of user interface elements. In building this application, you'll be exposed to the following:

- Processing text box events
- Processing radio button events
- Processing checkbox events
- Passing data to subprocedures
- Processing command button events

Laying Out the Form

Since you'll have several objects on this screen, let's start by taking a look at the basic layout of the objects on the page (see fig. 8.1).

FIG. 8.1

This is how the customer survey form will look.

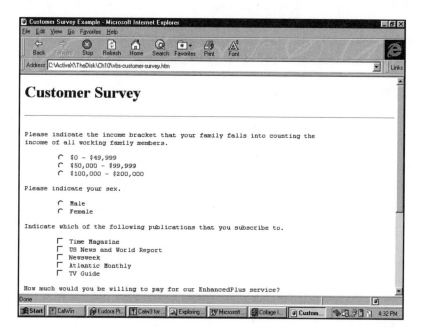

TIP All the examples in this chapter assume that you have a simple HTML template file.

To build this Customer Survey example, follow these steps:

1. Start the ActiveX Control Pad, and open your HTML template file.

2. Update the comment header, `<TITLE>` value, and `<H1>` tag pair to reflect the example name.

3. Save the file to a convenient working directory as VBS-CUSTOMER-SURVEY.HTM.

N O T E The next steps take you through the process of building the form. The complete listing of VBS-CUSTOMER-SURVEY.HTM is on the CD-ROM that accompanies this book, so you can check your work against that listing. ■

4. After the `<HR>` tag, add the HTML for the form. Your code now should look something like Listing 8.3.

Listing 8.3 *3VBS-CUSTOMER-SURVEY.HTM* HTML Code for the Customer Survey Form

```
<BODY BGCOLOR=#FFFFFF>
<H1>Customer Survey</H1>
<HR>
<! ------------------------------------------------------->
<! -- Form to collect customer survey data              >
<! ------------------------------------------------------->
<FORM NAME="customerSurvey">
<PRE>
```

Notice that we have not closed the `<BODY>` tag with a `</BODY>` tag. You'll take care of that a few steps later.

Use `<PRE>` (for preformatted) so that it's easy to lay out the form without messing with tables or fancy formatting. That way, you can concentrate on the VBScript aspects of this application. Let's take a look at all the form controls and how they invoke their associated functions.

5. The first form object we need is a radio button set. Typically, radio buttons are used for questions or input items that have a set of known, mutually exclusive answers. The `incomeBracket` radio button set invokes a method named `setIncome` when the `onClick` event fires. Notice that, unlike with JavaScript, the value of the radio button set here is passed as a string to the `setIncome()` function. Listing 8.4 shows how your code for the first radio button set might look.

Part

I

Ch

8

Listing 8.4 *4VBS-CUSTOMER-SURVEY.HTM* **The *IncomeBracket* Radio Button Set**

```
Please indicate the income bracket that your family falls into counting the
income of all working family members.

 <INPUT TYPE=radio NAME=IncomeBracket VALUE="IncomeBracket1"
onClick=setIncome("IncomeBracket1")> $0 - $49,999
 <INPUT TYPE=radio NAME=IncomeBracket VALUE="IncomeBracket2"
onClick=setIncome("IncomeBracket2")> $50,000 - $99,999
 <INPUT TYPE=radio NAME=IncomeBracket VALUE="IncomeBracket3"
onClick=setIncome("IncomeBracket3")> $100,000 - $200,000
```

6. The next form object also is a radio button set. The Sex radio button set invokes a method named `setSex` when the `onClick` event fires. Similar to the behavior of the `incomeBracket` control, the Sex control also passes the value of the selected radio button as a string (see Listing 8.5).

Listing 8.5 *5VBS-CUSTOMER-SURVEY.HTM* **The Sex Radio Button Set**

```
Please indicate your sex.

<INPUT TYPE=radio NAME=Sex VALUE="Male" onClick=SetSex("Male")> Male
<INPUT TYPE=radio NAME=Sex VALUE="Female" onClick=setSex("Female")> Female
```

7. Each of the magazines that a user can select is itself a checkbox control. Checkbox controls typically are used for input that has a set of known answers that are not mutually exclusive. Each checkbox invokes the same method in response to the `onClick` event (see Listing 8.6). This function, named `setMagazineText()`, takes two parameters.

Listing 8.6 *6VBS-CUSTOMER-SURVEY.HTM* **The Magazine Checkbox Set**

```
Indicate which of the following publications that you subscribe to.

 <INPUT TYPE=checkbox NAME=TimeMagazine VALUE="Time Magazine reading, "
onClick="setMagazineText TimeMagazine, 'Time Magazine reading, '" > Time Maga
        zine
 <INPUT TYPE=checkbox NAME=UsNews VALUE="US News scanning, "
onClick="setMagazineText UsNews, 'US News scanning, '" > US News and
        World Report
 <INPUT TYPE=checkbox NAME=Newsweek VALUE="Newsweek buying, "
onClick="setMagazineText Newsweek, 'Newsweek buying, '" > Newsweek
 <INPUT TYPE=checkbox NAME=AtlanticMonthly VALUE="Atlantic Monthly browsing, "
onClick="setMagazineText AtlanticMonthly, 'Atlantic Monthly browsing, '"   >
        Atlantic Monthly
 <INPUT TYPE=checkbox NAME=TvGuide VALUE="TV Guide opening, "
onClick="setMagazineText TvGuide, 'TV Guide opening, '" > TV Guide
```

continues

Listing 8.6 Continued

```
<INPUT TYPE="button" VALUE="Tell Us"   onClick=makeMessage>
<INPUT TYPE="reset"  VALUE="Reset">

</FORM>
```

Listing 8.7 gives you a closer look at a single checkbox item.

Listing 8.7   7VBS-CUSTOMER-SURVEY.HTM   Calling Functions with Multiple Parameters

```
<INPUT

TYPE=checkbox
NAME=TimeMagazine
VALUE="Time Magazine reading, "
onClick="setMagazineText TimeMagazine, 'Time Magazine reading, '"

> Time Magazine
```

Notice that the `onClick` attribute is enclosed in double quotes. The second parameter is the text value of the checkbox, passed as a string. You enclose strings like this within single quotes. The checkbox control also is passed as an object to the function. When a checkbox control is passed like this, the status of the box can be determined, in this example, by checking `TimeMagazine.Checked`. Try looking at `TimeMagazine.Name` as well—you should obtain the actual text included after the `NAME` attribute.

8. The remaining two questions presented to the user on the input form are really not new material, with one exception (see Listing 8.8). The `serviceCost` field has an `INPUT TYPE` of `text`. This field executes the `setPayAmount()` function in response to the `onChange` event. (The `onChange` event fires when the user changes a text field and then exits the field.)

Listing 8.8 8VBS-CUSTOMER-SURVEY.HTM   Finishing the Survey Questions in HTML

```
How much would you be willing to pay for our EnhancedPlus service?

 <INPUT TYPE=text NAME=ServiceCost onChange=setPayAmount(ServiceCost)>

Please rate the service you've received from our company.

 <INPUT TYPE=radio NAME=RateUs VALUE="excellent"
onClick=setRating("excellent")>
Excellent
  <INPUT TYPE=radio NAME=RateUs VALUE="good" onClick=setRating("good")> Good
  <INPUT TYPE=radio NAME=RateUs VALUE="fair" onClick=setRating("fair")> Fair
```

```
    <INPUT TYPE=radio NAME=RateUs VALUE="poor" onClick=setRating("poor")> Poor

</PRE>
<BR>
<BR>
```

Don't forget to use some space after closing out the <PRE> block. This separates the command buttons from the questionnaire.

9. Adding the command buttons is straightforward, as you can see in Listing 8.9. The action button executes makeMessage() when the onClick event fires.

On the CD

Listing 8.9 *9VBS-CUSTOMER-SURVEY.HTM* The Command Buttons

```
<INPUT TYPE="button" VALUE="Tell Us"    onClick=makeMessage>
<INPUT TYPE="reset"  VALUE="Reset">

</FORM>
```

Coding the Script

Okay, let's start putting together the script. Before you start coding, let's review what you need to build. Table 8.1 lists the necessary functions.

Table 8.1 Functions to Build for the Customer Survey Example

Function	Description
setSex()	Sets the text to be used by makeMessage() to report this customer's gender
setMagazineText()	Sets the text to be used by makeMessage() to report the magazines this customer reads
setIncome()	Sets the text to be used by makeMessage() to report the customer's income bracket
setRating()	Sets the text to be used by makeMessage() to report the customer's opinion of previous service
setPayAmount()	Sets the text to be used by makeMessage() to report what the customer would be willing to pay for a new service
makeMessage()	Formats the message to be reported for this survey

This application employs several global variables. Table 8.2 defines how these global variables will be used.

Table 8.2 Global Variables for the Customer Survey Application

Variable	Description
incomeText	Holds the text that describes the income bracket this customer has reported
sexText	Holds the text that describes this customer's gender
magazineText	Holds the list of magazines this customer reads
payAmountText	Stores the amount this customer would be willing to pay for a new service
ratingText	Holds the rating the customer has given for previous service

Now that you've been introduced to the major elements of this application, let's go ahead and start construction of the script. Perform the following steps:

1. To start the script portion of VBS-CUSTOMER-SURVEY.HTM, insert <SCRIPT> immediately following the <TITLE> tag pair (and before the </HEAD>). You can use the ActiveX Control Pad to insert this script element by choosing Tool, Script Wizard from the menu bar. Right-click the Global Variables entry in the Insert Actions box, then choose New Global Variable. Include the following global variables: incomeText, sexText, magazineText, payAmountText, and ratingText. Your code should look something like Listing 8.10.

On the CD

Listing 8.10 *10VBS-CUSTOMER-SURVEY.HTM* Declaring the Global Variables

```
<! ------------------------------------------------->
<! --                  >
<! --  Description:  Customer Survey Example      >
<! --                  >
<! --  Author:     Brian Farrar            >
<! --                  >
<! -- Date:       5/20/96      >
<! ------------------------------------------------->
<HTML>
<HEAD><TITLE>Customer Survey Example</TITLE>
<SCRIPT LANGUAGE="VBScript">

  Dim incomeText
  Dim sexText
  Dim magazineText
  Dim payAmountText
  Dim ratingText
```

2. Next, code the setSex() function that is executed when the NumPayments field is changed. Remember that setSex's job is to set the global sexText field with the desired text. To add setSex(), choose Procedures in the Script Wizard's Action List. Right-click, then choose New Procedure. For this procedure, you'll need to select Code View in order to enter the required VBScript code. Listing 8.11 shows the necessary code.

Listing 8.11 *11VBS-CUSTOMER-SURVEY.HTM* **The *setSex()* Function**

```
'----------------------------------------
' -- Set the sex text
'----------------------------------------
Sub setSex ( Sex )

  If Sex = "Male" Then
    sexText = "You're a girl !"
  Else
    sexText = "You're a boy !"
  End If

End Sub
```

Notice that this example sets the text to say "You're a girl" when the customer indicates that he's male. This is because the entire message in this example is tongue-in-cheek (as you'll see).

3. Next, code the `setMagazineText()` function, which builds a text item that lists the magazines the customer reads. Use the Script Wizard to add the new procedure as described in the previous step. Your code should look something like Listing 8.12.

Listing 8.12 *12VBS-CUSTOMER-SURVEY.HTM* **The *setMagazineText()* Function**

```
'----------------------------------------
' -- Set the Magazine text
'----------------------------------------


Sub setMagazineText(Magazine, Text)

  Dim Form

  Set Form = Document.CustomerSurvey

  If Magazine.Checked Then
    magazineText = magazineText + Text
  Else
    magazineText = ""
    Form.TimeMagazine.checked = false
    Form.UsNews.checked = false
    Form.Newsweek.checked = false
    Form.AtlanticMonthly.checked = false
    Form.TvGuide.checked = false
  End If

End Sub
```

Let's take a brief look at a couple of important items on this function. First, look at the difference between JavaScript and VBScript. Unlike the JavaScript version of this application, which uses an `Object.Form` style reference to fill in the local `form` variable, the VBScript implementation fills the local variable `Form` using a global reference like `Document.CustomerSurvey` to initialize.

Second, notice that the status of the checkbox associated with the passed object `Magazine` is verified by inspecting `Magazine.Checked`. (`Magazine.Checked` is set to `True` when the checkbox is checked, and `False` when it is not.)

4. Next, code the `setIncome()` function, which is very similar to the `setSex()` function. Use the Script Wizard to add the new procedure as described in step 2. Your code should look something like Listing 8.13.

Listing 8.13   _13VBS-CUSTOMER-SURVEY.HTM_   The _setIncome()_ Function

```
'------------------------------------------
' -- Set the Income text
'------------------------------------------
Sub setIncome(incomeBracket)

  If incomeBracket = "incomeBracket1" Then
    incomeText = "Modest Income"
  End If

  If incomeBracket = "incomeBracket2" Then
    incomeText = "Middle Income"
  End If

  If incomeBracket = "incomeBracket3" Then
    incomeText = "High Income"
  End If

End Sub
```

5. Next, code the `setRating()` function. Your code should look something like Listing 8.14.

Listing 8.14   _14VBS-CUSTOMER-SURVEY.HTM_   The _setRating()_ Function

```
'------------------------------------------
' -- Set the Rating text
'------------------------------------------
Sub setRating(Rating) ratingText = Rating
End Sub
```

6. Use the Script Wizard to add the `setPayAmount()` function, again using the process described in step 2. This function is similar to `setSex()`. Your code should look something like Listing 8.15.

On the CD

Listing 8.15   *15VBS-CUSTOMER-SURVEY.HTM*   The *setPayAmount() Function*

```
'---------------------------------------------
' -- Set the Pay Amount Text
'---------------------------------------------

Sub setPayAmount(Amount)

  If Amount.Value < 15 Then
    payAmountText = "Tight wad"
  End If
  If Amount.Value >= 15 And Amount.Value < 25 Then
    payAmountText = "Bargain hunter"
  End If
  If Amount.Value >= 25 Then
    payAmountText = "Sucker"
  End If

End Sub
```

7. Finally, code the `makeMessage()` function, which executes when the customer submits the survey. In this example, `makeMessage()` is a very simple `MsgBox` text message based on the customer's responses to the survey questions. Your code should look something like Listing 8.16.

On the CD

Listing 8.16   *16VBS-CUSTOMER-SURVEY.HTM*   The *makeMessage() Function*

```
'---------------------------------------------
' -- Make the message summarizing survey
'---------------------------------------------

Sub makeMessage

  Dim messageText

  If ratingText = "excellent" Then

    messageText = "So you gave us an excellent rating.
We find that a " _
        & payAmountText _
        & " seems to respond well to our service.
So we won't tell your mother that " _
        & sexText _
        & " And with a" _
        & incomeText _
        & " you can continue on as a " _
        & magazineText + "aficionado!!"
    MsgBox(messageText)
  End If

  If ratingText = "good" Then
    messageText = "So you gave us a good rating.  We find that a " _
        & payAmountText _
```

continues

Listing 8.16   Continued

```
          & " like you probably would.  Your mother tells us that " _
          & sexText _
          & " With a " _
          & incomeText _
          & " that often acts like a " _
          & magazineText + "genius!!"
      MsgBox(messageText)
    End If

    If ratingText = "fair" Then
      messageText = "So you gave us a fair rating.  We find that a " _
          & payAmountText _
          & " like you probably would.  But does your mother know that " _
          & sexText _
          & " People like you with a " _
          & incomeText _
          & " are known to be " _
          & magazineText + "IDIOTS!!!!"
      MsgBox(messageText)
    End If

    If ratingText = "poor" Then
      messageText = "So you gave us a poor rating.  Of course a " _
          & payAmountText _
          & " like you probably would.  But does your mother know that " _
          & sexText _
          & " People like you with a " _
          & incomeText _
          & " are known to be " _
          & magazineText + "IDIOTS!!!!"
      MsgBox(messageText)
    End If

  End Sub
</SCRIPT>
</HEAD>
```

Notice that many lines in this function are continued using the VBScript continuation string—a space followed by an underscore (" _").

10. Save your work as VBS-CUSTOMER-SURVEY.HTM.

Now that you've completed the HTML document, you can test your work using Microsoft Internet Explorer 3.0. The following steps walk you through the process of testing this HTML document:

1. Start Microsoft Internet Explorer 3.0.

2. Place the text cursor in the document text box, then type **VBS-CUSTOMER-SURVEY.HTM**. (Be sure to include the fully qualified path to your document.) Press Enter.

3. If you've done everything correctly, the HTML document looks something like what you saw in figure 8.1 in the beginning of the chapter.

> **CAUTION**
>
> If you have an error anywhere in your VBScript code, the entire script may fail to execute. MSIE 3.0 simply ignores malformed script data. Bear in mind that, sometimes, preceding HTML errors can cause an error in a script.

 An easy way to debug problems with your script is to use the MsgBox() function from VBScript. The MsgBox() function allows you to pop up a dialog box containing a string of text and an OK button. Use this feature to examine the values of any variables you're interested in testing.

Using VBScript—A Mortgage Calculator

You can use VBScript to implement forms that do calculations for your users. In this example, you'll be constructing a Web page to calculate mortgage payments.

In the following sections, you'll see the JavaScript implementation of the example and then the VBScript implementation. The review of the JavaScript will be cursory. The ActiveX sections will guide you step-by-step through the process of building the example. ■

Use VBScript for client-side scripting

Adding program functionality to your Web pages can be quite sophisticated using VBScripting.

Compare VBScript with JavaScript

If you've been using JavaScript with Netscape, a quick comparison to JavaScript will be an easy introduction to VBScript.

Building VBScript procedures

Breaking functions up into procedures is an important part of using VBScript.

Responding to events fired by <FORM> elements

User interface elements on the <FORM> tag can trigger events and execute procedures.

Building the Application

To calculate a mortgage payment, you need three factors:

- Number of payments
- Annual interest rate
- Amount to be borrowed

To process the form and calculate the payment, you'll build the following four functions:

- **Validate Payments**—This procedure insures that the payment entered by the user is greater than zero and less than or equal to 360.

- **Validate Interest Rate**—This procedure checks to make sure the interest rate is greater than zero and less than 100 percent. The user can enter either whole numbers or decimals (e.g., ten percent can be entered as either 10 or 0.10).

- **Validate Principal**—This procedure makes sure that the principal amount is less than $1 million and greater than zero.

- **Compute Payment**—This procedure calculates the monthly payment for a loan based upon the inputs.

Using JavaScript

Many Web developers will be making the transition from using JavaScript to using VBScript. So to help you get started quickly with VBScript, the following section briefly describes the construction of a mortgage calculator example in JavaScript with Netscape. The JavaScript is provided in Listing 9.1.

Listing 9.1 *JAVA-MORTGAGE-CALC.HTM* **JavaScript Implementation of the Mortgage Calculator**

```
<HTML>
<HEAD><TITLE>Mortgage Calculator</TITLE>
<SCRIPT LANGUAGE="JavaScript">

 function validatePayments(paymentEntered) {

  if ( paymentEntered.value > 0 && paymentEntered.value <= 360 ) {
   return true;
  }
  alert("Number of payments must be in the range of 1 to 360");
  paymentEntered.value = 0;
  return false;
 }
```

```
function validateInterestRate(rateEntered) {

  var interestRate = rateEntered.value;

  if (interestRate > 1.0 && interestRate <= 100) {
   return true;
  }
  if (interestRate > 0.01 && interestRate <= 1.0) {
   return true;
  }
  alert("Interest rate must be between .01 and 1.0 or 1 and 100");
  rateEntered.value = 0;
  return false;
}

function validatePrincipal(principalEntered) {

  if ( principalEntered.value > 0 && principalEntered.value < 1000000 ) {
   return true;
  }
  alert("Principal must be in the range of 1 to 1 Million");
  principalEntered.value = 0;
  return false;
}


function computePayment(form) {

  var interestRate = form.interest.value;
  var conversionFactor = 1;

  if ( interestRate > 1.0 )
   interestRate /= 100.0;

  interestRate /= 12

  for (var indx = 0; indx < form.numPayments.value; indx++)
   conversionFactor = conversionFactor * (1 + interestRate);
  form.payment.value = (form.principal.value * conversionFactor * interestRate)
/ (conversionFactor - 1)
}
</SCRIPT>
</HEAD>
```

Part

I

Ch

9

As with all scripting languages, you place your script code in the head of the Web document you're constructing (see Listing 9.2). Note that the script uses the (somewhat goofy) Java convention for variable naming (starting all variables with a lowercase word and capitalizing the second word, e.g., interestRate).

Listing 9.2 *2JAVA-MORTGAGE-CALC.HTM* The *<FORM>* for a Java Implementation of the Mortgage Calculator

```
<BODY BGCOLOR=#FFFFFF>
<H1>Mortgage Calculator</H1>
<HR>


<! -------------------------------------------------------->
<! -- Form collects parameters to calculate loan payment >
<! -------------------------------------------------------->

<FORM NAME="MCalcForm">
<PRE>
Number of payments       <INPUT TYPE=TEXT NAME=NumPayments  SIZE=5
onChange=ValidatePayments(NumPayments.value)>
Annual Interest rate     <INPUT TYPE=TEXT NAME=Interest  SIZE=6
onChange=ValidateInterestRate(Interest.Value)>
Principal                <INPUT TYPE=TEXT NAME=Principal SIZE=9
onChange=ValidatePrincipal(Principal.Value)>

Payment                  <INPUT TYPE=TEXT NAME=Payment   SIZE=9>
</PRE><BR>
<INPUT TYPE="button" VALUE="Calculate Payment"   onClick=ComputePayment>
<INPUT TYPE="reset"  VALUE="Reset">

</FORM>
</CENTER>

</BODY>
</HTML>
```

Using VBScript

In this section, you'll build a mortgage calculator. In the process, you'll be exposed to:

- Processing text box events
- Passing data to sub procedures
- Processing command button events

The process you'll follow is to first lay out the form. You'll find out about all the elements of the user interface, their names, and the procedures they execute when certain events occur. After the form has been built, you'll code the script. You'll learn the procedure names and the functions each must occur. Finally, you'll code each procedure.

Laying Out the Form

Since you'll have several objects on this screen, let's start by taking a look at the basic layout of the objects on the page (see fig. 9.1).

FIG. 9.1
VBScript mortgage
calculator example.

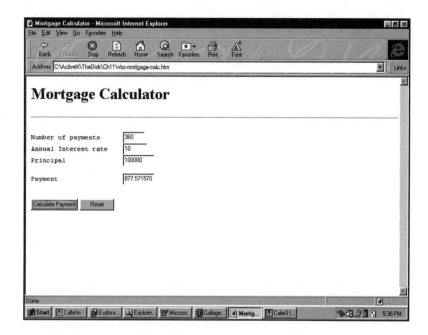

The form contains four fields, one for each of the following:

- **Number of Payments**—The VBScript variable name for this text box is `NumPayments`.
- **Annual Interest**—The VBScript variable name for this text box is `Interest`.
- **Principal**—The VBScript variable name for this text box is `Principal`.
- **Payment**—This field holds the resulting calculation based on the three values provided above.

 TIP All of the examples in this chapter assume that you have a simple HTML template file (the same template from Chapter 5 if you used it).

To build this Mortgage Calculator example, follow these steps:

1. Start the ActiveX Control Pad and open your HTML template file from Chapter 5.
2. Update the comment header, `TITLE` value, and H1 tag pair to reflect the example name.
3. Save the file to a convenient working directory as `VBS-MORTGAGE-CALC.HTM`.

   The next few steps take you through the process of building the form. The complete listing of `VBS-MORTGAGE-CALC.HTM` is on the CD so you'll want to check your work against it.

4. After the `<HR>` tag, add the HTML for the form. Your code should look something like Listing 9.3. Note that we have not closed the `<BODY>` tag with a `</BODY>`. You'll take care of that in a moment.

Listing 9.3 *VBS-MORTGAGE-CALC.HTM* **Mortgage Calculator Form Insertion**

```
<! ------------------------------------------------------>
<! -- Form collects parameters to calculate loan payment >
<! ------------------------------------------------------>

<FORM NAME="MCalcForm">
<PRE>
Number of payments       <INPUT TYPE=TEXT NAME=NumPayments  SIZE=5
onChange=ValidatePayments(NumPayments.value)>
Annual Interest rate     <INPUT TYPE=TEXT NAME=Interest   SIZE=6
onChange=ValidateInterestRate(Interest.Value)>
Principal                <INPUT TYPE=TEXT NAME=Principal SIZE=9
onChange=ValidatePrincipal(Principal.Value)>

Payment                  <INPUT TYPE=TEXT NAME=Payment    SIZE=9>
</PRE><BR>
<INPUT TYPE="button" VALUE="Calculate Payment"    onClick=ComputePayment>
<INPUT TYPE="reset"  VALUE="Reset">

</FORM>
```

Use the <PRE> (for preformatted) tag so that it's easy to lay out the form without messing with tables or fancier formatting. That way you can concentrate on the VBScript aspects of this application. Note that each of the three input fields uses the onChange event for validation of the data. The Calculate Payment button catches the onClick event in order to cause the payment to be generated. Notice that the procedures invoked due to the onChange events require parameters. These parameters are passed ByVal (e.g., the value held in the variable is passed and not the actual variable itself). But more on that when you build the procedures themselves.

Coding the Script

In building the form, you created a requirement for four functions. Table 9.1 summarizes the functions you'll need to build.

Table 9.1 **Functions to Build for the Mortgage Calculator Example**

Function	Description
ValidatePayments	This procedure insures that the payment entered by the user is greater than zero and less than or equal to 360.
ValidateInterestRate	This procedure checks to make sure the interest rate is greater than zero and less than 100 percent. The user can enter either whole numbers or decimals (e.g., ten percent can be entered as either 10 or 0.10).
ValidatePrincipal	This procedure makes sure that the principal amount is less than $1 million and greater than zero.

Function	Description
ComputePayment	This procedure calculates the monthly payment for a loan based upon the inputs.

These functions require some additional variables that are contained with brief explanation in Table 9.2.

Table 9.2 Additional Variables for Mortgage Calculator Example

Variable	Description
PaymentEntered	Used by ValidatePayment to check the number of payments entered.
RateEntered	Used by ValidateInterestRate to check the number of payments entered.
InterestRate	Used by ValidateInterest to check the number of payments entered. Used by ComputeForm to calculate the result.
PrincipalEntered	Used by ValidatePrincipal to check the number of payments entered.
ConversionFactor	Calculated by ComputeForm. Represents the loan discount factor.
Indx	Used to loop through the ConversionFactor calculation NumPayments number of times.

To finish coding the script, follow these steps:

1. To start the script portion of VBS-MORTGAGE-CALC.HTM, you'll insert a <SCRIPT> tag immediately following the <TITLE> tag set before the </HEAD> tag. You can use the ActiveX Control Pad to insert this script element by selecting Tools, Script Wizard from the menu bar. Your code should look something like Listing 9.4.

Listing 9.4 2VBS-MORTGAGE-CALC.HTM Script Header for Mortgage Calculator

```
<! ------------------------------------------------------->
<! --            >
<! -- Description: Mortgage Calculator Example     >
<! --         >
<! -- Author:  Brian Farrar                >
<! --          >
<! -- Date:    5/20/96     >
<! ------------------------------------------------------->
```

continues

Listing 9.4 Continued

```
<HTML>
<HEAD><TITLE>Mortgage Calculator</TITLE>
<SCRIPT LANGUAGE="VBScript">
```

2. Next, you'll code the ValidatePayments procedure that is executed when the NumPayments field is changed. Remember that ValidatePayment's job is to make sure that the the the number of payments is greater than zero and less than or equal to 360 payments. To add ValidatePayments, select the Procedures item in the Script Wizard's Action List. Press the right mouse button and select New Procedure. For this procedure, you'll need to select the Code View in order to enter the required VBScript code shown in Listing 9.5.

Listing 9.5 *3VBS-MORTGAGE-CALC.HTM* *ValidatePayments* Function for Mortgage Calculator

```
'------------------------------------------------
'-- Validate Payment data entry
'------------------------------------------------
Sub ValidatePayments(PaymentEntered)

 If PaymentEntered > 0 And PaymentEntered <= 360 Then
  Exit Sub
 End If

 MsgBox "Number of payments must be in the range of 1 to 360"
 Document.MCalcForm.NumPayments.Value = 0

End Sub
```

The PaymentEntered parameter is passed to the function by value, not by reference. A value for PaymentEntered is passed in to the procedure. If PaymentEntered fits within the appropriate range, the procedure is exited immediately. If PaymentEntered is not in the appropriate range, then the user is presented with a message box (an alert in JavaScript). Then the actual form field is cleared to zero.

Notice that the form field is changed by a global reference to the text input box (Document.MCalcForm.NumPayments.Value). This reference is required because the PaymentEntered field (which is set to the value of the field NumPayments when the field changes) is passed by value. A more elegant approach to deal with this situation would be to set PaymentEntered to zero where the PaymentEntered field is passed by reference. This would eliminate the jarring reference to the document name variable. VBScript includes support for pass by reference (e.g., the ByRef keyword). However, the alpha version of MSIE 3.0 used to construct this example only supports ByVal. That's why the reference to Document.MCalcForm.NumPayments.Value is required (see Table 9.3).

Table 9.3   Referring to a *<FORM>* Field Value From Within a Script

Reference	Explanation
Document	The document that the reference you're constructing is contained in.
MCalcForm	The NAME of the FORM where the textbox appears.
NumPayments	The NAME of the textbox INPUT object.
Value	The attribute of the textbox INPUT object to be referenced. In this case, the reference is to the VALUE attribute.

Part
I
Ch
9

3. Next code the ValidateInterestRate procedure. This function is very similar to the ValidatePayments field. Use the Script Wizard to add new procedures as described in the previous step. Your code should look something like Listing 9.6.

Listing 9.6   *4VBS-MORTGAGE-CALC.HTM   ValidateInterestRate* Function for the Mortgage Calculator

```
'-----------------------------------------------
'-- Validate Interest Rate data entry
'-----------------------------------------------
Sub ValidateInterestRate(RateEntered)

 If RateEntered > 0 And RateEntered <= 100 Then
  Exit Sub
 End If
 If RateEntered > 0.01 And RateEntered <= 1.0 Then
  Exit Sub
 End If

 MsgBox "Interest rate must be between .01 and 1.0 or 1 and 100"
 Document.MCalcForm.Interest.Value

End Sub
```

4. Using the Script Wizard as described in step 2, code the ValidatePrincipal procedure next. This function is very similar to the ValidatePayments field. Your code should look something like Listing 9.7.

Listing 9.7   *5VBS-MORTGAGE-CALC.HTM   ValidatePrincipal* Function for the Mortgage Calculator

```
'-----------------------------------------------
'-- Validate Principal data entry
'-----------------------------------------------
Sub ValidatePrincipal(PrincipalEntered)
```

continues

Listing 9.7 Continued

```
If PrincipalEntered > 0 And PrincipalEntered < 1000000 Then
 Exit Sub
End If

MsgBox "Principal must be in the range of 1 to 1 Million"
Document.MCalcForm.Principal.Value = 0

End Sub
```

5. Finally you'll code the ComputePayment function. This guy is the guts of the application. Once again, use the Script Wizard as explained in step 2. Your code should look something like Listing 9.8.

Listing 9.8 6VBS-MORTGAGE-CALC.HTM *ComputePayment* Function for the Mortgage Calculator

```
'-------------------------------------------------
'-- Compute the payment amount
'-------------------------------------------------
Sub ComputePayment

Dim InterestRate
Dim ConversionFactor
Dim Indx

InterestRate = Document.MCalcForm.Interest.Value
ConversionFactor = 1

If InterestRate > 1.0 Then
 InterestRate = InterestRate / 100.0
End If

InterestRate = InterestRate / 12

For Indx = 1 To Document.MCalcForm.NumPayments.Value
 ConversionFactor = ConversionFactor * (1 + InterestRate)
Next

Document.MCalcForm.Payment.Value = (Document.MCalcForm.Principal.Value *
     ConversionFactor *   InterestRate) / (ConversionFactor - 1)
End Sub
</SCRIPT>
</HEAD>
```

In this function, you'll declare three temporary variables: InterestRate, ConversionFactor, and Indx. First, you must adjust the representation of the InterestRate to a decimal value for use in the ConversionFactor calculation. Then, a for...next loop iterates Indx number of times to calculate the ConversionFactor. Finally, calculate the loan payment value based upon the ConversionFactor.

6. Save your work as VBS-MORTGAGE-CALC.HTM.

Now that you've completed the HTML document, you can test your work using Microsoft Internet Explorer 3.0. These next steps take you through testing out your HTML document.

1. Start Microsoft Internet Explorer 3.0.

2. Place the text cursor in the document text box and type **VBS-MORTGAGE-CALC.HTM**. Be sure to include the fully qualified path to your document. Hit Enter.

   If you've done everything correctly, the HTML document should look something like figure 9.1.

CAUTION

If you have an error anywhere in your VBScript, the entire script may fail to execute. MSIE 3.0 simply ignores malformed script data. Note that sometimes preceeding HTML errors can cause an error in a script.

 An easy way to debug problems with your script is to use the MSGBOX function from VBScript. The MSGBOX function allows you to pop up a dialog box with a string of text and an OK button. Use this feature to examine values of variables you're interested in testing.

CHAPTER 10

Using VBScript—A Cooking Measurement Converter

You can use VBScript to implement forms that calculate special numbers for users. In this chapter's example, you'll be constructing a Web page to convert all the various measurements used in cooking. You'll work with a number of different form elements including radio buttons, text fields, and command buttons. ■

Use VBScript for client-side scripting

Client-side scripting works very well for calculations of formulas where no interaction with a server is required.

Compare VBScript with JavaScript

To help you make the transition from JavaScript to VBScript, take a look at an implementation of this application in JavaScript.

Building VBScript procedures

Breaking functions up into procedures is an important part of using VBScript.

Responding to events fired by `<FORM>` elements

User interface elements on the `<FORM>` can trigger events and execute procedures.

Building the Application

You'll follow the same process as in the Mortgage Calculator example. First, you'll lay out the form. You'll find out about all the elements of the user interface, their names, and the procedures they execute when certain events occur. After the form has been built, you'll code the script. You'll learn the procedure names and the functions each must occur. Finally, you'll code each procedure.

To convert all of the cooking measures included in this example, you'll build four functions as follows:

- SetToIndx—This function fills in the ToIndx global variable.
- SetFromIndx—This function is used to set the FromIndx global variable.
- ValidateAmount—This function ensures that the value placed in the InAmount field is numeric.
- DoConvert—This function does the conversions among all the measurements on the form.

In the next two sections, you'll see the JavaScript implementation of the example and then the VBScript implementation. The review of the JavaScript will be cursory. The ActiveX sections will guide you step-by-step through the process of building the example.

Using JavaScript

Many Web developers will be making the transition from using JavaScript to using VBScript. So to help you get started quickly with VBScript, we'll show you the implementation in the JavaScript you're probably familiar with for comparison purposes with the VBScript version.

When you code this application in VBScript, there will be one major difference from JavaScript. In JavaScript, there is no array variable type. However, you can construct an array in JavaScript quite easily. In Listing 10.1, you'll see that the function makeArray is used to generate the necessary array. As you'll see in a moment, the VBScript implementation of this example uses the built-in ability to declare an array. Listing 10.1 shows the JavaScript version of the converter.

Listing 10.1 *JAVA-COOK.HTM* Java Implementation of the Cook's Converter

```
<HTML>
<HEAD><TITLE>Cook's Converter</TITLE>
<SCRIPT LANGUAGE="JavaScript">

    var fromIndx = 0;
    var toIndx = 0;
    var convertAmount = 0;

    function makeArray(arraySize) {
     this.length = arraySize;
```

```
    for (var indx = 1; indx <= arraySize; indx++) {
     this[indx] = 0
    }
         return this;
    }

function setFromIndx(anIndx) {
 fromIndx = anIndx.value;
}

function setToIndx(anIndx) {
 toIndx = anIndx.value;
}

function validateAmount(inputItem) {
 var str = inputItem.value;

 if (str.length == 0 || str == "" || str == null) {
   alert("You must enter a number.")
 }

 for (var i = 0; i < str.length; i++) {
  var ch = str.substring(i, i + 1)
  if ((ch < "0" || "9" < ch) && ch != '.' && ch != '$' && ch != ',') {
    alert("Invalid text in the field");
  }
 }
}

function doConvert(form) {

 conversionFactor = new makeArray(7);

 validateAmount(form.inAmount);
 convertAmount = form.inAmount.value;

 // Teaspoons to Tablespoons
 conversionFactor[0] = 3;

 // Tablespoons to Cup
 conversionFactor[1] = 16;

 // Cups to Pints
 conversionFactor[2] = 2;

 // Pints to Quarts
 conversionFactor[3] = 2;

 // Quarts to Gallons
 conversionFactor[4] = 4;

 // Gallons to Pecks
 conversionFactor[5] = 2;
```

Part

I

Ch

10

continues

Listing 10.1 Continued

```
// Pecks to Bushels
conversionFactor[6] = 4;

if ( fromIndx == toIndx) {
 return;
}

if ( fromIndx < toIndx ) {
 for (var indx=fromIndx; indx < toIndx; indx++) {
  convertAmount *= (1/conversionFactor[indx]);
 }
}
else {
 for (var indx=fromIndx; indx > toIndx; indx--) {
  convertAmount *= conversionFactor[indx-1];
 }
}

form.inAmount.value = convertAmount;
}

</SCRIPT>
</HEAD>
<BODY BGCOLOR=#FFFFFF>
<H1>Cook's Converter</H1>
<HR>

<FORM NAME="cookConvert">
<PRE>
<B>Amount:</B> <INPUT TYPE=text NAME=inAmount onChange=validateAmount(this)>

<B>Convert From:</B>
 <INPUT TYPE=radio NAME=convertFrom VALUE=0 onClick=setFromIndx(this)
CHECKED=true>
Teaspoons   <INPUT TYPE=radio NAME=convertFrom VALUE=4
onClick=setFromIndx(this)>
Quarts   <INPUT TYPE=radio NAME=convertFrom VALUE=1 onClick=setFromIndx(this)>
Tablespoons   <INPUT TYPE=radio NAME=convertFrom VALUE=5
onClick=setFromIndx(this)>
Gallons
 <INPUT TYPE=radio NAME=convertFrom VALUE=2 onClick=setFromIndx(this)>
Cups   <INPUT TYPE=radio NAME=convertFrom VALUE=6 onClick=setFromIndx(this)>
Pecks   <INPUT TYPE=radio NAME=convertFrom VALUE=3 onClick=setFromIndx(this)>
Pints   <INPUT TYPE=radio NAME=convertFrom VALUE=7 onClick=setFromIndx(this)>
Bushels

<B>Convert To:</B>
 <INPUT TYPE=radio NAME=convertTo VALUE=0 onClick=setToIndx(this) CHECKED=true>
Teaspoons   <INPUT TYPE=radio NAME=convertTo VALUE=4 onClick=setToIndx(this)>
Quarts
```

```
        <INPUT TYPE=radio NAME=convertTo VALUE=1 onClick=setToIndx(this)>
        Tablespoons    <INPUT TYPE=radio NAME=convertTo VALUE=5 onClick=setToIndx(this)>
        Gallons    <INPUT TYPE=radio NAME=convertTo VALUE=2 onClick=setToIndx(this)>
        Cups   <INPUT TYPE=radio NAME=convertTo VALUE=6 onClick=setToIndx(this)>
        Pecks   <INPUT TYPE=radio NAME=convertTo VALUE=3 onClick=setToIndx(this)>
        Pints   <INPUT TYPE=radio NAME=convertTo VALUE=7 onClick=setToIndx(this)>
        Bushels
        </PRE>
        <INPUT TYPE="button" VALUE="Calculate"   onClick=doConvert(this.form)>
        <INPUT TYPE="reset"  VALUE="Reset">

        </FORM>

        </CENTER>

        </BODY>
        </HTML>
```

Using VBScript

Now you'll build this in VBScript. First, you'll lay out the form. Next, you'll construct the various procedures that will carry out the conversion of the various measurements. Finally, you'll do some testing to ensure that your application works as advertised. By the time you're finished, you'll have the opportunity to exercise some of what you've learned so far. More particularly, in this example you'll get additional exposure to working with the following elements of VBScript:

- Processing text box events
- Processing radio button events
- Passing data to sub procedures
- Processing command button events

Laying Out the Form

This is a very simple form. You'll have one text field for amounts, two radio button sets for indicating the ConvertFrom and ConvertTo measures, and a couple of command buttons to tie everything together. Take a look at figure 10.1 to familiarize yourself with the form.

 TIP All of the examples in this chapter assume that you have a simple HTML template file (the same template from Chapter 5, "Including ActiveX Controls in Your Web Pages," if you used it).

To build this Cooking Conversion Tool example, follow these steps:

1. Start the ActiveX Control Pad and open your HTML template file from Chapter 5.
2. Update the comment header, TITLE value, and H1 tag pair to reflect the example name.

FIG. 10.1

This is the final Cook's Converter form.

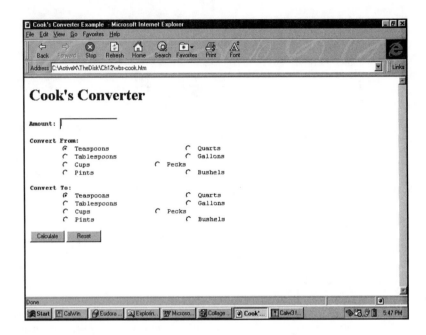

3. Save the file to a convenient working directory as VBS-COOK.HTM.

   The next few steps take you through the process of building the form. The complete listing of VBS-COOK.HTM is on the CD, so you'll want to check your work against it.

4. After the <HR> tag, add the HTML for the form. Your code should look something like Listing 10.2. Note that we have not closed the <BODY> tag with </BODY>. You'll take care of that in a moment.

On the CD

Listing 10.2   VBS-COOK.HTM   Starting the VBScript Implementation of the Cook's Converter

```
<BODY BGCOLOR=#FFFFFF>

<H1>Cook's Converter</H1>

<P>

<FORM NAME="cookConvert">
<PRE>
```

Use the <PRE> tag (for preformatted) so that its easy to lay out the form without worrying about tables and formatting. Concentrate on the VBScript aspects of this application. Let's take a look at each of the form controls and how they invoke their associated functions.

5. Next, you'll need to create a text entry box called InAmount. Typically, text boxes are used for questions or inputs that have any number of possible values. The InAmount text box invokes a method called ValidateAmount when the onChange event fires. Listing 10.3 shows an example of how your code might look.

Listing 10.3   *2VBS-COOK.HTM*   The Amount to Convert Text Box

```
<B>Amount:</B> <INPUT TYPE=text NAME=inAmount
onChange=validateAmount(inAmount.value)>
```

6. Finally, add the ConvertFrom and ConvertTo radio buttons which both invoke a similar method—one called SetFromIndx, the other SetToIndx—when the onClick event fires. Your code will look something like Listing 10.4.

Listing 10.4   *3VBS-COOK.HTM*   The Convert From And Convert To Radio Button Sets

```
<B>Convert From:</B>
 <INPUT TYPE=radio NAME=convertFrom VALUE=1 onClick=setFromIndx(1) CHECKED=true>
Teaspoons     <INPUT TYPE=radio NAME=convertFrom VALUE=5 onClick=setFromIndx(5)>
Quarts    <INPUT TYPE=radio NAME=convertFrom VALUE=2 onClick=setFromIndx(2)>
Tablespoons     <INPUT TYPE=radio NAME=convertFrom VALUE=6 onClick=setFromIndx(6)>
Gallons    <INPUT TYPE=radio NAME=convertFrom VALUE=3 onClick=setFromIndx(3)>
Cups    <INPUT TYPE=radio NAME=convertFrom VALUE=7 onClick=setFromIndx(7)>
Pecks    <INPUT TYPE=radio NAME=convertFrom VALUE=4 onClick=setFromIndx(4)>
Pints    <INPUT TYPE=radio NAME=convertFrom VALUE=8 onClick=setFromIndx(8)>
Bushels

<B>Convert To:</B>
 <INPUT TYPE=radio NAME=convertTo VALUE=0 onClick=setToIndx(1) CHECKED=true>
Teaspoons     <INPUT TYPE=radio NAME=convertTo VALUE=5 onClick=setToIndx(5)>
Quarts    <INPUT TYPE=radio NAME=convertTo VALUE=1 onClick=setToIndx(2)>
Tablespoons     <INPUT TYPE=radio NAME=convertTo VALUE=6 onClick=setToIndx(6)>
Gallons    <INPUT TYPE=radio NAME=convertTo VALUE=2 onClick=setToIndx(3)>
Cups    <INPUT TYPE=radio NAME=convertTo VALUE=7 onClick=setToIndx(7)>
Pecks    <INPUT TYPE=radio NAME=convertTo VALUE=3 onClick=setToIndx(4)>
Pints    <INPUT TYPE=radio NAME=convertTo VALUE=8 onClick=setToIndx(8)> Bushels
```

Notice that the formatting is quite strange. This is not exactly easily readable HTML. Since we're using <PRE> to simplify the HTML, the actual spacing of the code found in the <PRE> block above is the same code that generates the display in figure 10.1.

7. Adding the command buttons is straightforward. The action button executes the DoConvert when the onClick event fires as shown in Listing 10.5.

Part

I

Ch

10

On the CD

Listing 10.5   4VBS-COOK.HTM   Command Buttons for Cook's Converter

```
</PRE>
<INPUT TYPE="button" VALUE="Calculate"    onClick=doConvert>
<INPUT TYPE="reset"  VALUE="Reset">

</FORM>
```

Coding the Script

Now, let's start putting the script together. Before you start coding, let's review what you'll need to build. First, you'll be introduced to the functions required to do the cooking conversions. Then we'll review the global variables you'll need to construct.

The Cook's Converter employs several functions. Table 10.1 defines how these functions are used.

Table 10.1   Functions to Build the Cook's Converter Example

Function	Description
SetToIndx	Sets the ToIndx global variable.
SetFromIndx	Sets the FromIndx global variable.
ValidateAmount	Checks to be sure the amount field is numeric.
DoConvert	Converts one measure to another.

You'll also need to create a couple of global variables. The purpose of each of them is reviewed in Table 10.2.

Table 10.2   Global Variables for the Application

Variable	Description
FromIndx	The array index of the measure to be converted from.
ToIndx	The array index of the measure to be converted to.
ConvertAmount	The amount to be converted.

To start the script portion of VBS-COOK.HTM, follow these steps:

1. Insert a <SCRIPT> tag immediately following the <TITLE> tag set before the </HEAD> closing tag. You can use the ActiveX Control Pad to insert this script element by selecting Tool, Script Wizard from the menu bar. You'll also need to create the application's

global variables. To create a global variable, place the cursor over the Action window and press the right mouse button. Select New Global Variable. Enter **fromIndx** to create the `fromIndx` global variable. Repeat the process for `toIndx` and `convertAmount`. The Script Wizard will create code that looks something like Listing 10.6.

Listing 10.6   5VBS-COOK.HTM   Declaring Global Variables

```
<! -------------------------------------------------
<! --
<! -- Description: Cook's Converter Example
<! --
<! -- Author:  Brian Farrar
<! --
<! --   Date:  5/27/96
<! -------------------------------------------------

<HTML>

<HEAD>
<TITLE>Cook's Converter Example
</TITLE>
<SCRIPT LANGUAGE="VBScript">

'-------------------------------------------
'-- Declare and initialize globals
'-------------------------------------------
Dim fromIndx
Dim toIndx
Dim convertAmount

fromIndx = 1
toIndx = 1
```

2. Next, you'll code the `setFromIndx` and the `setToIndx` procedures that are executed when the `fromIndx` and `toIndx` fields are changed. To add `setFromIndx`, select the Procedures item in the Script Wizard's Action List. Press the right mouse button and select New Procedure. For this procedure, you'll need to select the Code View in order to enter the required VBScript code shown in the top half of Listing 10.7. Repeat the process for the `setToIndx` procedure using the code from the bottom half of Listing 10.7.

Listing 10.7   6VBS-COOK.HTM   The *SetIndex* Functions

```
'-------------------------------------------
'-- Set the convert from index value
'-------------------------------------------
Sub setFromIndx(anIndx)
 fromIndx = anIndx
End Sub
```

continues

Part

I

Ch

10

Listing 10.7   Continued

```
'-----------------------------------------
'-- Set the convert to index value
'-----------------------------------------
Sub setToIndx(anIndx)
 toIndx = anIndx
End Sub
```

3. Next code the `ValidateAmount` procedure. This function checks to be sure that the data entered in `InAmount` is a number. Use the Script Wizard to add this procedure as described in the previous step. Your code should look something like Listing 10.8.

Listing 10.8   *7VBS-COOK.HTM*   The *ValidateAmount* Function

```
'-----------------------------------------
'-- Validates the amount field
'-----------------------------------------
Sub validateAmount(inputItem)
 If IsNumeric(inputItem) Then
  Exit Sub
 Else
  MsgBox "This field must be numeric"
 End If
End Sub
```

Take a look at a difference between JavaScript and VBScript. Unlike the JavaScript version of this application, which uses a homegrown function determine whether the field is numeric, the VBScript implementation uses the built-in function `IsNumeric`.

4. Finally, you'll use the Script Wizard code view to add the `DoConvert` function. `DoConvert` executes when the customer presses the calculate button. Take a look at Listing 10.9 and then we'll discuss how it works.

On the CD

Listing 10.9   *8VBS-COOK.HTM*   The *DoConvert* Function

```
'-----------------------------------------
'-- Do the conversion
'-----------------------------------------
Sub doConvert

 Dim conversionFactor(7)
 Dim indx

 validateAmount(Document.cookConvert.inAmount.value)
 convertAmount = Document.cookConvert.inAmount.value

 ' Teaspoons to Tablespoons
 conversionFactor(1) = 3
```

```
' Tablespoons to Cup
conversionFactor(2) = 16

' Cups to Pints
conversionFactor(3) = 2

' Pints to Quarts
conversionFactor(4) = 2

' Quarts to Gallons
conversionFactor(5) = 4

' Gallons to Pecks
conversionFactor(6) = 2

' Pecks to Bushels
conversionFactor(7) = 4

If fromIndx = toIndx Then
  Exit Sub
End If

If fromIndx < toIndx Then

  For indx = fromIndx To toIndx-1
   convertAmount = convertAmount * (1/conversionFactor(indx))
  Next
Else
  For indx = toIndx To fromIndx-1
   convertAmount = convertAmount * conversionFactor(indx)
  Next
End If
Document.cookConvert.inAmount.value = convertAmount
End Sub


</SCRIPT>
</HEAD>
```

DoConvert keeps a list of conversion factors in an array called ConversionFactor. To calculate the conversion from any arbitrary units to any other units, simply multiply (or divide) all the conversion factors between the from unit and the to unit, times the amount you're converting.

5. Save your work as VBS-COOK.HTM.

Now that you've completed the HTML document, you can test your work using Microsoft Internet Explorer 3.0. Follow these steps:

1. Start Microsoft Internet Explorer 3.0.

2. Place the text cursor in the document text box and type **VBS-COOK.HTM**. Be sure to include the fully qualified path to your document. Press Enter.

3. If you've done everything correctly, the HTML document should look something like figure 10.1.

CAUTION

If you have an error anywhere in your VBScript, the entire script may fail to execute. MSIE 3.0 simply ignores malformed script data. Note that sometimes preceding HTML errors can cause an error in a script.

 An easy way to debug problems with your script is to use the MSGBOX function from VBScript. The MSGBOX function allows you to pop up a dialog box with a string of text and an OK button. Use this feature to examine values of variables you're interested in testing.

The ActiveX Internet Control Pack

Using the TCP Control in VB Applications

The *Transmission Control Protocol* (*TCP*) is the first of two principal methods for transmitting data over the Internet today. TCP is a connection-oriented protocol most often used for transmitting *Internet Protocol* (*IP*) packets over a network. Connection-oriented protocols like TCP are responsible for ensuring that a series of data packets sent over a network all arrive at the destination and are properly sequenced. The ActiveX TCP control allows you to easily handle TCP data packets in your applications, without knowing much about the details of the TCP protocol. ■

Learn the properties of the TCP ActiveX control

Properties are used to configure and customize an ActiveX control.

Learn the methods available to programmers using the TCP control

Methods take some sort of action, and ActiveX Controls use methods to add functionality to your applications.

Learn the events triggered by the TCP control

Event-driven programming with ActiveX Controls would be impossible without the events fired by a control.

Build an example Visual Basic application that employs the TCP control

Nothing makes learning a new control easier than building a practice application.

Properties

Table 11.1 summarizes all the properties available in the TCP control. Not surprisingly, all the data elements required to create a TCP connection are included as properties in this control.

Table 11.1 Properties in the TCP Control	
Property	**Purpose**
BytesReceived	The amount of data in the receive buffer
LocalHostName	The name of the local machine
LocalIP	The Internet Protocol (IP) address of the local machine
LocalPort	The TCP port used by the local machine for this communication
RemoteHost	The name of the remote machine
RemoteHostIP	The IP address of the remote machine
RemotePort	The TCP port used by the remote machine for this communication
SocketHandle	The handle used to communicate with the Winsock layer
State	The current status of the connection

Before we dive into the properties themselves, let's consider the basic components of a TCP connection. As shown in figure 11.1, a TCP connection requires that the client and the server each have an IP address and a port.

FIG. 11.1

This is a basic TCP connection between a client and a server.

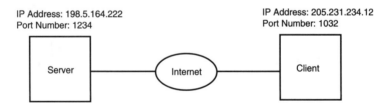

IP Address: 198.5.164.222
Port Number: 1234

IP Address: 205.231.234.12
Port Number: 1032

Server — Internet — Client

The specified port must not be used by any other application. Many ports already are defined as standard ports, and therefore are off-limits to your application. (For instance, Web browsers use port 80 to connect to Web servers.) Most books about TCP/IP contain a good list of port numbers that are already spoken for. A good rule of thumb is to use port numbers higher than 1000, for most of those are free.

Now, let's examine a few of these properties in more detail.

The *RemoteHost*, *RemotePort*, and *LocalPort* Properties

RemoteHost, RemotePort, and LocalPort are the properties you'll set in your programs most often. If the application you're writing is a client that will initiate connections with other applications, then you'll set the RemoteHost and RemotePort properties, respectively, to the appropriate host and port. RemoteHost should be a string with either a domain name (such as ftp.myhost.com) or a dot format IP address (such as 198.5.164.222). Set the RemotePort value to the port number that the server listens on.

If the application you're writing is a server that will listen for connections from another application, then you'll set Local Port to the port number you want to listen for connections on. For the hypothetical application shown in figure 11.1, the client would set RemoteHost = "198.5.164.222" and RemotePort = 1234. (The combination of an IP address and a host name is sometimes referred to as a *socket*.) The TCP control takes care of setting LocalHost on the client side, so on the server side, the server application must also set LocalHost = 1234.

The *State* Property

The State property stores the current state of the TCP connection. Since State is a read-only property, you never set the state of the connection. You will, however, want to use the value of State in all sorts of ways. Table 11.2 summarizes the values that State may contain.

Table 11.2   Possible Values for *State*

Value	Description
sckClosed	Socket is closed (default)
sckOpen	Socket is open
sckListening	Listening on the socket
sckConnectionPending	Connection is pending
sckResolvingHost	Resolving the host name to obtain an IP address
sckConnecting	Currently connecting
sckConnected	Connected
sckClosing	Another application is closing the socket
sckError	Socket has erred

Part
II
Ch
11

Most of the time, your programs will check to see if the connection is sckOpen or sckClosed.

Methods

The lifespan of a connection includes each of the following steps:

1. The server listens on a specific port.
2. The client requests a connection with the server.
3. The server accepts the connection.

4. Data is transferred between the client and the server.

5. Either the client or the server closes the connection.

As Table 11.3 shows, the TCP control has a method for each of these actions.

Table 11.3   Methods in the TCP Control

Method	Purpose
Accept	Accepts an incoming connection
Close	Closes a TCP connection
Connect	Makes a connection request to a distant machine
GetData	Obtains the current block of data
Listen	Creates and listens on a socket
PeekData	Obtains a copy of the current block of data
SendData	Sends data to a remote machine

Connecting Clients and Servers

To implement the server side of a TCP connection, you use the following methods:

- Listen
- Accept

Suppose that you have a TCP control named MyTCPControl. Your VB code to start the server looks like this:

```
MyTCPControl.LocalPort = 1252
MyTCPControl.Listen
```

When a client requests a connection to the server, the server must accept the connection. Your VB code for accepting a connection looks like this:

```
Private Sub MyTCPControl_ConnectionRequest(ByVal requestID As Long)

MyTCPControl.Accept requestID

End Sub
```

Note that you use a response function for the ConnectionRequest event to obtain the requestID for the connection.

To implement the client side of a TCP connection, your VB program must contain code like the following:

```
MyOtherTCPControl.RemotePort = 1252
MyOtherTCPControl.RemoteHost = "198.5.164.222"

MyOtherTCPControl.Connect
```

N O T E This assumes that your client program has a TCP control named
`MyOtherTCPControl.` ■

Sending and Receiving Data

Clients and servers use data transmission methods the same way. Your code to send data from one to the other looks something like this:

```
MyTCPControl.SendData "This is my message"
```

To obtain received data, you usually write a response to the `DataArrival()` event (more on `DataArrival()` in a moment). Your code looks something like this:

```
Private Sub sktStockServer_DataArrival(ByVal bytesTotal As Long)

Dim A

MyTCPControl.GetData A

    DoSomethingWith A

End Sub
```

Note that calling `GetData` causes the incoming buffer to be emptied. If you want to look at the incoming data without clearing the data, you can use `PeekData` in a similar manner.

Events

You've already seen how several of the most important events summarized in Table 11.4 are used. In the stock ticker example coming up, you'll learn how to respond to some of the others.

Table 11.4 Summary of Events in the TCP Control

Event	Description
`Close`	Triggered when the remote machine closes the connection
`Connect`	Signals that the connection is ready for data transfer
`ConnectionRequest`	Occurs when a distant machine requests a connection
`DataArrival`	Fires when new data has arrived in the receive buffer
`Error`	Signals a background processing error
`SendProgress`	Used to signal progress of data transfers

Part
II

Ch
11

The Stock Ticker Application

Your first introduction to using the ActiveX Internet Control Pack is going to be a stock ticker project that consists of two applications:

- **Stock Ticker Server**—Responsible for responding to requests from Stock Ticker Client for pricing updates.
- **Stock Ticker Client**—Responsible for displaying the ticker tape and requesting pricing updates from the server.

To understand how these two applications work together, you might want to run them before continuing. Be sure to start the server first—the client may fail to start correctly if the server isn't running.

The following sections take you through the process of building these two applications in a step-by-step manner.

Stock Ticker Server

Surprisingly, the server is the easier of the two applications to build. This example does an excellent job of demonstrating the ease and power of the ActiveX Internet Control Pack for including the Internet in your applications. To complete this example, you need to construct the following:

- frmStockServer—The startup form for the application, which contains the TCP control.
- sktStockServer—The TCP control to be used by the server.
- Status—A status bar control.

N O T E   These examples assume that you already know how to program in Visual Basic. ■

To construct Stock Ticker Server, complete the following steps:

1. Start Visual Basic 4.0.
2. Create a form named frmStockServer. Change the Caption property to Stock Ticker Server and the Name property to frmStockServer.
3. Resize frmStockServer to a smaller, more comfortable size, and then add a label to the center of the screen. Your label should be something like Stock Ticker Server.
4. Save the project to a convenient working directory.
5. Add the TCP control to the control toolbar. Choose Tools, Custom Controls, then select Microsoft Winsock Controls and click OK. This adds the TCP and UDP controls to your toolbar for this project.
6. Drag and drop the TCP control onto frmStockServer.
7. Drag and drop a StatusBar control onto frmStockServer. You want to use the simplest form of the StatusBar control, so set the Style property to 1 - Simple Text. Add some initializing text to the Simple Text property.

8. Add a menu item named `Server`, with three options: Restart (which is initially disabled), Stop, and Exit. Name these options `mnuServerRestart`, `mnuServerStop`, and `mnuServerExit`, respectively. When you're finished, the form should look something like figure 11.2.

FIG. 11.2

Here's how the
`frmStockServer`
form should appear.

9. Next, select the TCP control and change its `Name` property to `sktStockServer`. Change the `Index` property to `0` (you'll learn why in a moment).

10. Now, it's time to start coding the application. Open the code window by choosing View, Code. Declare two public variables, `gFirstTime` (used to initialize the stock ticker function named `SendStockQuotes`) and `gConnectionCount` (used to track the number of connections the server is supporting). Your code looks something like Listing 11.1.

On the CD

Listing 11.1 *STOCKSERVER.VBP* General Declarations for *frmStockServer*

```
Public gFirstTime As Boolean
Public gConnectionCount As Integer
```

11. Next, code the `Form_Load()` function for `frmStockServer`. When the form loads, you need to initialize `gFirstTime` and `sktStockServer.LocalPort`. Place the TCP control into Listen mode and update the Status bar to inform the user. Your code should look something like Listing 11.2.

On the CD

Listing 11.2 *2STOCKSERVER.VBP* *Form_Load()* Function

```
Private Sub Form_Load()

    gFirstTime = True
    gConnectionCount = 0
    '----------------------------------------------.-
    '-- Set the port to some arbitrary number high
    '-- numbered port.
    '----------------------------------------------
    sktStockServer(gConnectionCount).LocalPort = 1234

    '----------------------------------------------
    '-- Start the server listening for connects.
    '----------------------------------------------
    sktStockServer(gConnectionCount).Listen

    Status.SimpleText = "Waiting for a connection..."

End Sub
```

Part

II

Ch

11

In this application, the TCP control with an index of zero is the listener. That is, the server listens on sktStockServer(0) and then delegates requesting clients to new instances of sktStockServer (sktStockServer(1), sktStockServer(2), and so on).

12. As a safety measure, I like to add a Form_Terminate() response function that makes sure the connection has been closed. To avoid errors, you want to ensure that the socket hasn't already been closed by some other (polite!) function. Your code should look something like Listing 11.3.

Listing 11.3   3STOCKSERVER.VBP   Form_Terminate() Function

```
Private Sub Form_Terminate()

    For Jndx = 0 To gConnectionCount
        If sktStockServer(Jndx).State <> sktClosed Then
            sktStockServer(Jndx).Close
        If Jndx <> 0 Then
                Unload sktStockServer(Jndx)
            End If
        End If
    Next
End Sub
```

Notice that the termination procedure loops through all the open connections that the server is currently managing. As you'll see in a moment, the TCP control can be used to manage many connections simultaneously. Each connection is accessed by a specific index.

13. The mnuServerRestart menu option is initially disabled; however, when other events cause it to become enabled (for example, when the server has been stopped), you need to place the TCP control with an index of zero in Listen mode again. You also need to disable mnuServerRestart, enable mnuServerStop, and inform the user. Your code should look something like Listing 11.4.

Listing 11.4   4STOCKSERVER.VBP   mnuServerRestart_Click() Response Function

```
Private Sub mnuServerRestart_Click()
    sktStockServer(0).Listen
    Status.SimpleText = "Waiting for a connection..."
    mnuServerRestart.Enabled = False
    mnuServerStop.Enabled = True
End Sub
```

14. When the `mnuServerStop` menu option is clicked, you need to close all the connections. You also need to disable `mnuServerStop`, enable `mnuServerRestart`, and inform the user. Your code should look something like Listing 11.5.

On the CD

Listing 11.5 *5STOCKSERVER.VBP* *mnuServerStop_Click()* Response Function

```
Private Sub mnuServerStop_Click()

    For Jndx = 0 To gConnectionCount
        If sktStockServer(Jndx).State <> sktClosed Then
            sktStockServer(Jndx).Close
            If Jndx <> 0 Then
                Unload sktStockServer(Jndx)
            End If
        End If
    Next
    Status.SimpleText = "Server Stopped"
    mnuServerRestart.Enabled = True
    mnuServerStop.Enabled = False
    gConnectionCount = 0

End Sub
```

Notice that each `Close` is preceded by a verification that the TCP connection is not already closed. The other important thing to remember is to unload unused instances of the TCP control. Of course, VB won't let you unload the instance you included at design time, so you should only perform the Unload for an instance of `sktStockServer` where the index equals zero.

15. The `mnuServerExit()` function uses a simple call to `End`. Leave the connection-closing work to the `Terminate()` function.

You need to code the following response functions for the TCP control:

- `ConnectionRequest()`
- `DataArrival()`
- `Close()`
- `Error()`

Follow these steps to build the necessary response functions:

1. `ConnectionRequest()` fires when a client requests a connection on the port where your TCP control is listening. To complete the connection, you need to load a new instance of the TCP control, then accept the connection. Don't forget to notify the user. Your code should look something like Listing 11.6.

On the CD

Listing 11.6   6STOCKSERVER.VBP   ConnectionRequest() Response Function

```
Private Sub sktStockServer_ConnectionRequest(Index As Integer, ByVal requestID
As Long)

    Status.SimpleText = "Connection request received..."
    gConnectionCount = gConnectionCount + 1
    Load sktStockServer(gConnectionCount)
    sktStockServer(gConnectionCount).Accept requestID

End Sub
```

2. DataArrival() occurs when there is data in the incoming buffer to be obtained. Stock
   Ticker Server doesn't have much data to collect, because its job basically is to distribute
   data. Stock Ticker Client, however, does send a request to Stock Ticker Server that
   starts each new feed of updated stock prices. Your code should look something like
   Listing 11.7.

On the CD

Listing 11.7   7STOCKSERVER.VBP   The DataArrival Event Handler

```
Private Sub sktStockServer_DataArrival(Index As Integer, ByVal bytesTotal As Long)
    '----------------------------------------------------------
    '-- The Client will send a bit of data in order to trigger
    '-- another transmission of the quote. The server doesn't
    '-- care what the data is.
    '----------------------------------------------------------
    Dim vtTrashCan
    sktStockServer(Index).GetData vtTrashCan

    '----------------------------------------------------------
    '-- Send the quotes back to the
    '----------------------------------------------------------
    Status.SimpleText "Request for stock quote feed received..."
    SendStockQuotes Index
End Sub
```

The server doesn't care what kind of data the client sends. As long as something is sent,
the server starts sending the next round of stock quotations.

3. Close() occurs when the distant end closes the connection. You want the server to
   respond by closing the connection, so your code should look something like Listing 11.8.

On the CD

Listing 11.8   8STOCKSERVER.VBP   The Close Event Handler

```
Private Sub sktStockServer_Close(Index As Integer)

    Status.SimpleText "Connection closed by user client."
    sktStockServer(Index).Close

End Sub
```

4. When an error occurs, you want to report the error to the user, then close the open socket. Your code should look something like Listing 11.9.

On the CD

Listing 11.9   *9STOCKSERVER.VBP*   The Error Handler

```
Private Sub sktStockServer_Error(Index As Integer, Number As Integer,
Description As String, Scode As Long, Source As String, HelpFile As String,
HelpContext As Long, CancelDisplay As Boolean)

    MsgBox "Error [" & Number & "] " & Description
    If sktStockServer(Index).State <> sktClosed Then
        sktStockServer(Index).Close
    End If

End Sub
```

The Error event is nice enough to pass the proper error description and number to you, so this function is quite simple.

Stock Ticker Client

Building the client portion of this project is a bit more complicated than building the server portion. Have no fear, however—nothing here should stump you. To complete Stock Ticker Client, you must construct the following:

- frmStockClient—The startup form for the application, which contains the TCP control.
- sktStockClient—The TCP control to be used to connect to the server.
- Timer1—The control that will trigger the client to ask for another data feed from the server.
- txtTickerTape—The text box control to display the stock quotations received from the server.
- Status—A status bar control.

N O T E   Again, these examples assume that you already know how to program in Visual Basic. ■

To construct Stock Ticker Client, complete the following steps:

1. Start Visual Basic 4.0.
2. Create a form named frmStockClient. Change the Caption property to Stock Ticker Client and the Name property to frmStockClient.
3. Add a Timer control to the project. The default name of Timer1 is fine. Make sure that the Enabled property is set to True.
4. Add a Text box control to the center of the form. Change the Name property to txtStockTicker. Add some initialization text to the Text property (something like Waiting for market feed...).

Part
II

Ch
11

5. Resize `frmStockClient` to a smaller, more comfortable size.

6. Save the project to a convenient working directory.

7. Even if you added the TCP control to Stock Ticker Server, you probably need to do it again. To add the TCP control to the control toolbar, choose Tools, Custom Controls, and then select Microsoft Winsock Controls and click OK. This adds the TCP and UDP controls to your toolbar for this project.

8. Drag and drop the TCP control onto `frmStockClient`. Rename the TCP control `sktStockClient`.

9. Drag and drop a `StatusBar` control onto `frmStockClient`. Change the `Name` property to `Status`. You need to use the simplest form of the `StatusBar` control, so set the `Style` property to `1 - Simple Text`. Add some initializing text to the `Simple Text` property.

10. Add a menu item named `Client`, with two options: Restart (which is initially disabled) and Exit. Name these options `mnuRestart` and `mnuExit`, respectively. When you finish, the form should look something like figure 11.3.

FIG. 11.3

Your design view of the Stock Ticker Client form should resemble this.

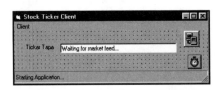

11. Now, it's time to start coding the application. Open the code window by choosing View, Code. Declare a public variable `strTickerText` (used to keep the current `Ticker Tape` string). Your code should look something like Listing 11.10.

Listing 11.10 10STOCKCLIENT.VBP Declaration of a Global Variable

```
'---------------------------------------------
'-- This global variable keeps the current
'-- value of the Ticker
'---------------------------------------------
Dim strTickerText As String
```

12. Next, code the `Form_Load()` function for `frmStockClient`. When the form loads, you need to initialize `Timer1.Interval`, `txtTickerTape.MaxLength`, `strTickerText`, `sktStockClient.RemotePort`, and `sktStockClient.RemoteHost`. Then place the TCP control into Connect mode. Your code should look something like Listing 11.11.

On the CD

Listing 11.11 *11STOCKCLIENT.VBP Form_Load() Function for frmStockClient*

```
Private Sub Form_Load()

    Timer1.Interval = 500

    txtTickerTape.MaxLength = 50

    strTickerText = "..."

    '-----------------------------------------
    '-- Set the client to connect on the port
    '-- that the server is listening on
    '-----------------------------------------
    sktStockClient.RemotePort = 1234

    '-----------------------------------------
    '-- Using this IP address allows testing
    '-- without connecting to a network.
    '-- 127.0.0.1 is often referred to as
    '-- local host. If you're using this app
    '-- over a network, you'll use a different
    '-- IP address here.
    '-----------------------------------------
    sktStockClient.RemoteHost = "127.0.0.1"

    sktStockClient.Connect
End Sub
```

Notice that the application connects to the port listened to by the server. The client application also employs a helpful feature of TCP/IP. The IP address 127.0.0.1 has special meaning. This address refers to the *local host*; that is, the computer on which the application is running. For more details, consult any TCP/IP reference. Knowing the details of how the local host address works is not as important as knowing what it allows you to do in this situation. By using this address, you can test both the client and server on your own machine.

13. As a safety measure, I like to add a Form_Terminate() response function that makes sure the connection has been closed. To avoid errors, you need to ensure that the socket hasn't already been closed by some other function. Your code should look something like Listing 11.12.

Listing 11.12   *12STOCKCLIENT.VBP*   *Form_Terminate() Function for frmStockClient*

```
Private Sub Form_Terminate()
    If sktStockClient <> sktClosed Then
        sktStockClient.Close
    End If
End Sub
```

14. The mnuRestart menu option is initially disabled. Other events will cause the client to enable this option (for example, when the server issues a Close command). In order to restart the client, you need to issue another Connect command. You also need to disable mnuRestart, enable Timer1, and inform the user. Your code should look something like Listing 11.13.

Listing 11.13   *13STOCKCLIENT.VBP*   *mnuRestart Response Function*

```
Private Sub mnuRestart_Click()
    Timer1.Enabled = True
    mnuRestart.Enabled = False

    sktStockClient.Connect
End Sub
```

15. The mnuServerExit() function uses a simple call to End. Leave the connection-closing work to the Terminate() function.

You need to code the following response functions for the TCP control:

- Connect()
- DataArrival()
- Close()
- Error()

Follow these steps to build the necessary response functions:

1. Connect() fires when a client's request for a connection is accepted. When a connection is made, the client must request the stock feed from the server. Remember that the server doesn't care what the request says, so you just need to send something. Don't forget to keep the user informed about what's happening from time to time. Your code should look something like Listing 11.14.

Listing 11.14   *14STOCKCLIENT.VBP*   *Connect() Response Function*

```
Private Sub sktStockClient_Connect()
    Status.SimpleText = "Connected to Stock Price Server"
    sktStockClient.SendData "Something"
End Sub
```

The call to send data is really quite simple, as you can see.

2. `DataArrival()` occurs when there is data in the incoming buffer to be obtained. Remember that the client's principal job is to collect and display stock price data. Your code should look something like Listing 11.15.

On the CD

Listing 11.15 *15STOCKCLIENT.VBP* *DataArrival()* **Response Function**

```
Private Sub sktStockClient_DataArrival(ByVal bytesTotal As Long)

    Status.SimpleText = "Getting Stock Data..."
    sktStockClient.GetData strTickerText, vbString

    ShowTickerTape (strTickerText)

End Sub
```

The client expects the data to be of type `String`. The `GetData()` function has an optional parameter allowing you to specify this. The response function finishes by passing the new `strTickerText` value to the `ShowTickerTape()` function for displaying.

3. You need to code `Close()` so that the client behaves appropriately when the connection is closed. This code should look something like Listing 11.16.

On the CD

Listing 11.16 *16STOCKCLIENT.VBP* *Close()* **Response Function**

```
Private Sub sktStockClient_Close()

    Status.SimpleText = "Connection closed by server"
    Timer1.Enabled = False
    mnuRestart.Enabled = True
    sktStockClient.Close

End Sub
```

4. When an error occurs, you want to report the error to the user, then close the open socket. Your code should look something like Listing 11.17.

On the CD

Listing 11.17 *17STOCKCLIENT.VBP* *Error* **Response Function**

```
Private Sub sktStockClient_Error(Number As Integer, Description As String,
Scode As Long, Source As String, HelpFile As String, HelpContext As Long,
CancelDisplay As Boolean)
    If sktStockClient.State <> sktClose Then
        sktStockClient.Close
    End If
    Status.SimpleText = Description
    mnuRestart.Enabled = True
End Sub
```

5. You now have all the communications set up, and you need to finish setting up the display of the stock ticker tape. This requires two functions. The first is a response to the Timer event of the Timer1 control. Each time the timer fires, a bit more of the ticker tape is displayed. This function is quite simple, and the code should look like Listing 11.18.

Listing 11.18   *18STOCKCLIENT.VBP   Timer1 Timer()* Response Function

```
Private Sub Timer1_Timer()
    ShowTickerTape strTickerText
End Sub
```

6. The second function you need is the ShowTickerTape() function. The ticker tape function takes the feed from the client and displays it in a left-to-right scrolling manner. When the full message has been displayed, another request is issued to the server. The code for this function should look like Listing 11.19.

Listing 11.19   *19STOCKCLIENT.VBP   ShowTickerTape()* Function

```
Public Sub ShowTickerTape(strTickerTape)

    Dim strTickerSoFar As String
    Static strCurrentDisplay As String
    Static Indx As Integer

    Indx = Indx + 1

    strTickerSoFar = Mid(strTickerTape, Len(strTickerTape) - (Indx - 1), 1)

    strCurrentDisplay = strTickerSoFar & strCurrentDisplay

    If Len(strCurrentDisplay) = txtTickerTape.MaxLength Then
        strCurrentDisplay = Left(strCurrentDisplay, txtTickerTape.MaxLength)
    End If

    txtTickerTape.Text = strCurrentDisplay

    If Indx = Len(strTickerTape) Then
        sktStockClient.SendData "Something"
        Indx = 0
    End If

End Sub
```

Testing the Applications

Finally, you're ready to test this project. Follow these steps to test both applications:

1. Start the Stock Ticker Server application. If you named the application as described in the example, the easiest way to do this is to click the Start button, then choose Run.

Enter **StockServer.exe** (with the appropriate path) and the server application will start. Figure 11.4 shows how the application should look.

FIG. 11.4

It's easy to check Stock Ticker Server for a successful startup.

Notice that the server's status bar indicates that it's waiting for a connection.

2. Next, start the Stock Ticker Client application. If you named the application as described in the example, click the Start button, then choose Run. Enter **StockClient.exe** (with the appropriate path) and the client application will start. Figure 11.5 shows how the application should look.

FIG. 11.5

This is how a healthy Stock Ticker Client looks at startup.

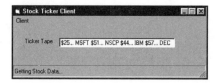

If all is well, the client will indicate on the status bar that it's Getting stock data.... The server's status bar will show the Request for stock quote feed received message.

You probably got everything to work perfectly on the first try. If you didn't, however, here are a couple of hints for debugging your code:

■ Determine if you have a communications problem or a problem with the ShowStockTicker() display. Try commenting out the ShowStockTicker() function and simply display the stock quote feed without scrolling it across the screen. This should be a matter of simply equating the txtTickerTape.Text property to the value obtained by GetData in the DataArrival() response function.

■ Make sure that the server is receiving the request for stock data from the client. The best way to do this is to run StockClient.exe from the command line and run StockServer.exe from VB. Set a break point in the DataArrival() response function for the server.

■ Use MsgBox() to display the value of sktStockServer.State and sktStockClient.State to ensure that the connection opens and closes properly.

CHAPTER 12

Using the UDP Control in VB Applications

The *User Datagram Protocol* (*UDP*) is the second of two principle methods for transmitting data over the Internet. UDP is a connectionless protocol most often used for transmitting Internet Protocol (IP) packets over a network. Connectionless protocols like UDP are typically employed for sending independent data packets—where one packet has no relationship to the next sequential packet—over a network. In the Stock Ticker example in the previous chapter, there is an obvious relationship between one request from the client to the server for stock price information and the next. In fact, the client would not even ask for the next stock ticker feed until it had finished processing the first one, and the server would not send another stock feed until the client had received the previous message and asked for the next feed. In essence, the requests for stock price information and the subsequent replies were part of an ongoing dialogue between client and server.

As you'll learn in this chapter, UDP often is used for network services that do not require an ongoing conversation between client and server. UDP senders typically don't care whether the receiver actually receives the message. Instead, UDP is used for discrete transmissions of information where the individual requests and replies are unrelated to one another. The best part about the ActiveX

Learn the properties of the UDP ActiveX control

Properties make configuring and using an ActiveX control easier.

Learn the methods available to programmers using the UDP ActiveX control

You'll use an ActiveX Control's methods to integrate ActiveX functionality into your applications.

Learn the events triggered by the UDP ActiveX control

ActiveX Controls also provide for certain events to be triggered. Reacting to these events can make your programs Internet-ready.

Build an example Visual Basic application that employs the UDP control

The best way to learn about UDP is to build an application that uses UDP for data communication. We'll put together a sample application in this chapter.

UDP control, however, is the ease with which you can implement these sorts of services without knowing much about the details of the UDP protocol. ■

Properties

Table 12.1 summarizes the properties available in the UDP control. All the data elements required to create a UDP connection are included as properties in this control.

Table 12.1   Properties of the UDP ActiveX Control

Property	Purpose
LocalHostName	Name of the local machine
LocalIP	Internet Protocol (IP) address of the local machine
LocalPort	TCP port used by the local machine for this communication
RemoteHost	Name of the remote machine
RemoteHostIP	IP address of the remote machine
RemotePort	TCP port used by the remote machine for this communication
SocketHandle	Handle used to communicate with the Winsock layer

Consider the basic components of a UDP connection. As shown in figure 12.1, a UDP connection (like a TCP connection) requires that the client and server each have both an IP address and a port.

FIG. 12.1

Examine this typical UDP connection.

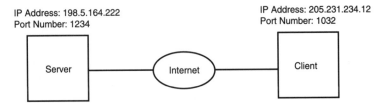

The specified port must not be used by any other application. Many ports already are defined as standard ports, and therefore are off-limits to your application. For instance, FTP servers use ports 20 and 21 to manage connections between clients and servers. A good rule of thumb is to use port numbers higher than 1,000, most of which are free.

Now, let's look at a few of these properties in more detail.

The *RemoteHost*, *RemotePort*, and *LocalPort* Properties

Just as with the TCP control, RemoteHost, RemotePort, and LocalPort are the properties of the UDP control you'll be setting most often. You'll set the RemoteHost and RemotePort properties to the host and port number, respectively, on which your application will be sending a message. On the receiving application, you'll set LocalPort to the port number where you want to receive the message. So, in the hypothetical application in figure 12.1, the client would set RemoteHost = "198.5.164.222" and RemotePort = 1234. (Note that the combination of an IP address and a host name is sometimes referred to as a "socket.")

Methods

Unlike the TCP control, the UDP control has only a couple of methods. This is because the connectionless UDP protocol is less involved than the TCP control. Table 12.2 summarizes the methods for the UDP control.

Table 12.2 Methods for the UDP Control

Method	Description
Connect	Makes a connection request to a distant machine
GetData	Obtains the current block of data
SendData	Sends data to a remote machine

Because the UDP protocol does not involve an ongoing conversation between two computers, there is no need for the Accept, Listen, and Close methods found in the TCP control. The reasons for this will become more obvious in a moment.

Connecting the Sending and Receiving Applications

To implement the receiving side of a UDP connection, you need to do the following:

- Set the LocalHost property.
- Employ the GetData method when data arrives (that is, when the DataArrival event is triggered).

Suppose that you have a UDP control named MyUDPControl. To program the receiver, your VB code should look something like the following:

```
MyUDPControl.LocalPort = 1252
```

You also need to provide an event handler for the DataArrival event (more on this in a moment) as follows:

```
Private Sub MyUDPControl_DataArrival(ByVal bytesTotal As Long)

    Dim ADatagram

    MyUDPControl.GetData ADatagram
        DoSomethingWith ADatagram

End Sub
```

Part
II

Ch
12

To implement the sender side of a UDP connection, you need to do the following:

- Set the `RemoteHost` property
- Set the `RemotePort` property
- Send data using the `SendData` method

When a sending application sends data over the network, you must initialize the `RemotePort` and `RemoteHost` properties, and then send data using the `SendData` method, with code similar to the following:

```
Dim ADatagram

MyOtherUDPControl.RemoteHost = "198.5.164.222"
MyOtherUDPCOntrol.RemotePort = 1252

MyOtherUDPControl.SendData ADatagram
```

N O T E The sample code shown here assumes that your sender program has a UDP control named `MyOtherUDPControl`. ▆

Events

Similar to the method list, the event list for the UDP control is quite sparse. Table 12.3 summarizes the events that are fired by the UDP control.

Table 12.3 Summary of Events in the UDP Control

Event	Description
DataArrival	Fires when new data has arrived in the receive buffer
Error	Signals a background processing error

These events are triggered the same way for the UDP control as they are for the TCP control (refer to the last chapter for details).

Building the Traffic Signal Project

To try out the UDP control, let's build a sample project that represents the workings of a traffic signal, along with someone's response to that traffic signal. This example actually consists of two applications:

- **Traffic Signal**—This application operates a normal traffic signal. The light is switched from green to yellow to red in a cycle based on a timer. When the light changes, the traffic signal sends out a UDP message indicating the color of the light.

■ **Automatic Pilot**—This application receives the current value of the traffic signal, then presses a vehicle's accelerator or brake pedal as appropriate.

To get an idea of how these two applications work together, you may want to run them before continuing. Recall that in the TCP example, you had to start the server first in order for the applications to work together correctly. The UDP example does not have the same restriction, thus emphasizing the point that the UDP is connectionless. First, the sender does not care whether the receiver actually gets the message. Second, the receiver doesn't care whether the sender ever sends a message.

The following sections walk you through the process of building these two applications in a step-by-step manner.

The Traffic Signal Application

This example does an excellent job of demonstrating the ease and power of the ActiveX Internet Control Pack for including the Internet in your applications. To complete this example, you'll construct the following:

■ frmTrafficSignal—The startup form for the application, which contains the UDP control

■ sktTrafficSignal—The UDP control to be used by the traffic signal to communicate the current status of the light

■ Timer1—The timer that causes the traffic signal to change

■ circRedLight—The graphic object that represents the red light of the traffic signal

■ circYellowLight—The graphic object that represents the yellow light of the traffic signal

■ circGreenLight—The graphic object that represents the green light of the traffic signal

N O T E These examples assume that you already know how to program in Visual Basic. ■

To build the Traffic Signal application, complete the following steps:

1. Start Visual Basic 4.0.

2. Create a form named frmTrafficSignal. Change the Caption property to Traffic Signal and the Name property to frmTrafficSignal.

3. Resize frmTrafficSignal to a smaller, more comfortable size.

4. Select the Shape control from the control toolbar and make a comfortably sized object, placed near the top of the form. Change its Shape property to 3 - Circle. Set the Name property to circRedLight. Set the FillColor property to a suitable color of red, and set the FillStyle property to 0 - Solid.

5. Draw another shape object the same size as the control you just completed, and place it below the circRedLight control. Again, change the Shape property to 3 - Circle. Set

the `Name` property to `circYellowLight`. Set the `FillColor` property to a suitable color of yellow, and set the `FillStyle` property to `0` - `Solid`.

6. Draw a third shape object the same size as the two controls you just completed, and place it below the `circYellowLight` control. Once more, change the `Shape` property to `3` - `Circle`. Set the `Name` property to `circGreenLight`. Set the `FillColor` property to a suitable color of green, and set the `FillStyle` property to `0` - `Solid`.

7. Save the project to a convenient working directory.

8. Add the UDP control to the control toolbar. Choose Tools, Custom Controls, and then select Microsoft Winsock Controls and click OK. This adds both the TCP and UDP controls to your toolbar for this project.

9. Drag and drop the UDP control onto `frmTrafficSignal`.

10. Drag and drop a Timer control onto `frmTrafficSignal`. Set the `Interval` property to a suitable delay (about 2000 milliseconds). When you finish, the form looks something like figure 12.2.

FIG. 12.2
This is the
`frmTrafficSignal`
form.

11. Next, select the UDP control and change the `Name` property to `sktTrafficSignal`.

12. Now, it's time to start coding the application. Open the code window by choosing View, Code. Declare four public variables: `gRed`, `gYellow`, `gGreen`, and `gCurrentColor`. The first three are simply constants that stand for the colors of the traffic signal. `gCurrentColor` is used to store the current state of the traffic signal. Your code looks something like Listing 12.1.

Listing 12.1 *TRAFFICSIGNAL.VBP* **General Declarations for *frmTrafficSignal***

```
'---------------------------------
'-- Global variable declarations
'---------------------------------
Public gCurrentColor As Integer
Public gRed As Integer
Public gYellow As Integer
Public gGreen As Integer
```

13. Next, code the `Form Load()` function for `frmTrafficSignal`. When the form loads, you need to initialize `gCurrentColor` as well as the `RemotePort` and `RemoteHost` for `sktTrafficSignal`. The necessary code looks like Listing 12.2.

On the CD

Listing 12.2 2TRAFFICSIGNAL.VBP   *Form Load()* **Function**

```
Private Sub Form_Load()

    '--------------------------------
    '-- Initialize the traffic signal
    '--------------------------------
    gRed = 0
    gYellow = 1
    gGreen = 2
    gCurrentColor = gRed
    ChangeLight gCurrentColor

    '--------------------------------
    '-- Initialize the UDP control
    '--------------------------------
    sktTrafficSignal.RemotePort = 1234
    sktTrafficSignal.RemoteHost = "127.0.0.1"

End Sub
```

Don't forget that the 127.0.0.1 refers to LocalHost (that is, the machine on which the application is running) and is used for testing. To allow this application to operate over a network, you need to set RemoteHost to an appropriate IP address.

14. Next, code the Timer event's response function. The traffic signal's light changes from red to green to yellow, and so on. Your code looks something like Listing 12.3.

On the CD

Listing 12.3 3TRAFFICSIGNAL.VBP   **Timer Response Function**

```
Private Sub Timer1_Timer()

    gCurrentColor = (gCurrentColor + 1) Mod 3
    ChangeLight gCurrentColor

    sktTrafficSignal.SendData gCurrentColor

End Sub
```

Part

II

Ch

12

Mod is used to rotate the value of gCurrentColor among 0, 1, and 2 (which you've already defined as gRed, gYellow, and gGreen, respectively). Then a procedure named ChangeLight (which manipulates the display of the lights) is executed. Finally, the current color of the light is sent via UDP.

15. Next, code the ChangeLight() function. This function simply changes which light is turned on and which lights are turned off. The code looks something like Listing 12.4.

Listing 12.4   4TRAFFICSIGNAL.VBP   *ChangeLight()* Function

```
Public Sub ChangeLight(ToColor As Integer)
    If ToColor = gRed Then
        circRedLight.FillStyle = 0
        circYellowLight.FillStyle = 1
        circGreenLight.FillStyle = 1
    End If
    If ToColor = gYellow Then
        circRedLight.FillStyle = 1
        circYellowLight.FillStyle = 0
        circGreenLight.FillStyle = 1
    End If
    If ToColor = gGreen Then
        circRedLight.FillStyle = 1
        circYellowLight.FillStyle = 1
        circGreenLight.FillStyle = 0
    End If

End Sub
```

16. Finally, let's code a simple error handler for `sktTrafficSignal`. The code looks like Listing 12.5.

Listing 12.5   5TRAFFICSIGNAL.VBP   Error Handler for the UDP Control

```
Private Sub sktTrafficSignal_Error(Number As Integer, Description As String,
Scode As Long, Source As String, HelpFile As String, HelpContext As Long,
CancelDisplay As Boolean)
    MsgBox "Error [" & Number & "] - " & Description
End Sub
```

The Automatic Pilot Application

The Automatic Pilot application gets messages from the Traffic Signal application. Depending on the color of the traffic signal, the Automatic Pilot changes its course of action. To construct the Automatic Pilot, you need the following objects in place:

- `frmAutoPilot`—The startup form for the application that contains the UDP control
- `sktAutoPilot`—The UDP control to be used to receive Traffic Signal messages
- `txtInstructions`—The text box control that displays the action to be taken based upon the color of the traffic signal

N O T E These examples assume that you already know how to program in Visual Basic. ▪

To build the Automatic Pilot application, complete the following steps:

1. Start Visual Basic 4.0.

2. Create a form named `frmAutoPilot`. Change the `Caption` property to `Automatic Pilot` and the `Name` property to `frmAutoPilot`.

3. Add a Text Box control to the center of the form. Change the `Name` property to `txtInstructions`. Add some initialization text to the `Text` property (for example, `Waiting for instructions...`).

4. Resize `frmAutoPilot` to a smaller, more comfortable size.

5. Save the project to a convenient working directory.

6. Even if you added the UDP control to the Traffic Signal application, you need to add it again here. Choose Tools, Custom Controls, then select Microsoft Winsock Controls and click OK.

7. Drag and drop the UDP control onto `frmAutoPilot`. Change the `Name` property to `sktAutoPilot`. When you finish, the form looks something like figure 12.3.

FIG. 12.3
This is how your design view of the Automatic Pilot form should appear.

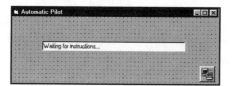

8. Now, it's time to start coding the application. Open the code window by choosing View, Code. Declare the same four global public variables you declared for the Traffic Signal application. Your code looks like Listing 12.6.

On the CD

Listing 12.6 *AUTOPILOT.VBP*   Declaration of Global Variables

```
'---------------------------------
'-- Global variable declarations
'---------------------------------
Public gCurrentColor As Integer
Public gRed As Integer
Public gYellow As Integer
Public gGreen As Integer
```

9. Next, code the `Form Load()` function for `frmAutoPilot`. When the form loads, you need to initialize the color constants and `gCurrentColor` as you did in the Traffic Signal application. You also need to initialize `sktAutoPilot.LocalPort` to `1234`. Your code looks something like Listing 12.7.

On the CD

Listing 12.7   2AUTOPILOT.VBP   *Form Load()* Function

```
Private Sub Form_Load()

    '---------------------------------
    '-- Initialize possible light colors
    '---------------------------------
    gRed = 0
    gYellow = 1
    gGreen = 2

    '---------------------------------
    '-- Initialize the UDP control
    '---------------------------------
    sktAutoPilot.LocalPort = 1234

End Sub
```

10. Now, you'll build the `DataArrival()` event response function. When the Traffic Signal light color packet is received, the Automatic Pilot application must react. This function can be very complicated or very simple, depending on your needs. The simple example in Listing 12.8 displays different text for each color.

On the CD

Listing 12.8   3AUTOPILOT.VBP   *DataArrival()* Event Response Function

```
Private Sub sktAutoPilot_DataArrival(ByVal bytesTotal As Long)

    Dim LightColor

    sktAutoPilot.GetData LightColor

    ' Actually GetData is treating LightColor as an
    ' array of vbByte so use the 0 subscript to get
    ' the current color of the light
    If LightColor(0) = gRed Then
        txtInstructions.Text = "Red Light! Pressing the brake..."
    End If
    If LightColor(0) = gYellow Then
        txtInstructions.Text = "Yellow Light! Proceeding with caution..."
    End If
    If LightColor(0) = gGreen Then
        txtInstructions.Text = "Green Light! Pressing the accelerator..."
    End If

End Sub
```

11. Finally, let's code a simple error handler for `sktAutoPilot`. You can use the same one you built for `sktTrafficSignal`, so your code looks like Listing 12.9.

On the CD

Listing 12.9 *4AUTOPILOT.VBP* Error Handler

```
Private Sub sktAutoPilot_Error(Number As Integer, Description As String,
Scode As Long, Source As String, HelpFile As String, HelpContext As Long,
CancelDisplay As Boolean)
    MsgBox "Error [" & Number & "] - " & Description
End Sub
```

Testing the Applications

Finally, you're ready to test the whole project. To test both sample applications, follow these steps:

1. Start the Traffic Signal application. If you named the applications as described in the example, the easiest way to do this is to click the Start button, then choose Run. Enter **TrafficSignal.exe** (along with the appropriate path, if necessary) and the server application starts up (see fig. 12.4).

FIG. 12.4

Your test of the Traffic Signal startup should look like this.

2. Next, start the Automatic Pilot application. If you named the applications as described in the example, click the Start button, then choose Run. Enter **AutoPilot.exe** (with the appropriate path, if necessary) and the application starts up (see fig. 12.5).

FIG. 12.5

This is a healthy startup of the Automatic Pilot application.

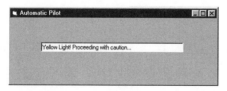

If all is well, the Automatic Pilot application indicates that it's waiting for instructions, then reacts to each change in color sent by the Traffic Signal application. ●

CHAPTER 13

Using the FTP Control in VB Applications

The File Transfer Protocol (FTP) provides a simple interface for moving text and binary files over the Internet. FTP is one of the most popular applications used on the Internet today. In fact, many Web browsers support the FTP protocol in addition to other more popular protocols like HTTP. Like most of the other Internet protocols, FTP requires both a client and a server to complete file transfers. The technical details of the FTP protocol are complicated, but the ActiveX FTP Client control allows us to avoid knowing much about FTP itself. ■

Learn the properties of the FTP Client ActiveX control

Using an ActiveX control often requires the use of the properties made available for configuring the control.

Learn the methods available to programmers using the FTP Client control

ActiveX Controls expose methods that allow you to integrate ActiveX functionality into your applications.

Learn the events triggered by the FTP Client control

ActiveX Controls each provide for certain events to be triggered, and reacting appropriately to these events can make your programs more sophisticated.

Build an example Visual Basic application that employs the FTP Client control

The best way to learn about FTP is to build an application that uses FTP to transfer files over the Internet. That's what this chapter helps you to do.

Work with FTPDirItem objects to read remote directories

ActiveX provides FTPDirItem objects to display directory entries in a manner independent of the operating system.

Properties

Table 13.1 summarizes the properties available in the FTP Client control. All the data elements required to transfer a file from an FTP server are included as properties in this control.

Table 13.1   Properties of the FTP Client ActiveX Control

Property	Purpose
AppendToFile	Tells whether file operations are appended or not
Busy	True if a command is currently in progress
DocInput	Refers to the DocInput object, which must be set before invoking the SendDoc method, and which conveys information about the progress of the data transfer
DocOutput	Refers to the DocOutput object, which must be set before invoking the GetDoc method, and which conveys information about the progress of the data transfer
EnableTimer	Tells the kind of timer that is fired by the TimeOut event
Errors	Refers to a collection detailing the last error
IsAuthenticated	True if authentication has been successfully completed
ListItemNotify	Tells how the ListItem event will pass an FTPDirItem object
LocalFile	Filename to be used in GetFile and PutFile operations
NotificationMode	Determines how notification of inbound data is provided
Password	Password to be used for logging on to an FTP server
ProtocolState	Indicates the state of the FTP client relative to the FTP server: not connected, waiting for authorization to connect, or connected
RemoteDir	Current directory on the remote server
RemoteFile	Filename to be used in GetFile and PutFile operations
RemoteHost	Host name or IP address of the server to be connected to
RemotePort	Port number used to connect to the FTP server
ReplyCode	Reply code sent by the server in response to a request from the client
ReplyString	Reply string sent by the server in response to a request from the client
State	Used to report the current state of the FTP connection
TimeOut	Tells how long to wait before firing the TimeOut event for the type of timer referred to by EnableTimer

Property	Purpose
URL	Uniform Resource Locator (for example, **ftp://myhost.com/ myfile.txt**)
UserID	User name to be used for logging on to an FTP server

Now, let's look at a few of these properties in more detail.

Properties of *DocInput* and *DocOutput*

DocInput and DocOutput objects allow you to control and monitor the incoming and outgoing documents from client to server. These objects also allow the output of one control to be streamed directly to the input of another control. These two objects and their associated properties are demonstrated in detail in the chapter on the HTTP protocol.

The *EnableTimer* Property

You'll often want to take some action after a timeout period has expired. For instance, you might want to ask the user to try again later if a connection takes more than 30 seconds to obtain. The EnableTimer property tells what kind of timer is enabled. The kinds of timers that can be enabled are listed in Table 13.2.

Table 13.2 *EnableTimer* Settings

Meaning	Value
prcConnectTimeout	This setting enables a connect timer. If a connection is not established within the timeout period, the TimeOut event is triggered.
prcReceiveTimeout	This setting enables a receive timer. If no data arrives within the timeout period, the TimeOut event is triggered.
prcUserTimeout	This setting provides a mechanism for adding user-defined timers. To implement such a timer, add an integer to prcUserTimeout.

To enable a connect timer, for instance, you use code like the following:

```
...
'---------------------------------------
'-- Define a custom timeout
'---------------------------------------
prcMyCustomTimeout = prcUserTimeout + 1


'---------------------------------------
'--- Enable the connect timeout
'---------------------------------------
MyFTPControl.EnableTimer(prcConnectTimeout) = True
```

Part
II

Ch
13

```
'------------------------------------
'--- Disable the receive timeout
'------------------------------------
MyFTPControl.EnableTimer(prcReceiveTimeout) = False

'------------------------------------
'--- Enable a user define timeout
'------------------------------------
MyFTPControl.EnableTimer(prcMyCustomTimeout) = True
...
```

It's easy to see that you can enable all, none, or any number of timers as required for your applications.

The *ListItemNotify* Property

The ListItemNotify property allows you to select whether requests for a directory listing are passed as an FTPDirItem object through the ListItem event, or as data blocks through the DocOutput event. As you'll see in the explanation of the ListItem event, the FTPDirItem object makes obtaining details about files and directory entries easy.

The *NotificationMode* Property

When you use the FTP Client control to transfer data, you can select when you will be notified that data has arrived. Table 13.3 shows the available modes.

Table 13.3 *NotificationMode* Settings	
Value	**Meaning**
0	Notify when the data transmission has been completed (this is the default)
1	Arrival of data causes an event to be continuously fired

The *ProtocolState* Property

The ProtocolState property provides protocol-specific information about the state of the connection. For the FTP control, there are three possible states for the protocol, as shown in Table 13.4.

Table 13.4 FTP *ProtocolState* Values	
Value	**Meaning**
ftpBase	The default state of the protocol prior to connecting to an FTP server
ftpAuthorization	Authorization using UserID and Password is currently underway
ftpTransaction	Authorization has been completed and the FTP client has identified itself to the FTP server

The *State* Property

The State property stores the current state of the FTP connection. Since State is a read-only property, you never set the state of the connection. You can, however, use the current value of State in all sorts of ways. Table 13.5 summarizes the values that State may contain.

Table 13.5 Possible Values for *State*

Value	Description
prcConnecting	This is the state of the FTP connection after requesting a connection and before receiving acknowledgment of the server.
prcResolvingHost	If the RemoteHost property is a domain name rather than an IP address, the connection reaches this state while the host name is being obtained as an IP address.
prcHostResolved	After the host name has been resolved to an IP address, this state is reached.
prcConnected	This is the state after the connection is established.
prcDisconnecting	This is the state when the close connection process has been initiated but not yet completed.
prcDisconnected	After the connection is closed and acknowledgment has been received, the state holds this value. This is also the initial state when you create a new instance of the FTP Client control.

Methods

Most of the action in an FTP session involves sending and receiving files. The methods to accomplish this work are summarized in Table 13.6.

Table 13.6 Methods for the FTP Client Control

Method	Use
Abort	Stops the last request for a data transfer
Account	Sends account information to the FTP server; checks the reply string to determine the results
Authentication	Authenticates the user through the UserID and Password properties
Cancel	Stops a pending request
ChangeDir	Requests that the directory on the FTP server change

continues

Table 13.6   Continued

Method	Use
Connect	Issues a request to the FTP server to open a connection; if a connection is established, the State property is set
CreateDir	Creates the specified directory on the FTP server (if the user is permitted)
DeleteDir	Deletes the specified directory on the FTP server (if the user is permitted)
DeleteFile	Deletes the specified file on the FTP server (if the user is permitted)
Execute	Executes a command directly on the server via the RFC-959 Quote command
GetDoc	Requests the retrieval of a document identified by a URL; can be used in conjunction with DocInput and DocOutput objects and events
GetFile	Obtains a file from the FTP server and places it in the current directory
Help	Obtains a help listing from the FTP server; the ReplyString property contains the results of the request
List	Returns a detailed listing of an FTP server directory; the ListItemNotify property indicates how and when this list is returned
ListSize	Lists files by size
Mode	Sets the FTP mode
NameList	Returns a list of filenames from the FTP server
NOOP	Causes the FTP server to reply with an OK value in the ReplyString property
ParentDir	Asks the FTP server to change the directory to the parent of the current directory
PrintDir	Asks the FTP server to reply with the current directory
PutFile	Places a file in the server's current directory
Quit	Closes the connection and fires the Quit event
ReInitialize	Issues a reinitialize request and obtains a reply in the ReplyString property
SendDoc	Requests that a document identified by URL be sent to the server; is used in conjunction with DocInput and DocOutput objects and events

Method	Use
Site	Obtains the type of file system supported by the remote system; the reply is placed in ReplyString
State	Obtains the state of the connection as defined in the RFC-959 STAT command
System	Requests that the server identify which operating system it requires; the reply is placed in ReplyString
Type	Specifies the type of data to be transferred

Most of these methods are self-explanatory; however, a few of them bear additional discussion in the following sections.

The *Type* Method

You'll use FTP to transfer files that contain all sorts of data. The FTP protocol requires that you identify the type of data contained in the transfer, to ensure that data is transferred reliably. The possible values to be passed to the Type method (for different types of file transfers) are shown in Table 13.7.

Table 13.7   Possible Values for the *Type* Method

Value	Type of File
ftpAscii	Text (this is the default)
ftpEBCDIC	Extended Binary Coded Decimal Interchange
ftpImage	Image
ftpBinary	Binary

Getting and Putting Files

The primary purpose of the FTP protocol is to transfer files from client to server, and back again. There are two methods to make this happen using the FTP Client control:

- Use DocInput and DocOutput objects and events with the SendDoc and GetDoc methods
- Use the GetFile and PutFile methods

As you'll see over the next couple of chapters, the DocInput and DocOutput approach is available in a number of different controls from the Internet Control Pack, including HTTP and NNTP. For variety, we'll use the GetFile and PutFile approach in the example program in this chapter.

To send a file from the FTP client to the server, you have to take several steps after connecting to the server. You need to set the LocalFile property to the filename that you want transferred. Next, you must set `RemoteFile` to the appropriate filename for the distant system. Finally, invoke the `PutFile` method to complete the transfer. The necessary code looks something like this:

```
...
'------------------------------------
'-- Set the two and from file names
'------------------------------------
MyFTPControl.LocalFile = "FileToSend.txt"
MyFTPControl.RemoteFile = "SendItHere.txt"

'------------------------------------
'-- Send the file
'------------------------------------
MyFTPControl.PutFile
...
```

Getting a file from the server to the client requires a very similar approach. You need to set `LocalFile` and `RemoteFile`, as appropriate, then invoke the `GetFile` method to complete the transfer. The necessary code looks something like this:

```
...
'------------------------------------
'-- Set the two and from file names
'------------------------------------
MyFTPControl.LocalFile = "SendItHere.txt"
MyFTPControl.RemoteFile = "FileToSend.txt"

'------------------------------------
'-- Get the file
'------------------------------------
MyFTPControl.GetFile
...
```

Events

The FTP Control provides numerous events on which your application can take action. Table 13.8 summarizes the events that may be fired by the FTP control.

Table 13.8   Summary of Events in the FTP Control

Event	Description
Abort	Fires when the Abort method is invoked
Account	Fires when the Account method is invoked
Authenticate	Fires when the Authentication method is invoked
Busy	Fires when a command is in progress
Cancel	Fires at the completion of the cancellation of a request

Event	Description
ChangeDir	Fires when a CWD is executed or the ChangeDir method is invoked
CreateDir	Fires when an MKD is executed or the CreateDir method is invoked
DelDir	Fires when an RMD is executed or the DeleteDir method is invoked
DelFile	Fires when a DELE is executed or the DeleteFile method is invoked
DocInput	Fires when data arrives at the control
DocOutput	Fires when data is sent from the control
Execute	Fires when the Execute method is invoked
Help	Fires when HELP is executed or the Help method is invoked
ListItem	If ListItemNotify is set to True, this event fires for every ListItem in a directory
Mode	Fires when the Mode method is invoked
NOOP	Fires when the NOOP method is invoked
ParentDir	Fires when a CDUP is executed or the ParentDir method is invoked
PrintDir	Fires when a PWD is executed or the PrintDir method is invoked
ProtocolStateChanged	Fires whenever the state of the FTP session changes
Reinitialize	Fires when a REINIT is executed or the ReInitialize method is invoked
Site	Fires when a SITE is executed or the Site method is invoked
State	Fires when the State method is executed
StateChanged	Fires whenever the state of the connection changes (that is, whenever the State property changes)
System	Fires when a SYST is executed or the System method is invoked
TimeOut	Fires when a given event fails to occur within the time period specified in the Timeout property
Type	Fires when the Type method is invoked

Part
II

Ch
13

Let's take a closer look at a few of these events.

The *ListItem* Event

The ListItem event is used to parse directory entries. If you set the ListItemNotify property to True, the ListItem event fires each time a new entry from a directory entry is returned. The ListItem event has an FTPDirItem object passed in as a parameter. Take a moment to look at Table 13.9, where the properties of the FTPDirItem object are summarized.

Table 13.9   Properties of the *FTPDirItem* Object

Property	Meaning
Attributes	Contains the file system attributes
Date	Stores the last-modified date of the file or directory entry
Details	Returns details about the file or directory entry
Filename	Keeps the name of the file
Size	Keeps the size of the file

When the ListItem event fires, you should format a text entry for display to the user. The code looks something like the following:

```
Private Sub MyFTPControl_ListItem(ByVal Item As FTPDirItem)
    Dim LineToDisplay As String
    Select Case Item.Attributes
        Case 1                  'If it's a directory
            LineToDisplay = Item.Filename & " " Item.Date
        Case 2              'If it's a file
     LineToDisplay = Item.Filename & " " Item.Size & " " Item.Date
    End Select
    ShowDirectoryListing LineToDisplay
End Sub
```

This code assumes that there is a ShowDirectoryListing procedure that populates a list box or some other control.

The *ProtocolStateChanged* Event

You may want to notify the user of changes to the state of the connection between the client and the server. The ProtocolStateChanged event is triggered when changes occur at the protocol level. When this event fires, you are passed an integer that represents the current ProtocolState. Refer to the discussion of the ProtocolState property for a list of possible values. Here's an example of how this event can be used:

```
Private Sub MyFTPControl_ProtocolStateChanged(ByVal ProtocolState As Integer)

        Select Case ProtocolState
            Case ftpAuthorization
```

```
                        Status.Panels(1).Text = "Authorization"
             Case ftpBase
                        Status.Panels(1).Text = "Base"
             Case ftpTransaction
                        Status.Panels(1).Text = "Transaction"
          End Select

End Sub
```

Of course, you need to have a `StatusBar` control named `Status` to use this code.

Building the FTP Client Application

To try out the FTP control, you'll construct a simple FTP client that provides the following functionality:

- Send files
- Receive files
- Select text and binary transfer types
- Change directories
- Obtain a directory listing

To get an idea of how this application works, you might want to run it before continuing. Of course, you need to have an FTP server available to actually use the application.

 T I P Working this example is much easier if you have an FTP server running locally on your computer. Since you probably don't have an FTP server application already, you should look for one on the Internet. One good place to look is **http://www.winsite.com**, but just about any FTP site that specializes in Windows 95 and Windows NT-based shareware and freeware will have one.

The following sections take you through the process of building the FTP Client application in a step-by-step manner.

Starting to Build the FTP Client Application

This example will show you how simple it is to integrate FTP functions into your own applications using the ActiveX Internet Control Pack. Since there will be quite a few controls on-screen, take a quick look at figure 13.1 to familiarize yourself with the form.

Before you start coding, take a look at the following summary tables that indicate the name of each control and its function within the application.

You need to create the seven command buttons shown in Table 13.10.

FIG. 13.1

Examine the FTP Client application's main form.

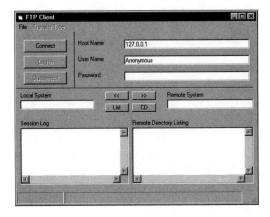

Table 13.10   Command Buttons for FTP Client

Button Name	Function
cmdConnect	Establishes the connection with an FTP server
cmdLogIn	Presents the user name and password to the server for authentication
cmdDisconnect	Closes the connection with an FTP server
cmdGet	Gets a file from the FTP server
cmdPut	Puts a file on the FTP server
cmdList	Gets a directory list
cmdChangeDir	Changes the directory on the remote server

You need to build seven text controls for this application. Table 13.11 summarizes the purpose of each of these.

Table 13.11   Text Controls for FTP Client

Control	Use
txtHostName	Stores the host to be connected to
txtUserName	Keeps the name of the user to log in as
txtPassword	Records the password to log in with
txtLocalFile	Name of the file on the local system
txtRemoteFile	Name of the file on the FTP server
txtSessionLog	Multiline text box to display ftpClient.ReplyString
txtDirBox	Multiline text box to display directory listings from the remote server

Your application needs to respond to the click event for the menu options shown in Table 13.12.

Table 13.12   Menu Options for FTP Client

Option	Action
mnuFileExit	Calls End to exit the application
mnuTransferBinary	Sets the transfer Type to ftpBinary
mnuTransferText	Sets the transfer Type to ftpText

Finally, you have to include the miscellaneous items shown in Table 13.13.

Table 13.13   Miscellaneous Controls for FTP Client

Control	Purpose
Status	Two-panel status bar to update the user with information
FtpClient	FTP Client ActiveX control that manages the connection with the server
frmFtpClient	Form for the application

To build the FTP client application, complete the following steps:

1. Start Visual Basic 4.0.
2. Create a form named frmFtpClient. Change the Caption property to Ftp Client and the Name property to frmFtpClient.
3. Resize frmFtpClient to a smaller, more manageable size.
4. Select the command button control and add the following command buttons: cmdConnect, cmdLogIn, cmdDisconnect, cmdGet, cmdPut, cmdList, and cmdChangeDir. Remember to give each one an appropriate caption. The Get, Put, List, and Change Directory buttons need to be quite small to fit between the txtRemoteFile and txtLocalFile text boxes. Use abbreviations if necessary.
5. Next, select the text box control and add the following text boxes: txtHostName, txtUserName, txtPassword, txtLocalFile, txtRemoteFile, txtSessionLog, and txtDirBox. Be sure to make the txtSessionLog and txtDirBox controls ready for multiline text by setting the Multiline property to True and the ScrollBars property to 3 - Both.
6. Add a status bar to the bottom of the form. Set the Name property to Status. Remember to create two panels on your status bar.
7. Next, add a menu to the application, with the following options: mnuFile, mnuFileExit, mnuTransferType, mnuTransferBinary, and mnuTransferText. Make sure to set mnuTransferType initially as disabled.

Part
II

Ch
13

8. Save the project to a convenient working directory.

9. Now, add the FTP control to the control toolbar. Choose Tools, Custom Controls, then select Microsoft FTP Client Control and click OK. This adds the FTP control to your toolbar for this project.

10. Drag and drop the FTP control onto frmFtpClient. When you finish, the form looks something like figure 13.2.

FIG. 13.2
Check your frmFtpClient against this figure for completeness.

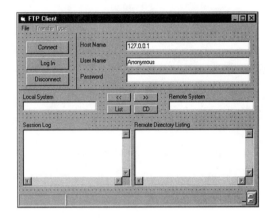

11. Select the FTP control and change its Name property to ftpClient.

12. Now, it's time to start coding the application. Start by working on the command buttons. The first one to code is cmdChangeDir. Your code looks something like Listing 13.1.

Listing 13.1 FTPCLIENT.VBP cmdChangeDir Click Response Function

On the CD

```
Private Sub cmdChangeDir_Click()

    ftpClient.ChangeDir txtRemoteFile.Text
    While ftpClient.Busy
        DoEvents
    Wend
    txtRemoteFile.Text = "*.*"
    txtDirBox.Text = ""
    ftpClient.ListItemNotify = True
    ftpClient.List txtRemoteFile.Text

End Sub
```

The txtRemoteFile.Text field contains the name of the directory to change to. Notice that you need to wait until the ChangeDir is done before getting a listing of the new directory. You use the Busy property to determine when the command has been completed. You set txtRemoteFile to "*.*" to ensure a complete directory listing.

13. Next, code the cmdConnect click response function. This button is used to connect to the FTP server specified in txtHostName.Text. Your code looks something like Listing 13.2.

Listing 13.2   2FTPCLIENT.VBP   cmdConnect Click Response Function

```
Private Sub cmdConnect_Click()

    If IsEmpty(txtHostName.Text) Then
        MsgBox "You must enter a host name"
    Else
        ftpClient.Connect txtHostName.Text
    End If

End Sub
```

Obviously, you cannot connect to a host if no host name is provided, so you have to check to be sure there's something in txtHostName.Text. Then you simply pass that value to the Connect method. Notice that you aren't notifying the user of anything in this code. You use a couple of events to keep the user informed of what's going on.

14. Now, code the cmdDisconnect response function. There's not much to this code, which looks something like Listing 13.3.

Listing 13.3   3FTPCLIENT.VBP   cmdDisconnect Click Response Function

```
Private Sub cmdDisconnect_Click()
    ftpClient.Quit
End Sub
```

15. The cmdGet click function is next. It invokes the GetFile method to transfer a file from the server. The code looks something like Listing 13.4.

Listing 13.4   4FTPCLIENT.VBP   cmdGet Click Response Function

```
Private Sub cmdGet_Click()

    If txtLocalFile.Text = "" Then
        txtLocalFile.Text = txtRemoteFile.Text
    End If

    ftpClient.GetFile txtRemoteFile.Text, txtLocalFile.Text

End Sub
```

The GetFile and PutFile functions each require that both the RemoteFile and LocalFile parameters be filled, even if the filenames are the same. It's easier for the user if you check for an empty txtLocalFile.Text field, and make the filenames equal if necessary.

Part
II

Ch
13

16. The `cmdList` click response function requires that the `ListItemNotify` property of `ftpClient` be set to `True`. Then the `List` method is invoked with `txtRemoteFile.Text` (which contains the directory you want listed). Listing 13.5 shows the necessary code.

Listing 13.5   *5FTPCLIENT.VBP*   cmdList Click Response Function

```
Private Sub cmdList_Click()
    ftpClient.ListItemNotify = True
    ftpClient.List txtRemoteFile.Text
    txtDirBox.Text = ""
End Sub
```

17. Next, code the `cmdLogIn` click response function. To get logged in to an FTP server, you set the `UserID` and `Password` properties to a valid user account and password, then invoke the `Authenticate` method. Your code looks like Listing 13.6.

Listing 13.6   *6FTPCLIENT.VBP*   cmdLogIn Click Response Function

```
Private Sub cmdLogIn_Click()

    If IsEmpty(txtUserName.Text) Or IsEmpty(txtPassword.Text) Then

        MsgBox "You must enter a User Name and Password to Login"

    Else

        ftpClient.UserID = txtUserName.Text
        ftpClient.Password = txtPassword.Text
        ftpClient.Authenticate

    End If
End Sub
```

It's good practice to save bandwidth wherever possible, so make sure that the user has entered something in the `txtUserName` and `txtPassword` text controls. Of course, you could let the server reject blank user name and password entries, but that would waste a call over the network to the server, plus a response from the server back to your client denying access.

18. The `cmdPut` click function is next. This function invokes the `PutFile` method to transfer a file to the server. Your code looks like Listing 13.7.

Listing 13.7   *7FTPCLIENT.VBP*   cmdPut Click Response Function

```
Private Sub cmdPut_Click()
    If txtRemoteFile.Text = "" Then
        txtRemoteFile.Text = txtLocalFile.Text
    End If
```

```
ftpClient.GetFile txtRemoteFile.Text, txtLocalFile.Text

End Sub
```

19. Now, let's code the menu click response functions. Code the mnuTransferBinary function first. Your code looks like Listing 13.8.

Listing 13.8 *8FTPCLIENT.VBP* *mnuTransferBinary* **Click Response Function**

```
Private Sub mnuTransferBinary_Click()
    ftpClient.Type ftpBinary
    mnuTransferText.Checked = False
    mnuTransferBinary.Checked = True
End Sub
```

Pass the constant ftpBinary as the parameter to the ftpClient object's Type method. Finish by putting a checkmark next to the Binary menu option and deselecting the Text menu option.

20. The mnuTransferText click function works just like mnuTransferBinary, as you can see in Listing 13.9.

Listing 13.9 *9FTPCLIENT.VBP* *mnuTransferText* **Click Response Function**

```
Private Sub mnuTransferText_Click()
    ftpClient.Type ftpAscii
    mnuTransferText.Checked = True
    mnuTransferBinary.Checked = False
End Sub
```

21. The mnuFileExit click function is a trivial End statement, as shown in Listing 13.10.

Listing 13.10 *10FTPCLIENT.VBP* *mnuFileExit* **Click Response Function**

```
Private Sub mnuFileExit_Click()
    End
End Sub
```

Part
II

Ch
13

22. Next, turn to the ftpClient control. The FTP client needs to respond to a number of events. Start by coding the Authenticate event response function. For authentication, the only thing you need to do is inform the user what's going on. Your code looks like Listing 13.11.

Listing 13.11 *11FTPCLIENT.VBP* ***Authenticate*** **Event Response Function**

```
Private Sub ftpClient_Authenticate()

    Status.Panels(1).Text = ftpClient.StateString
    Status.Panels(2).Text = ftpClient.ReplyString

End Sub
```

The FTP Client application uses `Status.Panels(1)` to display the `StateString` property, and `Status.Panels(2)` for `ReplyString`. This standard is adhered to throughout the application.

23. Now, add the `Busy` event response function. Busy gets fired every time a command finishes, so obviously this provides an excellent opportunity to give the user status information. Use `ReplyString` as the basis of your communication with the user. Your code looks like Listing 13.12.

Listing 13.12 *12FTPCLIENT.VBP* **Busy Event Response Function**

```
Private Sub ftpClient_Busy(ByVal isBusy As Boolean)
    txtSessionLog.Text = ftpClient.ReplyString
End Sub
```

Remember that `Status.Panels(2)` is the display space for `ReplyString`.

24. Next, write the `Connect` event response function. In order to keep the interface simple, most of the controls have remained disabled pending the client's connection to the FTP server. In this event response function, therefore, you enable all the appropriate controls. Your code looks like Listing 13.13.

Listing 13.13 *13FTPCLIENT.VBP* ***Connect*** **Event Response Function**

```
Private Sub ftpClient_Connect()

    cmdLogIn.Enabled = True
    cmdDisconnect.Enabled = True
    cmdConnect.Enabled = False
    mnuTransferType.Enabled = True

End Sub
```

25. The `Error` event response is a simple `MsgBox` function, as shown in Listing 13.14.

Listing 13.14 *14FTPCLIENT.VBP* ***Error*** **Event Response Function**

```
Private Sub ftpClient_Error(Number As Integer, Description As String,
Scode As Long, Source As String, HelpFile As String, HelpContext As Long,
```

```
CancelDisplay As Boolean)
    MsgBox Description
End Sub
```

26. The `ListItem` event response function is next. `ListItem` gets triggered when each line in a directory listing is received, as long as `ListItemNotify` is set to `True`. You should use this event to employ the passed `FTPDirItem` object and format output for the user, resulting in code that resembles Listing 13.15.

On the CD

Listing 13.15   *15FTPCLIENT.VBP*   *ListItem* Event Response Function

```
Private Sub ftpClient_ListItem(ByVal Item As FTPDirItem)

    txtDirBox.Text = txtDirBox.Text & Item.Size & vbTab
    Select Case Item.Attributes
        Case 1
            txtDirBox.Text = txtDirBox.Text & "[" & Item.filename & "]" & vbCrLf
        Case 2
            txtDirBox.Text = txtDirBox.Text & Item.filename & vbCrLf
    End Select
End Sub
```

For each line item, print the file's size and then tab over. If the entry is a directory (that's when the `Attribute` property equals 1), enclose the directory name in brackets. If the entry is a file, just print the name. Remember to include a carriage return and linefeed at the end of each directory item. Visual Basic supplies the handy constant `vbCrLf` for just this purpose.

27. The `Quit` event response is next. All you have to do is enable and disable controls as they were before the connection. The necessary code looks like Listing 13.16.

On the CD

Listing 13.16   *16FTPCLIENT.VBP*   *Quit* Event Response Function

```
Private Sub ftpClient_Quit()
    cmdDisconnect.Enabled = False
    cmdLogIn.Enabled = False
    cmdConnect.Enabled = True
    mnuTransferType.Enabled = False
End Sub
```

Part
II

Ch
13

28. Finally, code the `StateChanged` event response function. Two basic tasks must be accomplished. First, if the client and server are no longer connected, you need to reset the user interface elements to the proper enabled (or disabled) state. Second, you need to provide the user some status information. Your code for this function looks like Listing 13.17.

On the CD

Listing 13.17 *17FTPCLIENT.VBP* *StateChanged* Event Response Function

```
Private Sub ftpClient_StateChanged(ByVal State As Integer)
    If ftpClient.State <> prcConnected Then
        cmdDisconnect.Enabled = False
        cmdLogIn.Enabled = False
        cmdConnect.Enabled = True
        mnuTransferType.Enabled = False
    End If
    Status.Panels(1).Text = ftpClient.StateString
    Status.Panels(2).Text = ftpClient.ReplyString
End Sub
```

Testing the Application

Finally, it's time to test the application. Of course, you need access to an FTP server in order to run this test. As suggested earlier in the chapter, you may want to run an FTP server on the same computer as the FTP client to simplify testing. When you're ready to test the application, follow these steps:

1. Start the FTP Client application. If you named the application as described in the example, the easiest way to run it is to click the Start button, then choose Run from the menu. Type **FtpClient.exe** (with the appropriate path, if necessary) and the application starts up.

2. Next, click the Connect command button. The application connects to the server indicated, and the screen looks like figure 13.3.

FIG. 13.3

The application is running successfully!

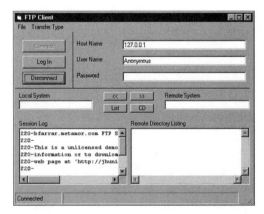

3. Enter a user name and password, then click the Log In command button. If you're an authorized user, the client completes authentication and the screen looks like figure 13.4.

4. Once you're logged in, try obtaining a directory listing. To do so, click the List command button. The screen resembles figure 13.5.

FIG. 13.4

Your test should include logging into an FTP server.

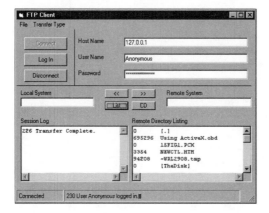

FIG. 13.5

Click the List command button to make sure that a directory listing comes up okay.

From here, you should be able to get and put files, as well as change directories. Remember that you've kept the interface simple, so you have to cut and paste filenames from the txtDirBox control into txtRemoteFile while testing the application. ●

Part

II

Ch

13

CHAPTER 14

Using the HTTP Client Control in VB Applications

The Hypertext Transmission Protocol (HTTP) is absolutely the most popular protocol on the Internet today. After all, HTTP is the protocol for the World Wide Web. Like most of the other Internet protocols, HTTP requires both a client and a server to complete document transfers. ∎

Learn the properties of the HTTP Client ActiveX control

Using an ActiveX control often requires the use of the properties made available for configuring the control.

Learn the methods available to programmers using the HTTP Client ActiveX control

ActiveX Controls expose methods that allow you to integrate ActiveX functionality into your applications.

Learn the events triggered by the HTTP Client ActiveX control

ActiveX Controls also provide for certain events to be triggered. Reacting to these events can make your programs Internet-ready.

Build an example Visual Basic application that employs the HTTP Client control

The best way to learn about HTTP is to build an application that uses HTTP to transfer files over the Internet.

Properties

Table 14.1 summarizes all the properties available in the HTTP Client control. All the data elements required to transfer a file from an HTTP server are included as properties in this control.

Table 14.1   Properties of the HTTP Client ActiveX control

Property	Purpose
Busy	`True` if a command is currently in progress.
DocInput	Refers to the `DocInput` object which must be set before invoking the `SendDoc` method and conveys information about the progress of the data transfer.
DocOutput	Refers to the `DocOuput` object which must be set before invoking the `GetDoc` method and conveys information about the progress of the data transfer.
Document	This property plus the `RemoteHost` identifies the target document.
EnableTimer	Tells the kind of timer that is fired by the `TimeOut` event.
Errors	Refers to a collection of errors detailing the last error.
Method	Sets the HTTP method to be used to request information from the HTTP server.
NotificationMode	Determines how notification of inbound data will be provided.
ProtocolState	Indicates whether the FTP client is not connected, waiting for authorization to connect, or connected to an FTP server.
RemoteHost	The host name or IP address of the server to be connected to.
RemotePort	The port number used to connect to the FTP server.
ReplyCode	The reply code sent by the server in response to requests from the client.
ReplyString	The reply string sent by the server in response to requests from the client.
State	Used to report the current state of the FTP connection.
TimeOut	Tells how long to wait before firing the `TimeOut` event for the type of timer referred to by `EnableTimer`.
URL	The Uniform Resource Locator, such as **http://myhost.com/ myfile.htm**.

Now let's take a look at a few of these properties in a bit more detail.

The *DocInput* Object

Controls that have the DocInput property can use properties of the DocInput object. Although it is somewhat counter intuitive, DocInput refers to data that will be sent from your application to a remote machine. As you'll see more clearly by the end of this chapter, the DocInput object is also passed through the DocInput event. With the DocInput object and the corresponding event working together control and action during document transfer can be quite robust. In the next few sections you'll be introduced to the key properties and methods of the DocInput object.

Properties of the *DocInput* Object The DocInput object makes many properties available for dealing with Internet documents. These properties are summarized in Table 14.2.

Table 14.2   Properties of the *DocInput* Object

Property	Value
BytesTotal	Returns either the size of the document to be passed or zero if the size is not known.
BytesTransferred	Returns the number of bytes already transferred.
DocLink	Allows data sent from a DocOutput object to be connected directly to this DocInput object.
Filename	Source from which DocInput data comes from. Valid only if DocLink is empty.
Headers	A reference to a DocHeaders collection.
State	Stores the current state of a document transfer.
Suspended	True if the document transfer has been suspended.

Let's take a moment and examine the Headers property and the State property a bit more closely.

The Headers *Property* The Headers property is a reference to a DocHeaders collection. The DocHeaders collection is basically a collection of DocHeader objects. The DocHeader object consists of a name and a value property. The Name property keeps the MIME header label (such as Content type) and the value property stores that MIME header's value (such as text/html). You'll find the Headers property to be quite useful in working with the DocOutput object as you'll see in a moment.

ON THE WEB

http://www.ncsa.uiuc.edu/SDG/Software/Mosaic/Docs   MIME stands for Multipurpose Internet Mail Extensions. MIME headers and values are employed in many applications on the Internet. To learn more about MIME headers, you should review RFC 1521 or check out this Web site.

Part
II
Ch
14

The* State *Property The DocInput object's State property provides information about the current state of the document transfer. There are several possible State properties that can be achieved and are summarized in Table 14.3.

Table 14.3 Values for the *State* Property in the *DocInput* Object

State	Meaning
icDocNone	No document transfer is in progress.
icDocBegin	A document transfer is being initiated.
icDocHeaders	Document headers are being transferred.
icDocData	A block of data is being transferred.
icDocError	An error has occurred during the document transfer.
icDocEnd	Document transfer has completed.

During the DocInput event response function, your application can take action based upon this State value.

Methods of the *DocInput* Object The DocInput object exposes several methods for use in your Visual Basic applications. Table 14.4 summarizes these methods and their functions.

Table 14.4 *DocInput* Object Methods

Method	Use
GetData	Retrieves the data currently being transferred when the DocInput event is fired.
SetData	Used to specify the data that will next be transferred when the DocInput event is fired.
Suspend	Suspends a transfer in progress.

The *DocOutput* Property

All controls that have the DocOutput property can access the properties of the DocOutput object. More importantly (as we'll discuss in more detail in a moment), the DocOutput object is passed through the DocOutput event. The DocOutput object and event provides all the necessary tools to do sophisticated processing of document transfer. Even though it seems backwards, DocOutput refers to data that will be received by your application from a remote machine. In the next few sections, you'll be introduced to the key properties and methods of the DocOutput object.

Properties of the *DocOutput* Object The properties made available by DocOutput are the same as those of the DocInput object with one exception. The DocOutput object does not have a DocLink property. These properties are summarized in Table 14.5.

Table 14.5 Properties of the *DocOutput* Object

Property	Value
BytesTotal	Returns either the size of the document to be passed or zero if the size is not known
BytesTransferred	Returns the number of bytes already transferred
Filename	Source from which data comes from
Headers	A reference to a DocHeaders collection
State	Stores the current state of a document transfer
Suspended	True if the document transfer has been suspended

Let's take a moment and examine the Headers property and the State property a bit more closely.

The Headers *Property* The Headers property in DocOutput is exactly the same as in the DocInput object. Using the Headers property in the DocOutput object will be a common task. So Listing 14.1 provides a brief demonstration of how to use this important property.

Listing 14.1 Using the *Headers* Property

```
Private Sub http_DocOutput(ByVal DocOutput As DocOutput)

    Dim hdr As DocHeader


    Select Case DocOutput.State

...

        Case icDocHeaders
            For Each hdr In DocOutput.Headers
                MsgBox "Name: " & CStr(hdr.Name) & " Value: " &
                CStr(hdr.Value)
            Next

...

    End Select

End Sub
```

Part

II

Ch

14

In this listing, each time a new header is received a message box is presented with the name and value of the header. Not a particularly useful function, but it demonstrates clearly how to use and access the Headers collection.

The State Property   DocInput and DocOutput both use the same values for the State property. So handling the various states of the data transfer will be handled with a Select Case statement for each of the states in DocOutput in the same manner as for DocInput. A simple example of such a statement is provided in Listing 14.1 in the section on the DocInput and DocOutput events.

Methods of the *DocOutput* Object   The DocOutput object exposes the same methods exposed by the DocInput object.

The *Method* Properties

The Method property allows you to set the type of request that will be issued to the Web server. Table 14.6 summarizes the types of requests available.

Table 14.6   *Method* Settings

Request	Meaning
prcGet	The HTTP GET request is used to obtain a document from the server.
prcHead	The HTTP HEAD request returns only the document header from the server.
prcPost	The HTTP POST request is issued to the server.
prcPut	The HTTP PUT request places a document on the server.

ProtocolState

The ProtocolState property provides protocol-specific information about the state of the connection. For the HTTP control, there are two states that the protocol can be in. These states are listed in Table 14.7.

Table 14.7   FTP *ProtocolState* Values

Value	Meaning
prcBase	The default state of the protocol prior to connecting to an HTTP server.
prcTransaction	Connection with the HTTP server has been obtained.

Methods

Most of the action in an FTP session involves sending and receiving files. The methods to accomplish this work are summarized in Table 14.8.

Table 14.8   Methods for the HTTP Client Control

Method	Use
Cancel	Stops a pending request.
Connect	Issues a request to the HTTP server to open a connection. If a connection is established, the State property is set.
GetDoc	Requests the retrieval of a document identified by a URL and can be used in conjunction with the DocInput and DocOutput objects and events.
PerformRequest	Like GetDoc, PerformRequest is another way to retrieve a document from the HTTP server.
SendDoc	Requests that a document identified by the URL to be sent to the server and can be used in conjunction with the DocInput and DocOutput objects and events.

Most of these methods are self-explanatory. However, a few of them bear additional discussion.

Events

The HTTP control provides numerous events on which your application can take action. Table 14.9 summarizes the events that are fired by the HTTP control.

Table 14.9   Summary of Events in the HTTP Control

Event	Description
Busy	Fires when a command is in progress and when a command is completed.
Cancel	Occurs at the completion of the cancellation of a request.
DocInput	Fired when data is sent from the control.
DocOutput	Triggered when data is sent to the control.
Error	Fires when an error is encountered.

continues

Part

II

Ch

14

Table 14.9   Continued

Event	Description
ProtocolStateChanged	Whenever the state of the HTTP session changes, this event is fired.
StateChanged	Occurs anytime the State of the connection changes, and therefore the State property changes.
TimeOut	Occurs when a given event fails to occur within the time period specified in the Timeout property.

DocInput and *DocOutput* Events

The DocInput and DocOutput events provide the programmer with a DocInput and DocOutput object. The properties and methods available in the DocInput and DocOutput objects allow you to control and monitor the incoming and outgoing documents from client to server. The most common way to use a DocInput or DocOutput event is to handle the various State properties in a Select Case statement. Listing 14.2 provides a basic skeleton for this approach.

Listing 14.2   Using *DocOutput State* Values

```
Private Sub http_DocOutput(ByVal DocOutput As DocOutput)

    Select Case DocOutput.State

        Case icDocBegin

        Case icDocHeaders

        Case icDocData

        Case icDocEnd

        Case icDocError

    End Select

End Sub
```

ProtocolStateChanged

You may want to notify the user of changes to the state of the connection between the client and the server. The ProtocolStateChanged event is triggered when changes occur at the protocol level. When the event fires, you'll be passed an integer that represents the current ProtocolState. Refer to the discussion of the ProtocolState property for a list of possible values. Listing 14.3 provides an example of how this event might be used.

Listing 14.3   Responding to the *ProtocolStateChanged* Event

```
Private Sub MyHTTPControl_ProtocolStateChanged(ByVal ProtocolState As Integer)

    Select Case ProtocolState
        Case prcBase
            Status.Panels(1).Text = "Base"
        Case prcTransaction
            Status.Panels(1).Text = "Transaction"
    End Select

End Sub
```

Of course, you would need to have a StatusBar control named Status to use this code.

The SourceViewer Application

To try out the HTTP control, you'll construct a simple HTTP client that allows you to download and view source HTML documents. The SourceViewer application provides the following functionality:

- Requests HTML documents from Web servers via HTTP
- Cancels requests for documents from Web servers
- Displays HTML source code downloaded from Web servers

To get an idea of how this application works, you may want to run it before continuing. Of course, you'll need to have an HTTP server available in order to actually use the application.

Working this example will be much easier if you have an HTTP server running locally on your computer. Since you probably don't have an HTTP server application already, you should look for one on the Internet. One good place to look is **http://website.ora.com**. Many of the Web server vendors have 90-day free trials. After you see how easy it is to develop custom Web browsers, you'll probably want to buy a good Web server application.

The following example takes you through the process of building the SourceViewer application in a step-by-step manner.

Building the SourceViewer Application

As you'll see in this example, integrating HTTP services into your own applications using the ActiveX Internet Control Pack adds pizzazz without too much programming headache. In this application, you'll need the following major components:

- frmSourceViewer—The main form for the application.
- cmdViewSource—A command button that initiates an HTTP request for the URL found in the txtURL control.

- ■ cmdStop—This cancels a pending HTTP request.
- ■ txtURL—A textbox for entering the URL to be retrieved.
- ■ txtDocumentWindow—A multiline text box used to display the HTML source retrieved from the Web server.

To build the SourceViewer application, follow these steps:

1. Start Visual Basic 4.0.
2. Create the form called frmSourceViewer. You'll need to change the Caption property to HTML SourceViewer and the Name property to frmSourceViewer.
3. Resize frmSourceViewer as appropriate.
4. Select the command button control and add the cmdViewSource button. Change the Caption property to View Source and the Name property to cmdViewSource. Also, add the cmdStop button and change its Caption and Name properties to Stop and cmdStop, respectively.
5. Now select the Textbox control and add the txtURL and txtDocumentWindow controls to frmSourceViewer. Be sure to make the txtDocumentWindow control ready for multiline text by setting the Multiline property to True and the ScrollBars property to 3 - Both.
6. Add the Status bar to the bottom of the form. Set the Name property to Status. Remember to make two panels on your Status bar.
7. Next add a simple menu to the application with just mnuFile and mnuFileExit as options.
8. Save the project to a convenient working directory.
9. Now add the HTTP control to the control toolbar. Select Tools, Custom Controls and choose Microsoft HTTP Client Control and click OK. This adds the HTTP control to your toolbar for this project. Since we'll be using the DocOutput object, you'll also need to add a reference to the support object library. Select Tools, References and choose Microsoft Internet Support Objects and click OK.
10. Drag and drop the HTTP control onto frmSourceViewer. When you're finished, the form should look something like figure 14.1.
11. Next select the HTTP control and change the Name property to http.
12. Now its time to start coding the application. Start by working on the command buttons. The first one you'll code is cmdViewSource. Your code will look something like Listing 14.3.

On the CD

Listing 14.3   *SOURCEVIEWER.VBP*   The *cmdViewSource* Click Response Function

```
Private Sub cmdViewSource_Click()

    txtDocumentWindow.Text = ""
```

```
If txtURL.Text <> "" Then
    http.URL = txtURL.Text
    http.GetDoc
Else
    MsgBox "You must enter a URL"
End If

End Sub
```

FIG. 14.1

Your SourceViewer application should look like this so far.

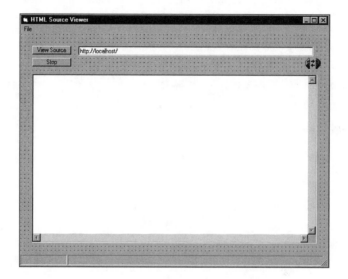

The txtDocumentWindow is cleared. Assuming that the user has entered something in the txtURL control, a call to GetDoc is executed to request a document. Notice that we have yet to notify the user of any activity. You'll use HTTP control events to take care of user messages.

13. Next you'll code the cmdStop click response function. Pressing this button stops any pending HTTP request. Your code will look like Listing 14.4.

On the CD

Listing 14.4 *2SOURCEVIEWER.VBP* *cmdStop* Response Function

```
Private Sub cmdStop_Click()
    http.Cancel
End Sub
```

Part
II

Ch
14

14. Now go ahead and get the simple menu out of the way. The only menu action in this application is the mnuFileExit click function, a trivial End statement (see Listing 14.5).

Listing 14.5   *3SOURCEVIEWER.VBP   mnuFileExit* Click Response Function

```
Private Sub mnuFileExit_Click()
    End
End Sub
```

15. Next turn to the `http` control. The SourceViewer application needs to respond to a number of events. You'll start by coding the `DocOutput` event response function. This response function constitutes the meat of the application. When the Web server sends data back to your SourceViewer application, this event response will place the HTML source code in `txtDocumentWindow` as well as notify the user of status changes as necessary (see Listing 14.6).

Listing 14.6   *FTPCLIENT.VBP*   Authenticate Event Response Function

```
Private Sub http_DocOutput(ByVal DocOutput As DocOutput)

    Dim htmlData As String

    Select Case DocOutput.State
        Case icDocBegin
            Status.Panels(2).Text = "Starting transfer"

        Case icDocData
            DocOutput.GetData htmlData
            txtDocumentWindow.Text = txtDocumentWindow.Text & htmlData
            Status.Panels(2).Text = DocOutput.BytesTransferred & " Bytes
                transferred"

        Case icDocEnd
            Status.Panels(2).Text = "Transfer complete"
    End Select

End Sub
```

For this application, you'll only need to worry about three values for the `State` property in the `DocInput` object—`icDocBegin`, `icDocData`, and `icDocEnd`. Both `icDocBegin` and `icDocEnd` are used solely for updating the Status bar. The `icDocData` state is used to obtain and format the HTML source code for display to the user.

16. Now you'll add the `Error` event response function. You'll use the `ReplyString` as the basis of your communication with the user. Your code will look like Listing 14.7.

Listing 14.7   *4SOURCEVIEWER.VBP*   *Error* Event Response Function

```
Private Sub http_Error(Number As Integer, Description As String, Scode As Long,
Source As String, HelpFile As String, HelpContext As Long, CancelDisplay As
Boolean)
```

```
    MsgBox http.ReplyString
End Sub
```

17. Finally you'll write the StateChanged event response function. All this function needs to do is update the Status bar. Your code will look like Listing 14.8.

On the CD

Listing 14.8 *2FTPCLIENT.VBP* Connect Event Response Function

```
Private Sub http_StateChanged(ByVal State As Integer)
    Status.Panels(1).Text = http.StateString
End Sub
```

Testing the Application

Finally, you're ready to test the application. Of course, you'll need access to an HTTP server in order to run this test. As suggested before, you may want to run an HTTP server on the same computer as the SourceViewer application to simplify testing. To test the application, follow these steps:

1. Start the SourceViewer application. If you named the applications as described in the example, the easiest way to do this is to press the Start button and then choose Run from the menu. Type **SourceViewer.exe** (with the appropriate path) and the server will start up. The application should look like figure 14.2.

FIG. 14.2

Start the SourceViewer application.

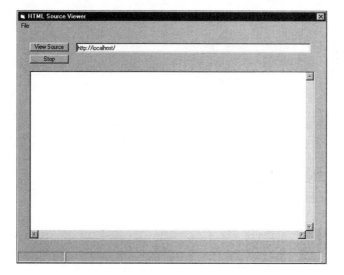

Part

II

Ch

14

2. Next, enter an URL and press the View Source command button. The application will retrieve the URL. Now the screen should look something like figure 14.3.

FIG. 14.3

See what you get after pressing View Source with a valid URL.

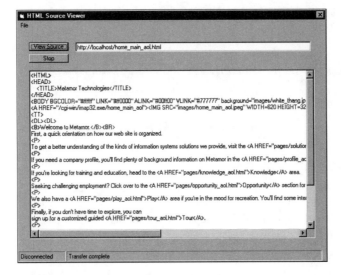

3. Now try entering an invalid URL. The Web server will send an error message and SourceViewer will show you the details. Your screen will look something like figure 14.4.

FIG. 14.4

This is how the screen looks after attempting to retrieve a bad URL.

CHAPTER 15

Using the HTML Control in VB Applications

The Hypertext Markup Language (HTML) is the code that describes how Web pages should look. After all, HTML documents are carried via the HTTP protocol over the World Wide Web between client and server. Now that you've obtained HTML documents over the Internet in the last chapter, you're ready to show them in a full-fledged Web browser. ■

Learn the properties of the HTML ActiveX control

Using an ActiveX Control often requires the use of the properties made available for configuring the control.

Learn the methods available to programmers using the HTML ActiveX control

ActiveX Controls expose methods that allow you to integrate ActiveX functionality into your applications.

Learn the events triggered by the HTML ActiveX control

ActiveX Controls also provide for certain events to be triggered. Reacting to these events can make your programs Internet ready.

Build a simple Web browser in Visual Basic that employs the HTML control

The best way to learn about using the HTML control in a Web browser is to build an application that renders Web pages from the Internet.

Properties

Table 15.1 summarizes all the properties available in the HTML control. All the data elements required to transfer and render an HTML document over the World Wide Web are included as properties in this control.

Table 15.1 Properties of the HTML ActiveX Control

Property	Purpose
BackImage	Stores the background image to be used in rendering the page.
BaseURL	Equal to the value of the <BASE> tag or URL if there is no <BASE>.
DeferRetrieval	True if embedded objects are not downloaded. False if embedded objects are downloaded.
DocBackColor	Keeps the BGCOLOR attribute of the <BODY> tag.
DocForeColor	Stores the TEXT attribute of the <BODY> tag.
DocInput	Refers to the DocInput object which must be set before invoking the SendDoc method and conveys information about the progress of the data transfer.
DocLinkColor	Equal to the value of the LINK attribute of the <BODY> tag.
DocOutput	Refers to the DocOuput object which must be set before invoking the GetDoc method and conveys information about the progress of the data transfer.
DocVisitedColor	Keeps the value of the VLINK attribute of the <BODY> tag.
ElemNotification	Used to parse each HTML element. Set to false unless you're using the HTML control as a parser in another application.
EnableTimer	Tells the kind of timer that is fired by the TimeOut event.
FixedFont	Identifies the font to be used for fixed width text.
Forms	Refers to an HTMLForms collection.
Heading1Font	The font to be used for text enclosed in H1 tags.
Heading2Font	The font to be used for text enclosed in H2 tags.
Heading3Font	The font to be used for text enclosed in H3 tags.
Heading4Font	The font to be used for text enclosed in H4 tags.
Heading5Font	The font to be used for text enclosed in H5 tags.
Heading6Font	The font to be used for text enclosed in H6 tags.
LayoutDone	True when the main HTML document has been rendered but embedded objects have not been downloaded.

Property	Purpose
LinkColor	The color used for text representing hypertext links.
ParseDone	True when the HTML has been parsed.
RedrawProperty	Set this property to false to make changes to the HTML document and avoid display defects. To cause the HTML control to be redrawn, set this property to true.
RequestURL	The URL that is currently being requested.
RetainSource	Set this to true to keep the source HTML code.
RetrieveBytesDone	Reports the number of bytes retrieved so far.
RetrieveBytesTotal	If available, the total number of bytes to be transferred.
SourceText	The HTML code currently rendered by the HTML control (read-only).
TimeOut	Tells how long to wait before firing the TimeOut event for the type of timer referred to by EnableTimer.
TotalHeight	The height in pixels of the complete document.
TotalWidth	The width in pixels of the complete document.
UnderlineLinks	True if hyptertext links should be underlined.
URL	The URL to be retrieved.
UseDocColors	If this is false, document specific color settings are ignored and the defaults are used.
ViewSource	Determines whether the HTML code should be rendered or shown as text.
VisitedColor	Renders the color of the visited links' text.

Now let's take a look at a few of these properties in a bit more detail.

URL versus RequestURL

At first glance, it might seem that these two properties are redundant. But, of course, they are not. The RequestURL property is set by the argument you pass to RequestDoc at execution. The URL property, on the other hand, is set during the process of fulfilling the request and thus may look a bit different from the original address you requested. For instance, the port number might be appended to the domain name. Listing 15.1 shows how these two properties are used.

Listing 15.1 Using *URL* and *RequestURL*

```
...

HTML.RequestDoc txtURL.Text

Status.Panel(2).Text = "Retrieving " & HTML.RequestURL
...

...
Private Sub HTML_EndRetrieval()

        Status.Panels(2).Text = "Document complete"

        txtURL.Text = HTML.URL

End Sub
```

While there are some methods and events you haven't seen yet here, you can see that the RequestURL property is used before the retrieval of the document and the URL property is used after completion of the document retrieval.

Forms Properties and Method

The Forms property points to an HTMLForms collection. The HTMLForms collection contains a number of HTMLForm objects. Table 15.2 details the properties of the HTMLForm object.

Table 15.2 Properties of the HTMLForm Object

Property	Value
Method	Must be one of prcGet, prcHead, prcPost, or prcPut HTML verbs.
URL	The ACTION URL from the form.
URLEncodedBody	Stores all the values of all of the form fields in text.

The HTMLForm object exposes only one method, the RequestSubmit function. RequestSubmit is used to send a form for processing. The RequestURL property of HTML object is set to the action URL for the form. The URL property is updated after processing of the request has successfully begun. The Method property refers to one of the HTTP methods that are represented by the constants prcGet, prcHead, prcPost, and prcPut.

Methods

The HTML control offers very few methods for execution. The three available methods are summarized in Table 15.3.

Table 15.3   Methods for the HTML Control

Method	Use
Cancel	Stops a pending request.
RequestAllEmbedded	Requests that all the embedded objects in the main document be downloaded.
RequestDoc	Requests that the main document be downloaded.

Most of the time you'll use RequestDoc. However, say that you had a configuration option that allowed the user to turn off the downloading of images and other embedded objects. (This is a common feature in most Web browsers so that you don't have to wait for big graphics to download if you don't want to.) You might then want the user to be able to download embedded objects on demand. This type of scenario would be an excellent situation for using the RequestAllEmbedded method.

Events

The HTML control provides numerous events on which your application can take action. Table 15.4 summarizes the events that are fired by the HTML control.

Table 15.4   Summary of Events in the HTML Control

Event	Description
BeginRetrieval	Occurs when the document transfer is initiated.
DocInput	Fired when data is sent from the control.
DocOutput	Triggered when data is sent to the control.
DoNewElement	Fires during HTML parsing when a new element is added.
DoRequestDoc	Triggered by either a call to RequestDoc or a click by the user on a hypertext link.
DoRequestEmbedded	Occurs when an embedded item is to be transferred.
DoRequestSubmit	Triggered by either a call to RequestSubmit or a user submitting a form.
EndRetrieval	Fires when the document and embedded objects have all been transferred.
LayoutComplete	Occurs when the entire main document has been transferred, although embedded objects may still be downloading.
ParseComplete	Fires when the HTML source has been parsed.

continues

Table 15.4 Continued	
Event	**Description**
TimeOut	Occurs when a given event fails to occur within the time period specified in the TimeOut property.

The Web Browser Application

To try out the HTML control, you'll construct a complete Web browser that allows you to download and view rendered HTML documents. The HTML control supports all HTML 2.0 tags, so the display of this application will be robust. The Web browser you build will provide the following functionality:

- Request HTML documents from Web servers via HTTP
- Cancel requests for documents from Web servers
- Render HTML 2.0 content downloaded from Web servers

To get an idea of how this application works, you may want to run it before continuing. Of course, you'll need to have an HTTP server available in order to actually use the application.

The following example takes you through the process of building the Web browser in a step-by-step manner.

Building the Web Browser Application

As you'll see in this example, integrating HTML browsing into your own applications using the ActiveX Internet Control Pack adds the World Wide Web to your application without requiring significant programming. In this application, you'll need the following major components:

- frmWebBrowser—The main form for the application.
- cmdHome—A command button that when pressed requests the default home page URL.
- cmdGetDocument—Command button that initiates a request for the URL found in the txtURL control.
- cmdBack—This command button requests the retrieval of the last page retrieved.
- cmdCancel—A command button used to cancel a pending HTTP request.
- txtURL—A text box for entering the URL to be retrieved.
- html—The ActiveX control that manages the HTTP session and renders the HTML code.

To build the Web browser application, follow these steps:

1. Start Visual Basic 4.0.

2. Create the form called `frmWebBrowser`. You'll need to change the Caption property to Web Browser and the Name property to `frmWebBrowser`. You may also want to set the form so that it cannot be resized at runtime.

3. Resize `frmWebBrowser` as appropriate.

4. Select the command button control and add the `cmdGetDocument`, `cmdHome`, `cmdBack`, and `cmdCancel` buttons. Set the Caption property of each of these buttons to an appropriate label. You'll also need to change the Name property to `cmdGetDocument`, `cmdHome`, `cmdBack`, and `cmdCancel`, respectively.

5. Now select the text box control and add the `txtURL` control to `frmWebBrowser`.

6. Add the Status bar to the bottom of the form. Set the Name property to `Status`. Remember to make two panels on your Status bar.

7. Next add a simple menu to the application with just `mnuFile` and `mnuFileExit` as options.

8. Save the project to a convenient working directory.

9. Now add the HTML control to the control toolbar. Select Tools, Custom Controls, Microsoft HTML Client Control and click OK. This adds the HTML Control to your toolbar for this project. You'll also need to add a reference to the support object library. Select Tools, References. Check Microsoft Internet Support Objects and click OK.

10. Drag and drop the HTML control onto `frmWebBrowser`. Size the control to a suitable size for browsing Web documents. When you're finished, the form should look something like figure 15.1.

FIG. 15.1
Review the layout of the `frmWebBrowser` form.

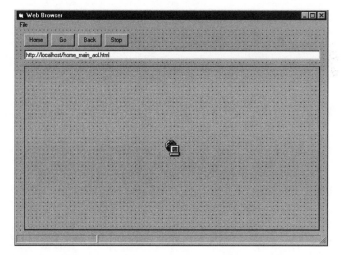

11. Next select the HTML control and change the Name property to `html`.

12. Now its time to start coding the application. Start by adding a couple of global variables you'll need to code the `cmdHome` and `cmdBack` button procedures. The global variables you'll need are `gLastURL` and `gHomeURL`. The code from the example is in Listing 15.2.

Listing 15.2 *WEBBROWSER.VBP* **Global Declarations**

```
Dim gLastURL As String
Dim gHomeURL As String
```

13. Code the cmdHome button next. This is a simple function that displays the browsers default home page. Your code will look like Listing 15.3.

Listing 15.3 *2WEBBROWSER.VBP* *cmdHome* **Response Function**

```
Private Sub cmdHome_Click()
    HTML.RequestDoc gHomeURL
End Sub
```

14. Next code the cmdGetDocument response function. The code is in Listing 15.4.

Listing 15.4 *3WEBBROWSER.VBP* *cmdGetDocument* **Response Function**

```
Private Sub cmdGetDocument_Click()
    If txtURL.Text <> "" Then
        HTML.RequestDoc txtURL.Text
    Else
        MsgBox "You must enter a URL"
    End If
End Sub
```

This function also calls RequestDoc to begin retrieving the page indicated by the txtURL Control.

15. Now add the cmdBack response function. The code is in Listing 15.5.

Listing 15.5 *4WEBBROWSER.VBP* *cmdBack* **Response Function**

```
Private Sub cmdBack_Click()
    HTML.RequestDoc gLastURL
End Sub
```

Rather than make a sophisticated Back button that uses a list of previous URL strings, the example keeps only the last URL.

16. Now go ahead and get the simple menu out of the way. The only menu action in this application is the mnuFileExit click function, a trivial End statement (see Listing 15.6).

Listing 15.6 *SOURCEVIEWER.VBP* *mnuFileExit* **Click Response Function**

```
Private Sub mnuFileExit_Click()
    End
End Sub
```

17. Next, code reponse functions for the events in the HTML control. The Web browser needs to respond to a number of events. First, you'll code the DoRequestDoc event response function. The DoRequestDoc event is triggered by a call to RequestDoc or by clicking a hypertext link. Your code should look like Listing 15.7.

Listing 15.7   5WEBBROWSER.VBP   DoRequestDoc Event Response Function

```
Private Sub HTML_DoRequestDoc(ByVal URL As String, ByVal Element As HTMLElement,
ByVal DocInput As DocInput, EnableDefault As Boolean)
    Status.Panels(2).Text = "Requesting " & URL
End Sub
```

Just a simple update of the Status bar is required.

18. Now you'll add the DoRequestEmbedded event response function, which is exactly the same as the DoRequestDoc function. The DoRequestEmbedded event fires when an embedded object in the main document is downloaded or by a call to RequestEmbedded (see Listing 15.8).

Listing 15.8   6WEBBROWSER.VBP   DoRequestEmbedded Event Response Function

```
Private Sub HTML_DoRequestEmbedded(ByVal URL As String, ByVal Element As
HTMLElement, ByVal DocInput As DocInput, EnableDefault As Boolean)
    Status.Panels(2).Text = "Requesting " & URL
End Sub
```

19. The DoRequestSubmit event occurs when the user presses a Submit button on a form or when the RequestSubmit method is invoked. The DoRequestSubmit response function is a simple Status bar update as well (see Listing 15.9).

Listing 15.9   7WEBBROWSER.VBP   DoRequestSubmit Event Response Function

```
Private Sub HTML_DoRequestSubmit(ByVal URL As String, ByVal Form As HTMLForm,
ByVal DocOutput As DocOutput, EnableDefault As Boolean)
    Status.Panels(2).Text = "Requesting " & URL
End Sub
```

20. The EndRetrieval event provides an opportunity to update the gLastURL variable and the txtURL control. The EndRetrieval event occurs when the requested document has been downloaded (see Listing 15.10). You'll also update the Status bar.

Listing 15.10   8WEBBROWSER.VBP   EndRetrieval Event Response Function

```
Private Sub HTML_EndRetrieval()
        Status.Panels(2).Text = "Document complete"
```

continues

Listing 15.10   Continued

```
         gLastURL = txtURL.Text
         txtURL.Text = html.URL
End Sub
```

Notice that txtURL.Text is updated with html.URL. Recall from previous that html.RequestURL is set by the string passed to RequestDoc. By the time the document has been completely retrieved and the EndRetrieval event fires, the html.URL property has been updated with the actual retrieved URL.

21. When the Error event occurs, you'll simply update the status bar with the error description (see Listing 15.11).

Listing 15.11   *9WEBBROWSER.VBP*   *Error* Event Response Function

```
Private Sub HTML_Error(Number As Integer, Description As String, Scode As Long,
Source As String, HelpFile As String, HelpContext As Long, CancelDisplay As
Boolean)

    Status.Panels(2).Text = Description

End Sub
```

22. The UpdateRetrieval event occurs after each block of data is read from the HTTP connection. This gives you the opportunity to tell the user how much data has been transferred. Your code should look like Listing 15.12.

Listing 15.12   *10WEBBROWSER.VBP*   *UpdateRetrieval* Event Response Function

```
Private Sub HTML_UpdateRetrieval()
    Status.Panels(1).Text = HTML.RetrieveBytesDone & " bytes retrieved"
End Sub
```

Of course, the RetrieveBytesDone property is updated before the UpdateRetrievel event occurs.

Testing the Application

Finally you're ready to test the Web browser. Of course, you'll need access to an HTTP server in order to run this test. As suggested before, you may want to run an HTTP server on the same computer as the Web browser to simplify testing. To test the applications, follow these steps:

1. Start the Web browser application. If you named the applications as described in the example, the easiest way to do this is to press the Start button and the choose Run from the menu. Type **WebBrowser.exe** (with the appropriate path) and the browser will start up. The application should look like figure 15.2.

FIG. 15.2

This is how the screen will look after starting the Web browser application.

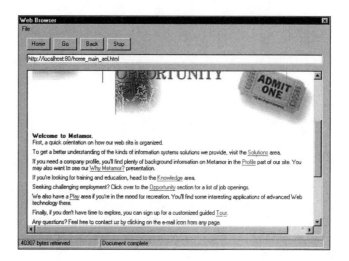

2. Next enter a URL and press the Go command button. The application will retrieve the URL. Now the screen should display the new Web page you've requested (see fig. 15.3).

FIG. 15.3

Your screen should look like this after selecting a new valid URL.

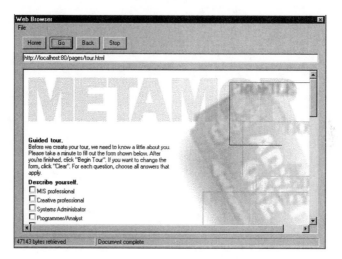

3. Now press the Back button. Your screen should return to the previous page. In this example, the screen would return to figure 15.2.

CHAPTER 16

Using the SMTP Control in VB Applications

E-mail is perhaps the most ubiquitous service on the Internet. Sure lots of people use the Web, but even my mother, father, and grandfather all use e-mail to communicate. So it makes sense that Microsoft has provided an ActiveX control to easily add e-mail functionality to your programs.

The Simple Mail Transport Protocol (SMTP) is responsible for carrying all of those electronic mail messages over the Internet. You'll encounter many cases where your applications need to send e-mail. Consider, for example, an application that copies files at night for use by users in the morning. You might want the application to fire off an e-mail in the event of an error. ■

Learn the properties of the SMTP ActiveX control

Add mail functionality to your programs using this control.

Learn the methods available to programmers using the SMTP ActiveX control

Implement functionality with the built-in methods supplied in this ActiveX control.

Learn the events triggered by the SMTP control

Respond to the various events that are fired by the ActiveX SMTP control.

Build a simple Mail application

Use ActiveX to send e-mail over the Internet in Visual Basic employing the SMTP control.

Properties

Table 16.1 summarizes all the properties available in the SMTP control. All the data elements required to send e-mail messages to an SMTP server are included as properties in this control.

Table 16.1   Properties of the SMTP Client ActiveX Control

Property	Purpose
Busy	True if a command is currently in progress.
DocInput	Refers to the DocInput object which must be set before invoking the SendDoc method and conveys information about the progress of the data transfer.
Errors	Refers to a collection of errors detailing the last error.
NotificationMode	Determines how notification of outbound data will be provided.
ProtocolState	Indicates whether the SMTP client is not connected, waiting for authorization to connect, or connected to an SMTP server.
RemoteHost	The host name or IP address of the SMTP server to be connected to.
RemotePort	The port number used to connect to the SMTP server.
ReplyCode	The reply code sent by the server in response to requests from the client.
ReplyString	The reply string sent by the server in response to requests from the client.
State	Used to report the current state of the SMTP connection.

You have seen all of these properties in previous controls. Recall from the Chapter 11, "Using the TCP Control in VB Applications," that all Internet services communicate on a TCP/IP port. In the case of e-mail, port 25 is standard for SMTP. Unless you need to run a special SMTP server on another port, the default value will be fine.

Methods

The SMTP control offers a couple of methods for programmers. The available methods are summarized in Table 16.2.

Table 16.2   Methods for the SMTP Client Control

Method	Use
Cancel	Stops a pending request.
SendDoc	Sends the mail message.

Your applications will make extensive use of SendDoc. To familiarize yourself with the elements of this handy function, take a look at each of the following parameters:

- URL—This optional parameter permits you to identify a remote document for sending.
- Headers—SMTP uses a number of headers to send mail including information such as the To and From addresses. So the SMTP control accepts a DocHeaders collection for passing these headers. This parameter is optional.
- InputData—This is an optional parameter for a buffer of data that holds the document to be sent.
- InputFile—This refers to a file on the local system. This file is the document to be sent and may optionally be set.

You'll always use the Headers parameter to set up SMTP headers as necessary. The example program at the end of this chapter uses the InputData parameter to pass message data to the SMTP server.

Events

The SMTP control provides numerous events on which your application can take action. Table 16.3 summarizes the events that are fired by the SMTP Client control.

Table 16.3   Summary of Events in the SMTP Client Control

Event	Description
Busy	This event is triggered when commands are in progress.
Cancel	This event is triggered when the Cancel method is executed.
DocInput	This event is fired when data is sent from the control.
Error	This event occurs when an error has been encountered.
ProtocolStateChange	When the state of the protocol changes, this event is fired.
StateChanged	When the state of the SMTP control changes, this event is thrown.
TimeOut	This event is triggered when a given event fails to occur within the time period specified in the TimeOut property.

The Mail Pad Application

To try out the SMTP control, you'll construct a simple mail sending program that allows you to jot down a message and send it via e-mail. The mail application you build will provide the following functionality:

■ Select an SMTP server

■ Select the mail account from which the message is sent

■ Select the address to deliver the message to as well as a courtesy copy recipient

■ Enter a subject heading and the text of the message

■ Send the mail message to the designated SMTP server

To get an idea of how this application works, you may want to run it before continuing. Of course, you'll need to have an SMTP server available in order to actually use the application.

 TIP Working this example will be much easier if you have an SMTP server running locally on your computer. Since you probably don't have an SMTP server application already, you should look for one on the Internet. One good place to look is **http://www.winsite.com**.

The following example takes you through the process of building the Mail Pad application in a step-by-step manner.

Building the Mail Pad Application

As you'll see in this example, integrating electronic mail functionality into your own applications using the ActiveX Internet Control Pack is fast and straightforward. In this application, you'll need the following major components:

■ `frmMail`—The main form for the application.

■ `cmdSendMessage`—A command button used to that initially requests the default home page URL.

■ `txtSMTPServer`—The server that will receive the message.

■ `txtToAddress`—A text box for entering the e-mail address of the recipient.

■ `txtFromAddress`—A text box for entering the e-mail address of the sender.

■ `txtCCAddress`—A text box for entering the e-mail address of a courtesy recipient.

■ `txtSubject`—A text box for entering a subject heading for the message.

■ `txtMessageBody`—A multiline text box for entering the mail message.

■ `SMTP1`—This is the ActiveX control that manages the SMTP session and sends the mail message.

To build the Mail Pad application, follow these steps:

1. Start Visual Basic 4.0.

2. Create the form called `frmMail`. You'll need to change the `Caption` property to `Mail Pad` and the `Name` property to `frmMail`. You may also want to set the form so that it cannot be resized at runtime.

3. Resize `frmMail` as appropriate.

4. Select the command button control and add the cmdSendMessage. Set the Caption property to an appropriate label like Send Message. You'll also need to change the Name property to cmdSendMessage.

5. Now select the text box control and add the following text controls: txtToAddress, txtFromAddress, txtSMTPServer, txtCCAddress, txtSubject, and txtMessageBody to frmMail. You'll also want to include a label for each of the text controls as appropriate.

6. Add the Status bar to the bottom of the form. Set the Name property to Status. Remember to make three panels on your Status bar.

7. Save the project to a convenient working directory.

8. Now add the SMTP control to the control toolbar. Select Tools, Custom Controls, Microsoft SMTP Client Control and click OK. This adds the SMTP control to your toolbar for this project. You'll also need to add a reference to the support object library. Select Tools, References. Check Microsoft Internet Support Objects and click OK.

9. Drag and drop the SMTP control onto frmMail. When you're finished, the form should look something like figure 16.1.

FIG. 16.1

Check your copy of the frmMail form.

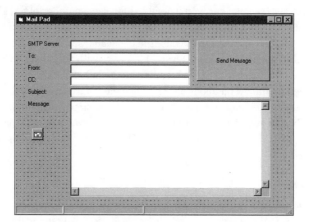

10. Next select the SMTP control and change the Name property to SMTP1.

11. Now its time to start coding the application. Start by coding the cmdSendMessage button. The heart of the mail application is in this button. Your code should look like Listing 16.1.

Listing 16.1   *MAILPAD.VBP*   cmdSendMessage Click Response Function

On the CD

```
Private Sub cmdSendMessage_Click()
    Dim MessageHeaders As DocHeaders

    Set MessageHeaders = SMTP1.DocInput.Headers
        MessageHeaders.Clear
```

continues

Part II

Ch 16

Listing 16.1   Continued

```
        MessageHeaders.Add "To", txtToAddress.Text
        MessageHeaders.Add "CC", txtCCAddress.Text
        MessageHeaders.Add "Subject", txtSubject.Text
        MessageHeaders.Add "Message-Id", "<" & App.Title & _
                           "." & Format(Date) & _
                           "." & Format(Timer) & _
                           "." & txtFromAddress.Text & ">"

        MessageHeaders.Add "Content-Type", "TEXT/PLAIN; charset=US-ASCII"
        MessageHeaders.Add "Content-Length", " " & Len(txtMessageBody.Text) + 2

    SMTP1.RemoteHost = txtSMTPServer.Text

    SMTP1.SendDoc , MessageHeaders, txtMessageBody

End Sub
```

This procedure starts by declaring MessageHeader as a DocHeaders collection. After declaring MessageHeader, you'll need to initialize a number of SMTP headers. A DocHeaders collection like MessageHeader is used to store each of these headers using the Add method. Be sure to execute the DocHeaders Clear method to the collection. (This is so the user can send several messages with a fresh set of SMTP headers.) Notice that a number of SMTP headers are included. Unlike some of the other controls, you need to know a bit about SMTP to use the control effectively. The only header that is required to send mail and have it arrive at the desired destination is the To header. The value that To equals must be of the form *username@hostname*. Finally, you'll set the RemoteHost property and call SendDoc. The message body itself is simply a parameter to SendDoc.

ON THE WEB

ftp://ds.internic.net/rfc   Explaining the details of SMTP headers is beyond the scope of this book. However, many other SMTP headers are clearly defined in RFC 821. You can find this document with the other RFCs at this FTP site.

12. Now let's work on the DocInput event for SMTP1. The DocInput event occurs as you send information by calling SendDoc. This event provides an excellent method for tracking the progress of the mail message as it is sent. The code is in Listing 16.2.

Listing 16.2   *2MAILPAD.VBP*   DocInput Event Response Function

On the CD
```
Private Sub SMTP1_DocInput(ByVal DocInput As DocInput)
    Select Case DocInput.State
        Case icDocBegin
            Status.Panels(3).Text = "SMTP session beginning."
        Case icDocHeaders
            Status.Panels(3).Text = "Sending SMTP message headers..."
        Case icDocData
```

```
                Status.Panels(3).Text = "Sending SMTP message data..."
        Case icDocEnd
                Status.Panels(3).Text = "SMTP session ended."
        Case icDocError
                Status.Panels(3).Text = "SMTP session error."
                MsgBox "Error"
    End Select
End Sub
```

The `DocInput` object exposes a `State` property that provides information about the status of the SMTP session in progress. When the document transfer begins, the `DocInput` object reaches the state `icDocBegin`. Next the headers are sent to the SMTP server. During this phase, the `DocInput.State` is `icDocHeaders`. The message body itself is then sent with the `DocInputState` equal to `icDocData`. If an error occurs, the `DocInput.State` is set to `icDocError`. Finally, whether the message send is successful or not, the `DocInput.State` is set to `icDocEnd`. As this process occurs, `Status.Panel(3)` is updated with a progress message.

TIP

If you get a runtime error with the message `User-defined type not defined`, you probably forgot to add a reference to the Internet Support Objects control set. `DocInput` and `DocOutput` are both defined in this library. To add the proper reference, select Tools, References. Check Microsoft Internet Support Objects and click OK.

13. Now lets code the `Error` event response function. The SMTP control is kind enough to supply the reply string from the SMTP server when an error occurs. You'll use `Status.Panel(2)` as the place to report these types of messages. The code is in Listing 16.3.

On the CD

Listing 16.3   *3MAILPAD.VBP*   *Error* Response Function

```
Private Sub SMTP1_Error(Number As Integer, Description As String, Scode As Long,
Source As String, HelpFile As String, HelpContext As Long, CancelDisplay As
Boolean)
    Status.Panels(2).Text = SMTP1.ReplyString
End Sub
```

14. Finally, you'll write the response function for the `State` event. You'll catch this event to update the user about the state of the connection with the SMTP server, using `Status.Panels(1)` to show the `StateString` property (see Listing 16.4).

On the CD

Listing 16.4   *4MAILPAD.VBP*   *State* Event Response Function

```
Private Sub SMTP1_StateChanged(ByVal State As Integer)
    Status.Panels(1).Text = SMTP1.StateString
End Sub
```

Testing the Application

Finally you're ready to test the Mail Pad application. Of course, you'll need access to an SMTP server in order to run this test. As suggested earlier, you may want to run an SMTP server on the same computer as the Mail Pad application to simplify testing. To test the applications, follow these steps:

1. Start the Mail Pad application. If you named the applications as described in the example, the easiest way to do this is to press the Start button and the choose Run from the menu. Type **MailPad.exe** (with the appropriate path) and the server will start up. The application should look like figure 16.2.

FIG. 16.2

Starting the Mail Pad application.

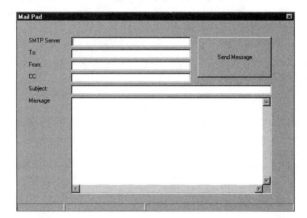

2. Next enter an SMTP server, a To address, a From address, a Subject, and a message body. If you're running an SMTP server on your local machine, your screen would look something like figure 16.3.

FIG. 16.3

This is how it looks when you send a message.

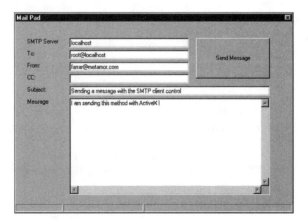

Of course, if you're connected to a network you can use the domain name of any handy SMTP server.

3. Now press the Send Message button. The application will connect to the SMTP server and send the message. When the send is complete, your screen will look something like figure 16.4.

FIG. 16.4
Check out the status after sending a message.

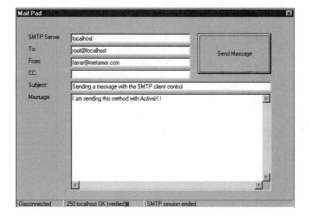

Using the POP Control in VB Applications

The Post Office Protocol (POP) is used to retrieve mail from a POP server. Typically, SMTP, which was discussed in the previous chapter, is used to transport mail to the appropriate POP server. The POP protocol is then used to retrieve and delete messages. The Post Office Protocol is handy for any applications that need to download mail messages from a server. ∎

Learn the properties of the POP ActiveX control

Add mail management functionality to your programs using this control.

Learn the methods available to programmers using the POP ActiveX control

Implement functionality with the built-in methods supplied in this ActiveX control.

Learn the events triggered by the POP ActiveX control

Respond to the various events that are fired by the ActiveX POP control.

Build a simple Mail Reader application

Use ActiveX to send and retrieve mail messages from a POP server over the Internet in Visual Basic.

Properties

Table 17.1 details the properties available in the POP control. All the data elements required to retrieve e-mail messages from a POP server are included as properties in this control.

Table 17.1 Properties of the POP Client ActiveX Control	
Property	**Purpose**
Busy	True if a command is currently in progress.
DocOutput	Refers to the DocOuput object that must be set before invoking the GetDoc method, and conveys information about the progress of the data transfer.
EnableTimer	Determines the kind of timer that is fired by the TimeOut event.
Errors	Refers to a collection of errors detailing the last error.
MessageCount	Stores the number of messages currently available on the POP server.
NotificationMode	Determines how notification of outbound data will be provided.
Password	Sets the password to be used for logging on to a POP server.
ProtocolState	Indicates whether the POP client is not connected, waiting for authorization to connect, or connected to an POP server.
RemoteHost	The host name or IP address of the POP server to be connected to.
RemotePort	The port number used to connect to the POP server.
ReplyCode	The reply code sent by the server in response to requests from the client.
ReplyString	The reply string sent by the server in response to requests from the client.
State	Used to report the current state of the POP connection.
TimeOut	Tells how long to wait before firing the TimeOut event for the type of timer referred to by EnableTimer.
TopLines	Keeps the number of lines to be returned in response to a TOP command.
TopSupported	Set to true when the server supports the TOP command.
URL	The URL of the document to be retrieved.
UserID	Sets the user name to be used for logging on to a POP server.

ON THE WEB

ftp://ds.internic.net/rfc Explaining the details of the POP protocol is beyond the scope of this book. However, you can find RFC 1081, which defines the POP protocol, with the other RFCs at this FTP site.

Methods

The POP control offers a few methods for programmers. The three available methods are summarized in Table 17.2.

Table 17.2 Methods for the SMTP Client Control

Method	Use
Authenticate	Authenticates the user using the UserID and Password properties.
Cancel	Stops a pending request.
Connect	Issues a request to the POP server to open a connection. If a connection is established, the State property is set.
Delete	Deletes the specified message on the POP server.
GetDoc	Requests the retrieval of a document identified by a URL, and can be used in conjunction with the DocInput and DocOutput objects and events.
Last	Initiates a LAST request.
MessageSize	Requests the size of the next message. The MessageSize event is fired when the request is successful.
NOOP	Causes the POP server to reply with an OK in the ReplyString property.
Quit	Closes the connection and fires the Quit event.
Reset	Issues a RSET command. Any messages marked for deletion are unmarked.
RetrieveMessage	Downloads the passed message number. The message is streamed through a DocOutput object.
TopMessage	Sends a Top of Message request for the message number passed through a DocOutput object.

Part

II

Ch

17

You've encountered most of these methods in previous chapters. There are a few, however, that are specific to the POP control and deserve a bit more attention.

The *MessageSize* Method

Sometimes you may want to know the size of a mail message before retrieving a message from the POP server. Perhaps you are concerned that some hacker has sent you a 2 GB mail message (yuck!). You might also build a specialized application that waits for a message of a certain size and then replies with a special message. Using `MessageSize` in your applications is simple. Take a look at Listing 17.1.

Listing 17.1 Using the *MessageSize* Method

```
...
...
Dim SizeOfThisMsg As Integer

Dim MsgOfInterest As Integer

MsgOfInterest = 1

MyPOPControl.MessageSize  MsgOfInterest
```

The call to `MyPOPControl.MessageSize` with a parameter of `MsgOfInterest` causes the `MessageSize` event to be fired. The size of the indicated message will be passed to you. Now your application can respond based upon this value.

The *RetrieveMessage* Method

Certainly the most important method exposed by the POP control is `RetrieveMessage`. Not suprisingly, `RetrieveMessage` is used to obtain a mail message from the POP server. When the POP control receives the message from the server, you have two options for the output. You can access the POP control's built-in `DocOutput` object, or you can pass `RetrieveMessage` your own `DocOutput` object. In most cases (including this chapter's example), you'll simply use the `DocOutput` object in the POP control. Listing 17.2 shows the alternative method of passing your own `DocOutput` object.

Listing 17.2 Using the *RetrieveMessage* Method

```
Dim MyOwnDocOutput As DocOutput
Dim MsgOfInterest As Integer
...
...
POP.RetrieveMessage MsgOfInterest, MyOwnDocOutput
...
...
```

Events

The POP control provides numerous events that your application can handle. Table 17.3 summarizes the events that are thrown by the POP Client control.

Table 17.3   Summary of Events in the POP Client Control

Event	Description
Authenticate	Triggered after the Authentication method is invoked.
Busy	This event is triggered when commands are in progress.
Cancel	This event is triggered when the Cancel method is executed.
DocOutput	This is fired when data arrives at the control.
Error	Occurs when an error has been encountered.
Last	This event is triggered when the Last method is called, and passes the last message accessed by the client.
MessageSize	Occurs in response to a call to the MessageSize method. The size of the message is passed.
ProtocolStateChange	When the state of the protocol changes, this event is fired.
Quit	Occurs after a call to the Quit method.
Reset	When a Reset call is successful, this event is triggered.
StateChanged	When the State of the POP control changes, this event is thrown.
TimeOut	Occurs when a given event fails to occur within the time period specified in the Timeout property.

Part

II

Ch

17

The Mail Reader Application

To try out the POP control in this step-by-step example, you'll construct a simple mail reader program that allows you to download a message from a POP server. The Mail application you build will provide the following functionality:

- Select a POP server
- Enter a user name and password
- Connect to the POP server
- Collect messages from the server and view them

To get an idea of how this application works, you may want to run it before continuing. Of course, you'll need to have an SMTP server available in order to actually use the application.

TIP Working with this Mail Reader application will be much easier if you have a POP server running locally on your computer. Since you probably don't have a POP server application already, you should look for one on the Internet. One good place to look is **http://www.winsite.com**.

The following example takes you through the process of building the Mail Reader application in a step-by-step manner.

Building the Mail Reader Application

As you'll see in this example, integrating POP client functionality into your own applications using the ActiveX Internet Control Pack is relatively easy. In the Mail Reader application, you'll need the following major components:

- frmReader—The main form for the application.
- cmdConnect—Connects to a POP server.
- cmdNextMessage—Retrieves the next mail message from the POP server.
- SSTab1—A tab control to keep the interface simple.
- txtPOPServer—The server that stores mail messages.
- txtUserName—The user name for logging on to the POP server.
- txtPassword—The password for logging on to the POP server.
- txtToAddress—A text box for showing the e-mail address of the recipient.
- txtFromAddress—A text box for showing the e-mail address of the sender.
- txtCCAddress—A text box for showing the e-mail address of a courtesy recipient.
- txtSubject—A text box for displaying the subject heading for the message.
- txtMessageBody—A multiline text box for displaying the mail message.
- txtMsgRemaining—A text box for showing the number of messages remaining to be read.
- POP1—Manages the POP session and retrieves the mail messages.

To build the Mail Reader application, complete the following steps:

1. Start Visual Basic 4.0.
2. Create the form called frmReader. You'll need to change the Caption property to Mail Reader, and the Name property to frmReader. You may also want to set the form so that it cannot be resized at runtime.
3. Resize frmReader as appropriate. You may also want to set the form so that it cannot be resized at runtime.
4. Select the command button control and add the cmdNextMessage. Set the Caption property to an appropriate label like Next Message. Also, change the Name property to cmdNextMessage.

5. Next, add the cmdConnect. Set the Caption property to an appropriate label like Connect. You'll also need to change the Name property to cmdConnect.

6. Select the SSTab control, and draw in a Tab control. You'll only need two tabs. Set the Caption of one to Configuration, and the Caption of the other to Read Mail.

7. On the Configuration tab, select the text box control, and add the following text controls: txtPOPServer, txtUserName, and txtPassword. Include a label for each of the text controls as appropriate.

8. Select the Read Mail tab and add the following text controls: txtFromAddress, txtToAddress, txtCCAddress, txtSubject, txtMessageBody, and txtMsgRemaining. Remember to include a label for each of the text controls.

9. Add the Status bar to the bottom of the form. Set the Name property to Status. Make three panels on your Status bar.

10. Next, add a simple menu with File and Exit as options. Name them mnuFile and mnuFileExit, respectively.

11. Save the project to a convenient working directory.

12. Now, add the POP control to the control toolbar. Select Tools, Custom Controls, and then select Microsoft POP Client Control and click OK. This adds the POP Control to your toolbar for this project. You'll also need to add a reference to the support object library. Select Tools, References, and check Microsoft Internet Support Objects, and click OK.

13. Drag and drop the POP control onto frmReader. When you're finished, the form should look something like figure 17.1.

FIG. 17.1
Review the frmReader form.

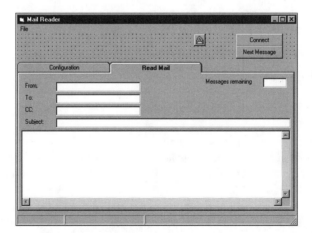

14. Next, select the POP control, and change the Name property to POP1.

15. Now it's time to start coding the application. Start by adding a global variable to store the current message number. Your code should look a bit like Listing 17.3.

Listing 17.3   *MAILREADER.VBP*   Global Variables

```
Dim gCurrentMsgNum As Integer
```

16. Remember to set gCurrentMsgNum equal to 0 during the frmReader's Load event (see Listing 17.4).

Listing 17.4   *2MAILREADER.VBP*   Form *Load* Event for *frmReader*

```
Private Sub Form_Load()

    gCurrentMsgNum = 0

End Sub
```

17. The first step in executing a POP session is connecting to the server. To connect to the server, use the Connect method. In the Mail Reader example, the cmdConnect button is used to trigger this action. The code is in Listing 17.5.

Listing 17.5   *3MAILREADER.VBP*   *cmdConnect Click* Event Response Function

```
Private Sub cmdConnect_Click()

    POP1.RemoteHost = txtPopServer.Text

    POP1.UserId = txtUserName.Text
]
    POP1.Password = txtPassword.Text

    POP1.Connect

End Sub
```

18. Next, code the cmdNextMessage response function. When the user presses the cmdNextMessage button, the application requests the next mail message from the POP server. To generate this request, call the RetrieveMessage method. Your code should resemble Listing 17.6.

Listing 17.6   *4MAILREADER.VBP*   Error Response Function

```
Private Sub cmdNextMessage_Click()

    gCurrentMsgNum = gCurrentMsgNum + 1

    POP1.RetrieveMessage gCurrentMsgNum
```

```
If txtMsgRemaining > 0 Then

    txtMsgRemaining = txtMsgRemaining - 1

End If

If txtMsgRemaining = 0 Then

    cmdNextMessage.Enabled = False

End If

End Sub
```

First, you'll increment the gCurrentMsgNum global variable. The call to RetrieveMessage requires the message number (gCurrentMsgNum) to return a mail message. Next, you'll decrement the txtMsgRemaining text box. Of course, you'll need to make sure that the decrement won't make txtMsgRemainer a negative number. When txtMsgRemaining reaches zero, go ahead and disable the cmdNextMessage control.

19. The mnuFileExit click function is a trivial End statement (see Listing 17.7).

Listing 17.7 *5MAILREADER.VBP* *mnuFileExit* Click Response Function

```
Private Sub mnuFileExit_Click()

    End

End Sub
```

20. Now, let's turn to the POP control. The first event you'll work on is the Authenticate event. Authenticate fires after a call to the Authenticate method successfully logs on to the POP server (see Listing 17.8).

Listing 17.8 *6MAILREADER.VBP* *Authenticate* Event Response Function

```
Private Sub POP1_Authenticate()

    txtMsgRemaining = POP1.MessageCount

    If POP1.MessageCount > 0 Then

        cmdNextMessage.Enabled = True

    End If

    cmdConnect.Enabled = False

End Sub
```

Part
II

Ch
17

Once connected, you'll use the MessageCount to set txtMsgRemaining. As long as there is at least one mail message, the cmdNextMessage command button is enabled. Since you're now connected, the cmdConnect button should be disabled.

21. The DocOutput event is thrown when a mail message is received from the POP server. In this event, you'll manage the process of filling out the frmReader form (see Listing 17.9).

On the CD

Listing 17.9   *7MAILREADER.VBP*   Filling out the *frmReader* Form

```vb
Private Sub POP1_DocOutput(ByVal DocOutput As DocOutput)

    Dim Msg As Variant
    Dim MsgHdr As DocHeader

    Select Case DocOutput.State

        Case icDocBegin
            Status.Panels(2).Text = "Starting message download."
            txtMessageBody.Text = ""
            txtFromAddress.Text = ""
            txtMessageBody.Text = ""
            txtToAddress.Text = ""
            txtCCAddress.Text = ""
            txtSubject.Text = ""

        Case icDocHeaders
            For Each MsgHdr In DocOutput.Headers

                Status.Panels(2).Text = "Getting " & MsgHdr.Name & " header..."

                Select Case LCase(MsgHdr.Name)
            Case "from"
                txtFromAddress.Text = MsgHdr.Value
            Case "to"
                txtToAddress.Text = MsgHdr.Value
            Case "cc"
                txtCCAddress.Text = MsgHdr.Value
            Case "subject"
                txtSubject.Text = MsgHdr.Value
            Case Else
                txtMessageBody.Text = txtMessageBody.Text & MsgHdr.Name & ":" _
                                    & MsgHdr.Value & vbCrLf
            End Select
        Next

        Case icDocData
            DocOutput.GetData Msg
            Status.Panels(2).Text = "Getting message body..."
            txtMessageBody.Text = txtMessageBody.Text & Msg

        Case icDocEnd
            Status.Panels(2).Text = "Message downloaded."
```

```
    Case icDocError
        Status.Panels(2).Text = "Download Error."

    Case icDocNone

End Select

End Sub
```

Like DocInput, the DocOutput object has a State property that provides information about the status of the POP session in progress. When the document transfer begins, the DocOutput object enters the icDocBegin state. When the State property is icDocHeaders, the message headers are received from the POP server. If the current MsgHeader.Name is one of the text box fields (for example, txtFromAddress, txtToAddress, txtCCAddress, txtSubject, txtMessageBody), that text body is updated. The message body itself is then retrieved when DocOutput.State is equal to icDocData. If the message is large, the icDocData code may be executed a number of times, so Msg is appended to the existing value txtMessageBody. If an error occurs, the DocOutput.State is set to icDocError. Finally, whether the message send is successful or not, the DocOutput.State is set to icDocEnd. As this process occurs, Status.Panel(2) is updated with a progress message.

22. Finally, you'll code the ProtocolStateChanged response function. When the connection reaches the prcAuthorization state, invoke the Authenticate method (see Listing 17.10).

Listing 17.10 *8MAILREADER.VBP* *ProtocolStateChanged* Event Response Function

```
Private Sub POP1_ProtocolStateChanged(ByVal ProtocolState As Integer)

    If ProtocolState = prcAuthorization Then

        POP1.Authenticate

    End If

    Status.Panels(1).Text = POP1.ProtocolStateString

End Sub
```

Testing the Application

You're ready to test the Mail Reader application. Of course, you'll need access to a POP server in order to run this test. As suggested earlier, you may want to run a POP server on the same computer as the Mail Reader application to simplify testing. To test the application, follow these steps:

1. Start the Mail Reader application. If you named the application as described in the example, the easiest way to do this is to press the Start button and the choose Run from the menu. Type **MailReader.exe** (with the appropriate path) and the server will start up. The application should look like figure 17.2.

FIG. 17.2
The Mail Reader application starts as shown.

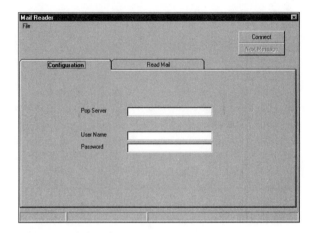

2. Next, enter the address or domain name of a nearby POP server that you have an account on. If you're running a POP server on your local machine, your screen would look something like figure 17.3.

FIG. 17.3
How to log on to the POP server.

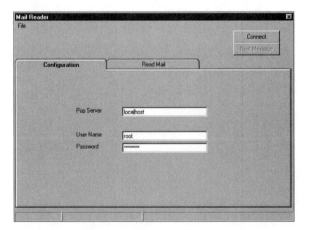

Of course, if you're connected to a network, you can use the domain name of any handy POP server.

3. Select the Read Mail tab and press the cmdConnect button. If your user name and password are correct, and the login occurs, the txtMsgRemaining field is updated with the number of messages. Your screen looks something like figure 17.4.

FIG. 17.4

The interface state after connecting to the POP server.

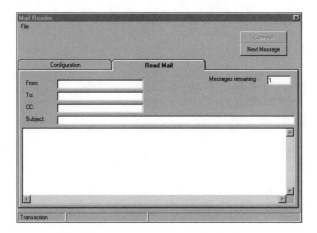

4. Now press the cmdNextMessage button. When the message downloads, the fields on-screen are filled out, and the txtMsgRemaining field is one lower. Your screen should look like figure 17.5.

FIG. 17.5

How the interface looks after downloading a message.

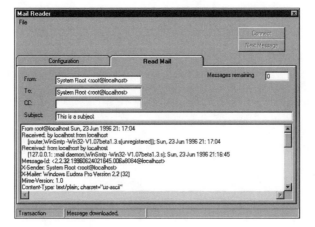

CHAPTER 18

Using the NNTP Control in VB Applications

The Network News Transmission Protocol (NNTP) is used to read from and post to the UseNet news network. You'll find many uses for newsgroups and news article retrieval in your own applications. For instance, say your workgroup needs to check a certain newsgroup each day for articles related to your company. Using the NNTP control, you can easily implement your own program to download the articles automatically. You could even combine the NNTP control with the SMTP and have your application mail the articles directly to your e-mail account. ■

Learn the properties of the NNTP ActiveX control

Add newsreader functionality to your programs using this control.

Learn the methods available to programmers using the NNTP ActiveX control

Implement functionality with the built-in methods supplied in this ActiveX control.

Learn the events triggered by the NNTP ActiveX control

Respond to the various events that are fired by the ActiveX NNTP control.

Build a simple newsreader application to retrieve news articles from a newsserver over the Internet in Visual Basic

Use ActiveX to retrieve news articles from UseNet newsservers over the Internet in Visual Basic employing the NNTP control.

Properties

Table 18.1 details the properties available in the NNTP control. All the data elements required to retrieve and post news articles to an NNTP server are included as properties in this control.

Table 18.1 Properties of the NNTP Client ActiveX Control

Property	Purpose
ArticleNumbersSupported	If this property is true, the GetArticleNumbers method properly returns a list of article numbers.
Busy	True if a command is currently in progress.
DocInput	Refers to the DocInput object that must be set before invoking the SendDoc method, and conveys information about the progress of the data transfer.
DocOutput	Refers to the DocOuput object that must be set before invoking the GetDoc method, and conveys information about the progress of the data transfer.
EnableTimer	Tells the kind of timer that is fired by the TimeOut event.
Errors	Refers to a collection of errors detailing the last error.
LastUpdate	The date used by newgroups and newnews to decide what is new.
NotificationMode	Determines how notification of outbound data is provided.
OverviewSupported	True if the GetOverviewFormat and GetOverview methods return headers stored in the server's overview database.
PostingAllowed	When the server permits posting of messages, this property is set to true.
ProtocolState	Indicates whether the POP client is not connected, waiting for authorization to connect, or connected to an NNTP newsserver.
RemoteHost	The host name or IP address of the NNTP server to be connected to.
RemotePort	The port number used to connect to the NNTP server.
ReplyCode	The reply code sent by the server in response to requests from the client.
ReplyString	The reply string sent by the server in response to requests from the client.

Property	Purpose
State	Used to report the current state of the NNTP connection.
TimeOut	Tells how long to wait before firing the TimeOut event for the type of timer referred to by EnableTimer.
URL	The URL of the document being retrieved.

Although explaining the details of the NNTP protocol is beyond the scope of this book, you should take note of the LastUpdate property explained below. In addition, you can find RFC 977, which defines the NNTP protocol with the other RFCs at **http://ds.internic.net/ds/rfc-index.html**.

The *LastUpdate* Property

NNTP provides a mechanism for deciding which articles and groups are to be transmitted (for example, which things are new). A call to the ListNewGroups method uses this property as the date the group list was last updated. For example, the LastUpdate property is equal to 7/3/96 and on 7/4/96 a new group **comp.new.group** is added. A call to ListNewgroups made on 7/5/96 in your application can obtain the **comp.new.group** during the DocOutput event.

Methods

The NNTP control offers a number of methods for programmers. These methods are summarized in Table 18.2.

Table 18.2   Methods for the NNTP Client Control

Method	Use
Cancel	Stops a pending request.
Connect	Issues a request to the POP server to open a connection. If a connection is established, the State property is set.
GetAdministrationFile	Sends the NNTP XMOTD command and retrieves the server's administrator data.
GetArticleByArticleNumber	Requests an article from the newsserver using the article number. Successful requests fire the DocOutput event.
GetArticleByMessageID	Requests an article from the newsserver using the message ID. The DocOutput event is triggered on success.

continues

Table 18.2 Continued

Method	Use
GetArticleHeaders	Obtains specific headers from a list of articles.
GetArticleNumbers	Gets a list of article numbers from the newsserver. Triggers the DocOutput event on success.
GetBodyByArticleNumber	Obtains the body of an article based on the article number. Fires the DocOutput event on success.
GetBodyByMessageID	Obtains the body of an article based on the message ID. Causes the DocOutput event to occur on success.
GetDoc	Requests the retrieval of a document identified by a URL and can be used in conjunction with the DocInput and DocOutput objects and events.
GetHeaderByArticleNumber	Obtains the header of an article based on the article number. Fires the DocOutput event on success.
GetHeaderByMessageID	Obtains the header of an article based on the message ID. Causes the DocOutput event to occur on success.
GetOverView	Returns information from the overview database for the specified article.
GetOverViewFormat	Retrieves a list of headers in the order they appear in the overview database.
GetStatByArticleNumber	Requests the stat of an article.
ListGroupDescriptions	Requests a list of group descriptions and triggers the DocOutput event.
ListGroups	Requests a list of groups and fires the DocOutput event.
ListNewGroups	Requests a list of new groups from the NNTP server. The DocOutput event occurs on success.
Quit	Closes the connection and fires the Quit event.
SelectGroup	Requests a list of articles from the newsserver. Triggers the DocOutput event on success.
SendDoc	Requests the transmission of a document identified by a URL to the server. Used in conjunction with the DocInput event.
SetLastArticle	Selects a newsgroup's last article.
SetNextArticle	Selects a newsgroup's next article.

The NNTP control is rich with methods to make the interface with the newsserver simple and flexible. To fully exploit the power of the NNTP control, you'll need to learn a bit about some of these functions shown in Table 18.2.

Referencing the Current Article Pointer

The newsserver keeps a current article pointer that refers to the article that is acted on by the server unless an article number is passed. There are several functions that rely on this current article pointer including:

- SetLastArticle
- SetNextArticle
- The GetArticle methods

SetLastArticle moves the article pointer to the last article in a news group. The SetNextArticle advances the article pointer to the next article in the newsgroup. All of the GetArticle functions act on the current article unless an appropriate reference is passed. For instance, take a look at Listing 18.1.

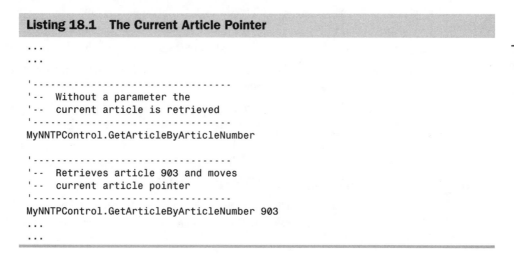

Listing 18.1 The Current Article Pointer

```
...
...

'---------------------------------
'--  Without a parameter the
'--  current article is retrieved
'---------------------------------
MyNNTPControl.GetArticleByArticleNumber


'---------------------------------
'--  Retrieves article 903 and moves
'--  current article pointer
'---------------------------------
MyNNTPControl.GetArticleByArticleNumber 903
...
...
```

Imagine that the article pointer was referencing article 847. The first call would return article 847, while the second call returns article 903 and advances the current article pointer.

Responding to the NNTP Control's Events

The NNTP Control provides numerous events that your application can handle. Table 18.3 summarizes the events that are thrown by the NNTP Client control.

Part
II

Ch
18

Table 18.3   Summary of Events in the POP Client Control

Event	Description
AuthenticateRequest	Triggered when the news server requests authentication.
AuthenticateResponse	Occurs after an authentication response is received from the newsserver.
Banner	Fires when the server's welcome banner is received.
Busy	Triggered when commands are in progress.
Cancel	Triggered when the Cancel method is executed.
DocInput	Fired when data is sent from the control.
DocOutput	Fired when data arrives at the control.
LastArticle	Occurs when the last article in a list is reached.
NextArticle	Triggered by selecting the next article in the list.
ProtocolStateChange	When the state of the protocol changes, this event is fired.
SelectGroup	Occurs when the SelectGroup method is successful.
StateChanged	When the State of the NNTP control changes, this event is thrown.
TimeOut	Occurs when a given event fails to occur within the time period specified in the Timeout property.

Trying the NewsReader Application

To try out the NNTP control, you'll construct a simple newsreader program that allows you to download a message from a newsserver. The NewsReader application you build will provide the following functionality:

- Select a newsserver
- Connect to the newsserver
- Obtain a list of newsgroups from the newsserver
- Select a newsgroup for obtaining an article list
- Read articles from the newsserver
- Post articles to the newsserver

To get an idea of how this application works, you may want to run it before continuing. Of course, you'll need to have a newsserver available in order to actually use the application.

T I P There are many public access newsservers available on the Internet. You can find them by using one of the many search engines on the World Wide Web. Try **www.yahoo.com**, for instance.

The following example takes you through the process of building the NewsReader application in a step-by-step manner.

Building the NewsReader Application

As you'll see in this example, integrating NNTP client functionality into your own applications using the ActiveX Internet Control Pack is straightforward. In this application, you'll need the following major components:

- frmNewsReader–he main form for the application.
- cmdConnect–onnects to a newsserver.
- cmdListNewsgroups—Lists the newsgroups available on the server.
- cmdSelectNewsgroup—Displays the articles for a given newsgroup.
- cmdGetArticle—Returns the body of an article from the newsserver.
- cmdPostArticle—Sends an article to the newsserver.
- SSTab1—A tab control to keep the interface simple.
- txtNewsServer—The server that stores mail messages.
- txtNewsGroup—The newsgroup selected.
- txtArticleNumber—The article number selected.
- txtArticle—A rich text box to display the body of the article.
- txtName—The name of the person posting the article.
- txtEmailAddress—A text box for showing the e-mail address of the person posting the article.
- txtPostToNewsgroup—The newsgroup to which the entered article is posted.
- txtSubject—A text box for displaying the subject heading for the article.
- txtMessageToPost—A multiline text box for entering the article text.
- NNTP—Manages the NNTP session, retrieves, and posts news articles.

To build the NewsReader application, you'll complete the following steps:

1. Start Visual Basic 4.0.
2. Create the form called frmNewsReader. You'll need to change the Caption property to newsreader, and the Name property to frmNewsReader.
3. Resize frmNewsReader as appropriate. You may also want to set the form so that it cannot be resized at runtime.
4. Select the SSTab control, and draw in a tab control. You'll need three tabs as follows: a Connect tab, a Read News tab, and a Post tab. Identify each of these tabs by changing the Caption property to the appropriate text.

Part
II

Ch
18

5. Select the Command Button control from the toolbar. On the Connect tab, add the cmdConnect and cmdDisconnect buttons to the form. Set the Caption properties to appropriate labels like Connect and Disconnect. You'll also need to change the Name properties to cmdConnect and cmdDisconnect.

6. Go ahead and draw in the txtNewsServer control as well. Set the Name property to txtNewsServer. Add an appropriate label.

7. Move on to the Read News tab. Add the cmdListNewsgroups, cmdSelectNewsgroup, and cmdGetArticle buttons to the form. Set the Caption properties of each control to an appropriate label. You'll also need to change the Name property to cmdListNewsgroups, cmdSelectNewsgroup, and cmdGetArticle, respectively.

8. Next add the txtNewsGroup, txtArticleNumber, and txtArticle text controls. Remember to make the txtArticle a rich text box control. (The List Groups command can return a large result set.)

9. Now select the Post tab and add the following text controls: txtName, txtEmailAddress, txtPostToNewsgroup, txtSubject, and txtMessageToPost. Include a label for each of the text controls as appropriate.

10. There's only one button on the Post tab, the cmdPostArticle button. Change its Name and Caption properties to Post Article and cmdPostArticle, respectively.

11. Add the Status bar to the bottom of the form. Set the Name property to Status. You'll need to make two panels on your Status bar.

12. Next, add a simple menu with File and Exit as options. Name them mnuFile and mnuFileExit, respectively.

13. Save the project to a convenient working directory.

14. Now add the NNTP control to the control toolbar. Select Tools, Custom Controls and choose Microsoft NNTP Client Control and click OK. This adds the NNTP Control to your tool bar for this project. You'll also need to add a reference to the support object library. Select Tools, References and choose Microsoft Internet Support Objects and click OK.

15. Drag and drop the NNTP control onto frmNewsReader. When you're finished, the form should look something like figures 18.1, 18.2, and 18.3.

16. Next, select the NNTP control and change the Name property to NNTP.

17. The first step in executing an NNTP session is connecting to the server. To connect to the server, you'll use the connect method. In this example, the cmdConnect button is used to trigger this action. The code is in Listing 18.2.

On the CD

Listing 18.2 *NEWSREADER.VBP* **cmdConnect_Click Event Response Function**

```
Private Sub cmdConnect_Click()
    NNTP.Connect txtNewsServer.Text
End Sub
```

FIG. 18.1
Check your
frmNewsReader
Connect tab.

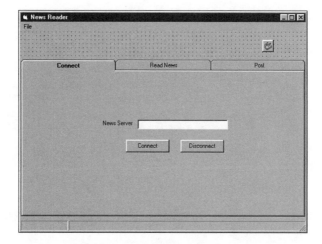

FIG. 18.2
Check your
frmNewsReader
Read News tab.

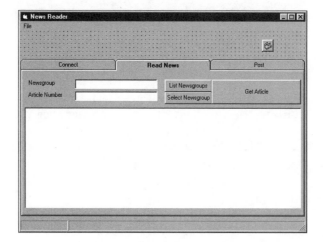

Part
II

Ch
18

18. Next, code the cmdDisconnect response function. When the user presses the
cmdDisconnect button, the application will shut down an open NNTP session. Your code
should resemble Listing 18.3.

On the CD

Listing 18.3 2NEWSREADER.VBP cmdDisconnect_Click Response Function

```
Private Sub cmdDisconnect_Click()
    NNTP.Quit
End Sub
```

19. The mnuFileExit click function is a trivial End statement (see Listing 18.4).

FIG. 18.3

Check your
frmNewsReader
Post tab.

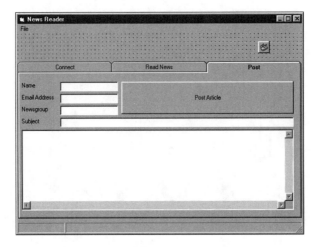

On the CD

Listing 18.4   *3NEWSREADER.VBP   mnuFileExit_Click* **Response Function**

```
Private Sub mnuFileExit_Click()
     End
End Sub
```

20. Now, let's turn to the Read News tab. Three command buttons must be coded. Work on the cmdListNewsgroups function first. Listing 18.5 shows how your code should look.

On the CD

Listing 18.5   *4NEWSREADER.VBP   cmdListNewsgroups_Click* **Response Function**

```
Private Sub cmdListNewsgroups_Click()
    NNTP.ListGroups
    Status.Panels(2).Text = "Requesting list of newsgroups..."
End Sub
```

You'll use the ListGroups method to request that the newsserver return a list of available newsgroups. Use Status.Panel(2) to update the user.

21. The cmdSelectNewsgroup button triggers a request to the server to select a newsgroup. You'll use the txtNewsGroup control to select the newsgroup as shown in Listing 18.6.

On the CD

Listing 18.6   *5NEWSREADER.VBP   cmdSelectNewsgroup_Click* **Response Function**

```
Private Sub cmdSelectNewsgroup_Click()
    NNTP.SelectGroup txtNewsGroup.Text
End Sub
```

The cmdSelectNewsgroup functions trigger the SelectGroup event. The newsserver keeps track of the article and newsgroup currently selected. When you retrieve an article, this server-based article and group pointer is advanced. The SelectGroup method causes this pointer to be moved.

22. The cmdGetArticle button triggers a request to the server to retrieve an article from the newsserver. You'll use the txtArticleNumber control to select the desired article. Your code should look like Listing 18.7.

On the CD

Listing 18.7 6NEWSREADER.VBP *cmdGetArticle_Click* Response Function

```
Private Sub cmdGetArticle_Click()
    NNTP.GetArticleByArticleNumber txtArticleNumber.Text
End Sub
```

Both the cmdListNewsgroups and the cmdGetArticle functions trigger the DocOutput event to obtain and display the results of these requests.

23. Next, work on the NNTP control. There are a number of events to which the newsreader application responds. There are a couple of simple ones, so get them out of the way first. When the StatusChanged event is thrown, you'll update the user with the current connection status. Your code looks like Listing 18.8.

On the CD

Listing 18.8 7NEWSREADER.VBP *StateChanged* Event Response Function

```
Private Sub NNTP_StateChanged(ByVal State As Integer)
    Status.Panels(1).Text = NNTP.StateString
End Sub
```

24. After a successful execution of the SelectGroup method, the SelectGroup event is triggered. Once the group has been selected, you can call GetArticleHeaders to build a list of subjects to show the user the articles currently available. Your code will look like Listing 18.9.

On the CD

Listing 18.9 8NEWSREADER.VBP *SelectGroup* Event Response Function

```
Private Sub NNTP_SelectGroup(ByVal groupName As String, ByVal firstMessage As
Long, ByVal lastMessage As Long, ByVal msgCount As Long)

    NNTP.GetArticleHeaders "Subject", Trim$(Str$(firstMessage)),
Trim$(Str$(lastMessage))
    Status.Panels(2).Text = "Downloading subjects for " & msgCount & " mes
    sages..."

End Sub
```

The first parameter to GetArticleHeaders indicates which header you want to retrieve. The second two parameters to the GetArticleHeaders call determine the range of articles for which headers are requested. So, in this case, the application asks for the subject header for every article available in the newsgroup. You'll also update the Status bar to notify the user as to the number of messages being downloaded.

25. The DocOutput event is thrown when a response from the newsserver is received. The newsreader does not require that you pay attention to the kind of output you're receiving. Some special processing is required when article headers are received (see Listing 18.10).

On the CD

Listing 18.10   *9NEWSREADER.VBP*   *DocOutput* Event Response Function

```
Private Sub NNTP_DocOutput(ByVal DocOutput As DocOutput)

    Dim ArticleBody As String
    Dim ArticleHeader As Object

    Select Case DocOutput.State

        Case icDocBegin
            txtArticle.Text = ""

        Case icDocHeaders
            For Each ArticleHeader In DocOutput.Headers

                Select Case LCase(ArticleHeader.Name)

                    Case "subject"
                        txtSubject.Text = ArticleHeader.Value

                    Case "from"
                        txtName.Text = ArticleHeader.Value
                        txtEmailAddress.Text = ArticleHeader.Value

                    Case "newsgroups"
                        txtNewsGroup.Text = ArticleHeader.Value
                        txtPostToNewsgroup.Text = ArticleHeader.Value

                End Select

            Next

        Case icDocData
            DocOutput.GetData ArticleBody
            txtArticle.Text = txtArticle.Text & ArticleBody

        Case icDocEnd
            Status.Panels(2).Text = "Process complete."

        Case icDocError
            Status.Panels(2).Text = "Error occurred."
    End Select

End Sub
```

Recall that the DocOutput object has a State property that provides information about the status of the NNTP session in progress. When the document transfer begins, the DocOutput object enters the icDocBegin state. When State is icDocHeaders, the article headers are received from the NNTP server. If the current ArticleHeader.Name is one of the text box fields (for example, txtSubject, txtName, txtNewsGroup), the text is updated. The article body itself is then retrieved when the DocOutput.State is equal to icDocData. If the message is large, the icDocData code may be executed a number of times so ArticleBody is appended to the existing value, txtArticle. If an error occurs, the DocOutput.State is set to icDocError. Finally, whether the message send is successful or not, the DocOutput.State is set to icDocEnd.

26. Because you'll be finishing up the Post part of the application, go ahead and get the DocInput event response function done now. No sophisticated header processing is required in this function, just some status update for the user (see Listing 18.11).

On the CD

Listing 18.11   *10NEWSREADER.VBP*   DocInput Event Response Function

```
Private Sub NNTP_DocInput(ByVal DocInput As DocInput)
    Select Case DocInput.State
        Case icDocEnd
            Status.Panels(2).Text = "Process complete."

        Case icDocError
            Status.Panels(2).Text = "Error occurred."
    End Select
End Sub
```

Part

II

Ch

18

27. Next, switch to the Post tab's cmdPostArticle command button. You'll construct appropriate headers for the article, and then use the SendDoc method to transmit the article to the newsserver (see Listing 18.12).

Listing 18.12   *11NEWSREADER.VBP*   cmdPostArticle_Click Event Response Function

```
Private Sub cmdPostArticle_Click()

    Dim ArticleHeader As DocHeaders
    Dim ArticleBody As String
    Dim TheDate As String
    Dim TheTime As String

    Set ArticleHeader = NNTP.DocInput.Headers
    ArticleHeader.Clear
    ArticleHeader.Add "From", txtName.Text & " <" & txtEmailAddress.Text & ">"

    TheDate = Format(Date, "ddd, dd mmm yyyy ")
    TheTime = Format(Time, "hh:mm:ss") & " CST"
```

continues

Listing 18.12   Continued

```
ArticleHeader.Add "Date", TheDate & TheTime
ArticleHeader.Add "Newsgroups", txtNewsGroup.Text
ArticleHeader.Add "Subject", txtSubject.Text

TheDate = Format(Date, "mmddyyyy")
TheTime = Format(Time, "hhmmss")

ArticleHeader.Add "Message-ID", "<" & TheDate & TheTime &
txtEmailAddress.Text & ">" ArticleHeader.Add "Path", NNTP.RemoteHost

ArticleBody = vbCrLf & txtMessageToPost.Text & vbCrLf
Status.Panels(2).Text = "Posting article..."
NNTP.SendDoc , ArticleHeader, ArticleBody
```

End Sub

Most newsservers require a minimum set of headers in order to allow an article to be posted. This minimum set includes: a date, newsgroup, subject, path, and message-id header. The form of these headers is specified in RFC 1036. While explaining this RFC in detail is beyond the scope of this book, the formatting code above properly formats the minimum header set.

Testing the Application

Finally, you're ready to test the NewsReader application. Of course, you'll need access to a newsserver in order to run this test. To test the application, follow these steps:

1. Start the NewsReader application. If you named the applications as described in the previous example, the easiest way to start the NewsReader application is to press the Start button, and then choose Run from the menu. Type **NewsReader.exe** (with the appropriate path), and the server starts up. The application should look like figure 18.4.

FIG. 18.4

Starting the NewsReader application.

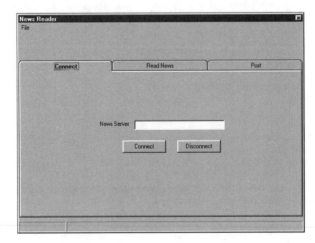

2. Next, enter the address or domain name of a nearby newsserver and press the cmdConnect button. Your screen sould look something like figure 18.5.

FIG. 18.5

Logging on to the newsserver.

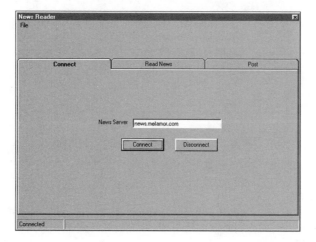

3. Select the Read News tab, and press the cmdListNewsgroups button. A list of available newsgroups is displayed (see fig. 18.6).

FIG. 18.6

Use the NewsReader application to list newsgroups.

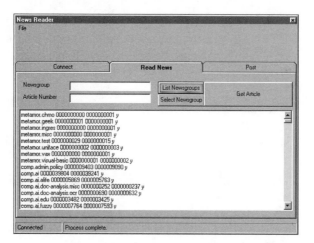

Part

II

Ch

18

4. Now, enter a newsgroup name like **comp.admin.policy,** and press the cmdSelectNewsgroup button. Your screen should display a list of articles in the selected newsgroup (see fig. 18.7).

FIG. 18.7

Selecting a newsgroup.

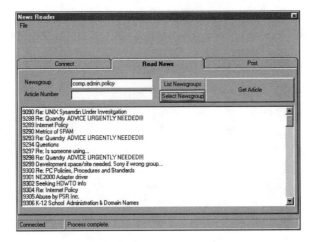

5. Enter an article number and press the `cmdGetArticle` button. Your screen should display the selected article (see fig. 18.8).

FIG. 18.8

How to read an article with the NewsReader application.

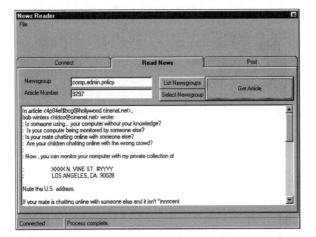

6. Select the Post tab and enter your name, e-mail address, newsgroup, subject, and article text appropriate for the newsgroup. Press the `cmdPostArticle` button; your screen should look like figure 18.9.

FIG. 18.9

You can post an article using the NewsReader application.

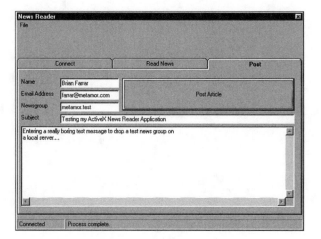

The ActiveX Server Framework

CHAPTER 19

ActiveX Security Issues

Perhaps one of the most pernicious issues affecting the growth and development of Internet-based applications is security. The dynamic document revolution that ActiveX is a part of brings with it the downloadable, executable objects. Unlike when you go to your local software store and buy a shrink-wrapped software package, you can't be sure of the intentions of the software provider on the Internet. One of the greatest things about the Internet is that even the little guy can distribute software to the masses. However, it's harder to know all the little guys well enough to trust the software that their Web sites ask you to download.

The ActiveX framework addresses this more risky environment with an API, tools, and processes that give clients (Web browsers, for instance) the ability to permit downloads from trusted software providers and deny download to untrusted or unknown sources. ∎

ActiveX security architecture

Learn the security architecture for downloading ActiveX controls over the Internet.

Internet component download

Explore an approach for downloading and verifying executable objects over the Internet.

Windows trust verification services

Overview the `WinVerifyTrust()` API which provides a framework for certifying downloaded code.

Use `DIAGNTZ` to make cabinet files

Executable content can be packaged together for download using cabinet files.

Internet Component Download

Web browsers, such as Microsoft Internet Explorer 3.0 and other similar client applications, rely heavily on the Internet Component Download process (see fig. 19.1). The `WinVerifyTrust` API provides the low-level support for these services.

FIG. 19.1
Examine the architec-
ture of ActiveX security.

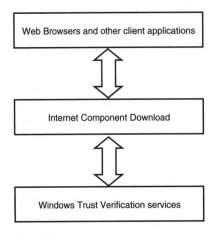

The Internet Component Download specification provides for a safe mechanism to download executable content such as ActiveX Controls into Web browsers. Microsoft defines the Internet Component Download as a process consisting of the following steps:

- Download the necessary files
- Call `WinVerifyTrust` API before permitting installation
- Self-register OLE components
- Add entries to the system registry to keep track of downloaded code
- Call `CoGetClassObject` for the appropriate `CLSID`

Let's take a few moments with each of these steps and look at a few details.

Packing Files For Download

In the typical Web browser download scenario, the `<OBJECT>` tag triggers a request for a downloadable component. The `<OBJECT>` tag includes a `CODE` attribute that indicates the location of the component to be downloaded. The Internet Component Download anticipates three different types of downloadable files as shown in Table 19.1.

Table 19.1 Types of Files to Download

File Type	Description
Portable executable	A single file OLE control
Cabinet file	A multiple file OLE control package with set-up instructions
`.INF` file	A text file describing download and installation instructions

Working with Portable Executable Files The *portable executable*, or *PE*, is a stand-alone `.OCX` or `.DLL` file. Of course, because the file is itself executable, no additional file compression can be used. You'll use this method for compact, simple ActiveX Controls.

Note that the Internet Component Download process can rely on the MIME type to determine the appropriate treatment of the PE file. Table 19.2 summarizes the appropriate MIME types.

Table 19.2 MIME Types for PE Files

MIME Type	Description
`application/x-pe_win32_x86`	A portable executable built for Windows NT or Windows 95 on the Intel x86 platform
`application/x-pe_win32_ppc`	A portable executable built for Windows NT or Windows 95 on the PowerPC platform
`application/x-pe_win32_mips`	A portable executable built for Windows NT or Windows 95 on the MIPS platform
`application/x-pe_win32_alpha`	A portable executable built for Windows NT or Windows 95 on the DEC Alpha platform
`application/x-pe_mac_ppc`	A portable executable built for Macintosh on the PowerPC platform

Part
III

Ch
19

Working with Cabinet Files Some ActiveX control applications will require more than one file. Installation instructions may be somewhat involved. For situations like this, the Internet Component Download process provides for the so-called "cabinet file" (`.CAB`). Cabinet files must include an `.INF` information file that describes the installation procedure. Best of all, the cabinet file permits file compression reducing bandwidth requirements during download.

Note that the Internet Component Download process can rely on the MIME type to determine the appropriate treatment of the cabinet file. Table 19.3 summarizes the appropriate MIME types.

Table 19.3   MIME Types for .*CAB* Files

MIME Type	Description
application/x-cabinet_win32_x86	A cabinet file built for Windows NT or Windows 95 on the Intel x86 platform
application/x-cabinet_win32_ppc	A cabinet file built for Windows NT or Windows 95 on the x86 platform
application/x-cabinet_win32_mips	A cabinet file built for Windows NT or Windows 95 on the MIPS platform
application/x-cabinet_win32_alpha	A cabinet file built for Windows NT or Windows 95 on the DEC Alpha platform
application/x-cabinet_mac_ppc	A cabinet file built for Macintosh on the PowerPC platform

Making cabinet files is really quite simple. The ActiveX SDK includes a utility called DIANTZ.EXE built for just this purpose. Listing 19.1. shows the command line prototype for the DIANTZ.EXE.

Listing 19.1   Command Line for the *DIANTZ.EXE* Application

```
DIANTZ [/V[n]] [/D var=value ...] [/L dir] source [destination]
DIANTZ [/V[n]] [/D var=value ...] /F directive_file [...]

   source        File to compress.
   destination   File name to give compressed file.  If omitted, the
                 last character of the source file name is replaced
                 with an underscore (_) and used as the destination.
   /F directives A file with Diamond directives (may be repeated).
   /D var=value  Defines variable with specified value.
   /L dir        Location to place destination (default is current directory).
   /V[n]         Verbosity level (1..3).
```

Generally, you'll construct a directive file (with an extension of .DDF) that holds the instructions for creating the cabinet file. Listing 19.2 shows an example of such a directive file.

Listing 19.2   Directive File for *DIANTZ.EXE*

```
;----------------------------------------------------
;-- Directive file for generating Cabinet file
;----------------------------------------------------
.Option Explicit
.Set CabinetNameTemplate=MyCabinet.CAB
.Set Cabinet=on
.Set Compress=on
MyInfFile.INF
MyActiveXControl.OCX
```

You can try building a .CAB file by taking the following steps.

1. Create a new directory as a temporary working space for creating your cabinet file. The directory \activex\thedisk\NewCh19 was used in this example.

2. Put an ActiveX control file in your temporary working directory. Any .OCX file will do. In this example, a fictitious ActiveX control file called MyActiveXControl.OCX was used.

3. Next, create a file called MyInfFile.INF. Using Notepad or some other text editor, enter the code as shown in Listing 19.3. Save your .INF file.

Listing 19.3 *MYINFFILE.INF* Contents of the *MyInfFile.INF* File

```
;------------------------------------
;-- MyInfFile INF file
;------------------------------------
[Add.Code]
MyActiveXControl.ocx=MyActiveXControl.ocx


;------------------------------------------------
;-- MyActiveXControl.OCX can be found at
;-- the provided URL
;------------------------------------------------
[MyActiveXControl.ocx]
file=http://www.somewhere.com/over/the/rainbow/MyCabinet.cab
FileVersion=1,0,0,0
```

4. Next, create a file ecalled MyCabinet.ddf. Using Notepad, enter the code shown in Listing 19.4.

Listing 19.4 *MYCABINET.DDF* A Cabinet Definition File

```
;----------------------------------------------------------
;-- Directive file for generating Cabinet file
;----------------------------------------------------------
.Option Explicit
.Set CabinetNameTemplate=MyCabinet.CAB
.Set Cabinet=on
.Set Compress=on
MyInfFile.INF
MyActiveXControl.OCX
```

5. From the command line, enter the DIANTZ command as shown in Listing 19.5. Press Enter and DIANTZ will build your cabinet file for you.

Listing 19.5 Starting the *DIANTZ* Command

```
C:\MSDEV\INETSDK\BIN\DIANTZ.EXE /F MyCabinet.ddf
```

Part

III

Ch

19

FIG. 19.2

Check the output of DIANTZ.EXE.

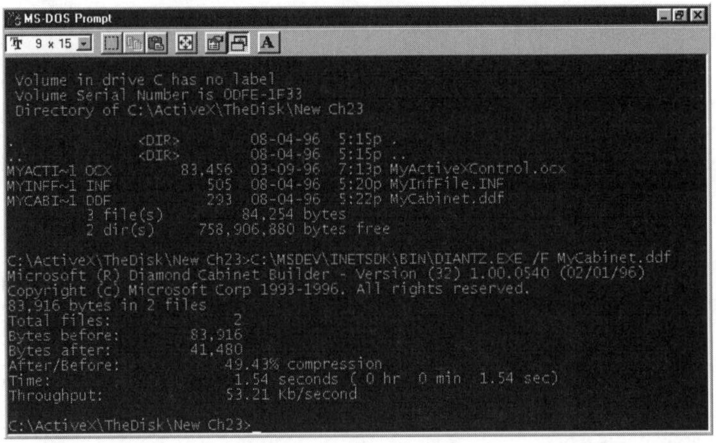

If you've done everything correctly, your DOS window should look something like figure 19.2.

The DIANTZ executable creates two diagnostic files (setup.inf and setup.rpt) as well as a directory called disk1 where the new cabinet file is stored. The setup files show various statistics concerning the cabinet file.

Working with .INF Files   The .INF installation file describes which files need to be downloaded or retrieved from the cabinet. This file also provides installation instructions for the files contained in the cabinet.

Note that the Internet Component Download process can rely on the MIME type to determine the appropriate treatment of the .INF file. The MIME type for a stand-alone .INF file is application/x-setupscript.

Take a look at Listing 19.6 which shows a sample .INF file.

Listing 19.6   An Example of a *.INF* File

```
;-----------------------------------
;-- Sample INF file
;-----------------------------------
[Add.Code]
MyActiveXControl.ocx=MyActiveXControl.ocx
NeedsThis.dll=NeedsThis.dll
mfc40.dll=mfc40.dll


;-------------------------------------------------
;-- MyActiveXControl.OCX can be found in the
;-- in the cabinet file at the provided URL
;-------------------------------------------------
[MyActiveXControl.ocx]
file=http://www.somewhere.com/over/the/rainbow/MyCabinet.cab
clsid={94EF87GG-634R-929C-23FE-00444ECE293}
FileVersion=1,0,0,0


;-------------------------------------------------
```

```
;-- NeedsThis.dll can be found in the
;-- in the cabinet file at the provided URL
;-------------------------------------------------
[NeedsThis.dll]
file=http://www.somewhere.com/way/up/high/NeedsThis.dll
FileVersion=
DestDir=10


;-------------------------------------------------
;-- mfc40.dll must be present, if not the
;-- the installation will fail
;-------------------------------------------------
[mfc40.dll]
file=
FileVersion=4,0,0,5
```

Notice the `DestDir` parameter used in the `NeedsThis.dll` section of the `.INF` file. This parameter can be set to either 10 or 11. The number 10 indicates that this file should be downloaded to the `\WINDOWS` directory. If you select the number 11, the downloaded files will be placed in the `\WINDOWS\SYSTEMS` directory.

The other important thing to notice in the `.INF` file is the `file=` notation in the `mfc40.dll` section. This entry implies that `mfc40.dll` version 4.0.0.5 is required to use the downloadable component. However, if this DLL is not available on the local system, the required DLL will not be downloaded. Instead, the download operation will fail.

Regardless of which type of file you choose to use for your downloaded objects, the download will occur asynchronously.

Using *WinVerifyTrust* to Permit Installation

Once the proper information and files have been obtained for installation, the next step in the process is to obtain verification that the components are trustworthy. The `WinVerifyTrust` API is really an extension of the Win32 API. The trust verification services provided are used to determine whether an object can be trusted based upon local administrative policy. The trust model on which `WinVerifyTrust` is based begins with three basic concepts:

- Trusted authority
- Trust administrator
- Trust provider

A *trusted authority* is an organization or entity that can be trusted to provide safe objects. For instance, your corporate MIS department would be considered a trusted authority to provide business applications for employees. You might also consider companies that sell shrink-wrapped products to be trusted to deliver safe copies of the products they sell.

Part
III

Ch
19

A *trust administrator* holds the decision-making power to determine whether a given organization or entity will be considered a trusted authority. The trust administrator may even decide not to trust entities that include digital certificates that guarantee the identity of entity. Say, for example, a certain software vendor is known to have an infected application in distribution. The trust administrator might decide that local policy will prevent software from that vendor to be downloaded and installed.

A *trust provider* is a software implementation for local trust policy. In essence, a trust provider supplies the logic for determining whether a particular action is permissible via local policy. We'll discuss this a bit more carefully in a moment.

Trust verification services are actually implemented for "subjects" and "actions." The service evaluates the trustworthiness of a subject based upon the action that's requested using the WinVerifyTrust function. Listing 19.7 shows the declaration of this important function for the WinBASE.h file in the ActiveX SDK.

On the CD

Listing 19.7   *WINBASE.H*   Declaration of *WinVerifyTrust*

```
////////////////////////////////////////////////////////////////
//                                                            //
//            Trust API and Structures                        //
//                                                            //
////////////////////////////////////////////////////////////////

WINBASEAPI
LONG
WINAPI
WinVerifyTrust(
    HWND    hwnd,
    DWORD   dwTrustProvider,
    DWORD   dwActionID,
    LPVOID  ActionData
    );
```

There are four parameters supplied to WinVerifyTrust function. If user intervention (and therefore, a user interface) is needed to determine whether trust should be granted, the hWnd parameter is expected to be the handle to the appropriate interactive window. Note that determination of trust is intended to be a largely transparent exercise. Use of direct user interaction should be discouraged. The dwTrustProvider specifies the trust provider is to be utilized to determine whether the subject should be trusted for the requested action. The requested action is specified in the dwActionID parameter. The possible values for the dwActionID are dependent upon the individual trust provider making the decision. Any additional information required by the trust provider must be passed in the dwActionData parameter. The content and meaning of the information passed is determined by the value of dwActionID and the individual trust provider. ●

CHAPTER 20

The Common Gateway Interface

Before you leap into ISAPI programming, take a minute to review the next two chapters concerning CGI applications. ISAPI and ISAPI filters provide many advantages over CGI applications in certain circumstances. You'll find that understanding the details of both CGI and ISAPI will help you choose between ISAPI and CGI for each situation. If you've never programmed CGI applications before, these two chapters give you a quick primer as well. ∎

Learn the CGI architecture

CGI is the current standard for server side scripts on the World Wide Web. Review the architectural concepts of CGI for comparison with the new ActiveX ISAPI technology.

Understand and use CGI environment variables

The CGI provides for a number of environment variables that can be used to communicate with server side scripts. Review the purpose and use of these environment variables.

Handling the GET method

The HU»P protocol provides two methods for starting a CGI script. The GET method is the more simple of the two. Review how to process GET requests in a CGI script.

Handling the POST method

The HTTP protocol provides two methods for starting a CGI script. The POST method is more robust than GET. Review how to process POST requests in a CGI script.

Understanding the CGI Architecture

The Common Gateway Interface (CGI) provides a simple mechanism for a Web browser to ask the Web server to execute a program. This CGI program is free to access system resources and then write results in HTML format back to the Web browser. Figure 20.1 graphically demonstrates the CGI architecture.

FIG. 20.1
An architecural look at the CGI architecture.

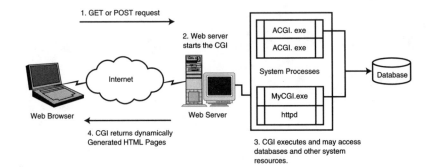

Let's walk through the figure step-by-step, and the process step-by-step. Each step is numbered in the figure, and then described in detail below:

1. A Web browser asks the Web server to execute a CGI program. The Web browser has two methods of making the request—POST and GET. These methods are described in detail later in the chapter.

2. The Web server invokes the CGI application. The Web server starts the execution of the CGI program by asking the operating system to create a new process in which to run the CGI program. If you're used to UNIX, think of this as a call to fork. If you're familiar with the Win32 API, think of this as a call to CreateProcess. When the operating system creates this process, it must do things like allocating process memory space and duplicating (or not duplicating) the parent process's environment. The CGI specifies that when the CGI's process environment is created, a set of CGI environment variables must be set. These environment variables contain a wealth of information about the request to run the CGI. You'll review each of these variables in detail later in this chapter. In addition, take special note of this step, because when you turn to ActiveX ISAPI applications, this step is significantly different.

3. The CGI application executes as a separate process in system memory. The CGI application can access relational databases, text files, fax machines, toasters, and any resource that it has access and permission to use. Because any number of different instances of the CGI application can be running in memory, special care must be taken when writing a CGI application to make sure that temporary filenames that might be created during the execution of the application are process specific. (Here again is an area where the ActiveX ISAPI process is different.)

4. When results need to be communicated back to the user, the CGI application simply writes to the stdout in its process space. Anything written out to stdout is passed to the

Web browser, so CGI applications need to send HTTP compliant headers. In addition, all output to be read by the user must be formatted in HTML.

Understanding CGI Environment Variables

The CGI provides a number of environment variables that can be used by applications to govern processing and set parameters. Table 20.1 briefly summarizes the CGI environment variables.

Table 20.1   CGI Environment Variables

Environment Variable	Purpose
SERVER_SOFTWARE	The name and version of the Web server servicing the request in name/version format.
SERVER_NAME	The domain name of the server.
GATEWAY_INTERFACE	The revision of the CGI standard that the server servicing this request is in compliance with.
SERVER_PROTOCOL	The protocol (on the Web it is always HTTP) and revision supported by this server.
SERVER_PORT	The port number the request received on.
REQUEST_METHOD	Indicates the type of request made by the Web browser. Usually, it is GET or POST.
PATH_INFO	Other information appearing in the request URL after the name of the executable.
PATH_TRANSLATED	The actual path after resolving any virtual path information.
SCRIPT_NAME	The virtual path to the CGI application.
QUERY_STRING	A string that contains the fields and value from an HTML form during a GET request.
REMOTE_HOST	The host name of the machine making the request.
REMOTE_ADDR	The IP address of the machine making the request.
AUTH_TYPE	For servers that support authentication, the types of authentication are reported here.
REMOTE_USER	The user name supplied during authentication.
REMOTE_IDENT	Servers that support the RFC 931 identification standard report the retrieved user name.
CONTENT_TYPE	The content type of the attached information.
CONTENT_LENGTH	The number of bytes in the body of the HTTP transaction.

Part

III

Ch

20

continues

Table 20.1 Continued	
Environment Variable	**Purpose**
HTTP_USER_AGENT*	The browser used to generate the request.
HTTP_REFERRER*	The page viewed by the user prior to making this request.

These two are actually so-called extra headers (see **http://hoohoo.ncsa.edu/cgi/). However, they are both very useful fields as described in the following section.*

Let's take a look at a couple of these CGI environment variables in more detail.

Using the *QUERY_STRING*

QUERY_STRING is the most often used environment variable. The QUERY_STRING is passed to a CGI program in an encoded form. To make use of it, your application has to parse the name value pairs passed through this variable. If you have an HTML form with three fields named— BarnAnimal1, BarnAnimal2, and BarnAnimal3—and the user has placed the text, The Pig, The Dog, and The Cat, the encoded QUERY_STRING would look like Listing 20.1.

Listing 20.1   An Encoded Query String
BarnAnimal1=The+Pig&BarnAnimal2=The+Dog&BarnAnimal3=The+Cat

The CGI observes the following rules concerning query strings:

- Field name and value pairs are separated by an ampersand (&).
- Field names are separated from their associated values by an equal sign (=).
- Spaces in the value field are converted to plus signs (+).
- Special characters may be *escaped*. That is, encoded as a percent sign (%) followed by the hexadecimal ASCII value of the desired character.

You could write your own functions to deal with query strings if you wanted to. However, there are many freely available libraries on the Internet that make writing your own seem like a waste of time. The examples in this book use the **util.c library** available from **http:// hoohoo.ncsa.uiuc.edu/cgi/**.

Using the *HTTP_USER_AGENT*

The HTTP_USER_AGENT field is used in a number of different ways. Many times, you may be forced to provide different versions of the same HTML page for different Web browsers. Although HTML is supposed to be standard, Web browser developers often provide custom features. The HTTP_USER_AGENT variable tells what browser generated the request. Your CGI programs can use this information to decide what kind of HTML to return. The form of the HTTP_USER_AGENT is *software/version library/version*. Standards are only useful when they are followed. Unfortunately, the HTTP_USER_AGENT variable is followed only loosely. In fact, there is an entire Web site (**http://www.browserwatch.com**) dedicated to documenting the values of HTTP_USER_AGENT and other fields. Listing 20.2 shows the value of these variables for MSIE 3.0.

Listing 20.2   Environment Variables for MSIE 3.0

```
SERVER_SOFTWARE=WebSite/1.0g
SERVER_NAME=localhost
SERVER_ADMIN=farrar@metamor.com
GATEWAY_INTERFACE=CGI/1.2 (DOS)
SERVER_PORT=80
GMT_OFFSET=-21600
DEBUG_MODE=NO
SERVER_PROTOCOL=HTTP/1.0
REQUEST_METHOD=GET
HTTP_ACCEPT=c:\temp\bws.acc
SCRIPT_NAME=/cgi-shl/GetEnvironment.exe
OUTPUT_FILE=c:\temp\bws.out
QUERY_STRING=NumPayments=&Interest=&Principal=
REMOTE_ADDR=127.0.0.1
HTTP_REFERER=http://localhost/INDEX.html
AUTH_TYPE=Basic
AUTH_NAME=Web Server
ACCEPT_LANGUAGE=en
PRAGMA=no-cache
HTTP_USER_AGENT=Mozilla/2.0 (compatible; MSIE 3.0B; Windows 95;800,600
HOST=localhost
```

Some servers set the name of the environment variable as USER_AGENT rather than HTTP_USER_AGENT.

Handling a *GET* Request

The simplest CGI program uses the GET method. The GET method relies on filling the QUERY_STRING environment variable with field name and value pairs. If you were going to implement the mortgage calculator from Chapter 9 as a CGI application, your form would look something like Listing 20.3.

Listing 20.3   A CGI-Based Mortgage Calculator Form

```
<HTML>
<HEAD>
<TITLE>Your Home Page Goes Here</TITLE>
</HEAD>
<BODY>
<H1>Mortgage Calculator</H1>
<p>
<FORM METHOD="GET" ACTION="/cgi-shl/MortgageCalculator.exe">
Number of payments      <INPUT TYPE=TEXT NAME=NumPayments  SIZE=5><BR>
Annual Interest rate    <INPUT TYPE=TEXT NAME=Interest   SIZE=6><BR>
Principal               <INPUT TYPE=TEXT NAME=Principal SIZE=9> <BR>
<INPUT TYPE=Submit>
```

Part
III

Ch
20

continues

Listing 20.3   Continued

```
</FORM>
</BODY>
</HTML>
```

Processing the GET involves parsing the QUERY_STRING variable. The first step in a GET method request application is to ensure that calling HTML document has properly launched the application using the GET method. Listing 20.4 shows the code for making this happen.

Listing 20.4   Checking for the *GET* Method

```
/*---------------------------------------------
 *-- Make sure the FORM tag included the
 *-- GET method
 *---------------------------------------------*/
if(strcmp(getenv("REQUEST_METHOD"),"GET")) {

       printf("You must use <FORM METHOD=\"GET\"...> in your HTML document\n");
       exit(1);
}
```

The next step in processing the request is to ensure that there is some value in the QUERY_STRING field. Listing 20.5 demonstrates a method for accomplishing this goal.

Listing 20.5   Ensuring That the *QUERY_STRING* Has Data

```
/*---------------------------------------------
 *-- Make sure the QUERY_STRING has some data
 *---------------------------------------*/
pstrRawQueryString = getenv("QUERY_STRING");
if(pstrRawQueryString == NULL) {

       printf("Empty QUERY_STRING.\n");
       exit(1);

}
```

The value of the QUERY_STRING environment variable has now been referenced in the pstrRawQueryString variable. Of course, you might not need to evaluate the QUERY_STRING at all (if, for example, your application required no user input). But, in most cases, you'll want to get user input.

The pstrRawQueryString must be parsed into name and value pairs. This is a four step process. Recall that the form of the QUERY_STRING follows four basic requirements. Field name and value pairs are separated by an ampersand. The field names themselves are separated from their associated values by an equal sign. The value part of the name/value pair will have all spaces converted to plus signs, and any other special characters may be escaped (for example, encoded as a percent sign followed by the hexadecimal ASCII value of the desired character). Listing 20.6 shows the code for this process.

Listing 20.6 Parsing the *QUERY_STRING*

```
/*-----------------------------------------------
 *-- Parse the QUERY_STRING and save the
 *-- name/value pairs.
 *-----------------------------------------*/
for(indx = 0; pstrRawQueryString[0] != '\0'; indx++) {

    // Get the name value pair into the szVal filed
    getword(cgiEntry[indx].szVal, pstrRawQueryString,'&');

    // Change the '+' signs to spaces
    plustospace(cgiEntry[indx].szVal);

        //Convert escaped characters
    unescape_url(cgiEntry[indx].szVal);

    //Get the name part of the pair into the szName field
    getword(cgiEntry[indx].szName, cgiEntry[indx].szVal, '=');
}
```

Note that the cgiEntry variable used in the previous listing is a structure defined as shown in Listing 20.7.

Listing 20.7 The Name/Value Pair for the CGI

```
typedef struct {
    char szName[128];
    char szVal[128];
} CGI_TUPLE;
```

As mentioned before, you could write your own versions of the getword, plustospace, and unescape_url function, but the NCSA Web server, called httpd, has these functions available free for your use. You can also get these library tools at the **http://hoohoo.ncsa.edu/cgi/** Web site.

Handling a *POST* Request

More complex CGI programs use the POST method. The POST method passes form field name/value pairs through the stdin, where the GET method relies on filling the QUERY_STRING environment variable if your form has lots of fields, or if the value passed in a single field may be large, you may run out of environment space. For those situations, the POST method is a better choice. Again, return to the mortgage calculator from Chapter 9 as a CGI application. Your form would look something like Listing 20.8.

Listing 20.8   Another CGI-Based Mortgage Calculator Form

```
<HTML>
<TITLE>Your Home Page Goes Here</TITLE>
<H1>Mortgage Calculator</H1>
<p>
<FORM METHOD="POST" ACTION="/cgi-shl/MortgageCalculator.exe">
Number of payments        <INPUT TYPE=TEXT NAME=NumPayments  SIZE=5><BR>
Annual Interest rate      <INPUT TYPE=TEXT NAME=Interest  SIZE=6><BR>
Principal                 <INPUT TYPE=TEXT NAME=Principal SIZE=9> <BR>
<INPUT TYPE=Submit>
</FORM>
</HTML>
```

Processing the POST involves reading the POST data from stdin, and parsing the information. The first step in the POST method request application is to ensure that the calling HTML document has properly launched the application using the POST method. Listing 20.9 shows the code for making this happen.

Listing 20.9   Checking for the *POST* Method

```
/*--------------------------------------------
 *-- Make sure the FORM tag included the
 *-- POST method
 *-------------------------------------------*/
if(strcmp(getenv("REQUEST_METHOD"),"POST")) {

      printf("You must use <FORM METHOD=\"POST\"...> in your HTML document\n");
      exit(1);
}
```

The next step in processing the CGI request is to allocate enough memory for the POST data. Check the CONTENT_LENGTH environment variable for this information. Listing 20.10 demonstrates this process.

Listing 20.10   Using the *CONTENT_LENGTH* Variable

```
// Determine the size of the post data block
iSizeOfPostData = atoi(getenv("CONTENT_LENGTH"));

// Allocate memory to read the block into
pstrRawPostData = (char *) malloc(iSizeOfPostData);

// Read the data from stdin
fread(pstrRawPostData, iSizeOfPostData, 1, stdin);

// Inserts a null character at the end of the string.
pstrRawPostData[iSizeOfPostData] = '\0';
```

From here, you can treat pstrRawPostData just as in the GET request. Parse the pstrRawPostData into name and value pairs. Listing 20.11 shows the code for this process.

Listing 20.11 Parsing the *QUERY_STRING*

```
/*-----------------------------------------
 *-- Parse the QUERY_STRING and save the
 *-- name/value pairs.
 *-----------------------------------------*/
for(indx = 0; pstrRawPostData[0] != '\0'; indx++) {

    m = indx;

    // Get the name value pair into the szVal filed
    getword(cgiEntry[indx].szVal, pstrRawPostData,'&');

    // Change the '+' signs to spaces
    plustospace(cgiEntry[indx].szVal);

       //Convert escaped characters
    unescape_url(cgiEntry[indx].szVal);

    //Get the name part of the pair into the szName field
    getword(cgiEntry[indx].szName, cgiEntry[indx].szVal, '=');
}
```

Part

III

Ch

20

CHAPTER 21

Example CGI Programs

So far, our review of CGI has focused on elements of the CGI and not applications. In this chapter, you'll construct a couple of applications using the CGI. Both the POST and GET methods will be reviewed in the construction of these applications. The final section of this chapter is devoted to a discussion of some of the drawbacks of CGI. The ActiveX Server Framework ISAPI standard offers some distinct advantages over CGI for certain types of applications. Understanding the strengths and weaknesses of the CGI helps you decide on the right technology for your Internet applications. ▪

Construct a CGI application using GET

In this chapter, you'll construct a server-side CGI implementation.

Construct a CGI application using POST

In this chapter, you'll construct a CGI implementation.

Drawbacks of the CGI architecture

For some applications, CGI is not the best choice. The ActiveX Server Framework standard ISAPI provides a high-end alternative to the CGI for some situations. Here, we'll discuss some of the situations where CGI is not well-suited.

The Mortgage Calculator

Recall from Chapter 9 that the Mortgage Calculator was quite simple to implement as a VBScript application. Of course, before client-side scripting was available, all applications, such as the Mortgage Calculator, had to be implemented as CGI applications. So in many cases, the Mortgage Calculator is implemented as a client-side script with the advent of the ActiveX environment. However, say that you wanted to keep a list of the rates that were entered in the interest rate field (to get a sense of what rates people expected to be able to borrow money, for instance). You may still want to implement the Mortgage Calculator as a CGI script. In this section, you'll construct the skeleton of a server-side Mortgage Calculator.

Laying Out the Form

Since you'll have several objects on-screen, let's start by taking a look at the basic layout of the objects on the page (see fig. 21.1).

FIG. 21.1

CGI Mortgage Calculator example.

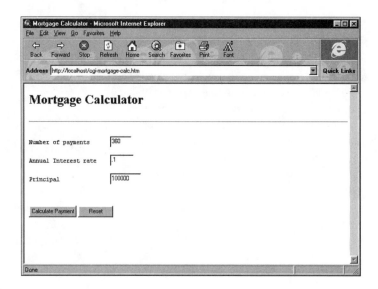

The form contains three fields, one for each of the following:

- **Number of Payments**—The name of this text box is NumPayments.
- **Annual Interest**—The name of this text box is Interest.
- **Principal**—The name of this text box is Principal.

To build the Mortgage Calculator example, follow these steps:

1. Using the ActiveX Control Pad, or your favorite text editor, open your HTML template file.
2. Update the comment header, TITLE value, and H1 tag pair to reflect the name of the example.

3. Save the file to a convenient working directory, giving it a name like
   CGI-MORTGAGE-CALC.HTM.

4. Now add the FORM to the body of the HTML document. Go ahead and add the three form
   fields, and the Submit and Reset buttons. When you're finished, your code should look
   like Listing 21.1.

On the CD

Listing 21.1 *CGI-MORTGAGE-CALC.HTM* **Mortgage Calculator Form Insertion**

```
<!------------------------------------------------------>
<!--                      >
<!-- Description: Mortgage Calculator Example     >
<!--        >
<!-- Author:  Brian Farrar             >
<!--        >
<!-- Date:   7/14/96                  >
<!------------------------------------------------------>
<HTML>
<HEAD><TITLE>Mortgage Calculator</TITLE>
</HEAD>
<BODY BGCOLOR=#FFFFFF>
<H1>Mortgage Calculator</H1>
<HR>

<!------------------------------------------------------>
<!-- Form collects parameters to calculate loan payment >
<!------------------------------------------------------>

<FORM METHOD="GET" ACTION="/cgi-shl/MortgageCalculator.exe" NAME="MCalcForm">
<PRE>
Number of payments      <INPUT TYPE=TEXT NAME=NumPayments  SIZE=5 >

Annual Interest rate    <INPUT TYPE=TEXT NAME=Interest   SIZE=6 >

Principal               <INPUT TYPE=TEXT NAME=Principal SIZE=9 >

</PRE><BR>
<INPUT TYPE="submit" VALUE="Calculate Payment" >
<INPUT TYPE="reset"  VALUE="Reset">

</FORM>
</CENTER>

</BODY>
</HTML>
```

Use <PRE> (for preformatted) so that it's easy to lay out the form without messing with tables
or fancier formatting. The <FORM> tag uses some additional attributes that weren't used in the
VBScript version of this application. The method for this application is GET and the action is the
server root relative path to the executable you'll construct in just a moment.

Coding the Script

Now that the HTML portion of this application is complete, let's turn to the server side of the equation. CGI scripts can be created in any programming language that supports a stdin and stdout concept. For the examples in this book, you'll use the C programming language. The examples are compiled using Microsoft Visual C++ 4.1. If you use any other C compiler, the examples should work without modification. Follow these steps:

1. Open your C compiler and start a new project. The first thing you'll need is a small header (.h) file that defines the CGI_TUPLE structure. CGI_TUPLE stores the name/value pairs that arrive via the QUERY_STRING when the application is started by the Web server. Your code should look like Listing 21.2.

On the CD

Listing 21.2   *UTIL.H*   Header File to Define *CGI_TUPLE* Structure

```
/*---------------------------------------------
 *-- Header file for util.c
 *---------------------------------------*/
typedef struct {
    char szName[128];
    char szVal[128];
} CGI_TUPLE;


void getword(char *word, char *line, char stop);
char x2c(char *what);
void unescape_url(char *url);
void plustospace(char *str);
```

As mentioned in the previous chapter, the functions declared in this header file are freely available from **http://hoohoo.ncsa.edu/cgi/**. These routines are used in the examples, and can be found on the CD as well.

2. Save the file as util.h, and start a new file in the project. This file (called MortgageCalculator.c) contains main for the CGI application, as well as any functions needed to calculate the mortgage payment. The first thing to do in MortgageCalculator.c is to declare the header files required. Your code should look like Listing 21.3.

On the CD

Listing 21.3   *MORTGAGECALCULATOR.C*   Declare Required Header Files

```
/*-------------------------------------------------------------------
 *--
 *--    Include required header files
 *--
 *-------------------------------------------------------------*/
#include <stdio.h>
#include <stdlib.h>
#include <string.h>
#include "util.h"
```

3. Next, code the CalculatePayment function. This function takes an array of CGI_TUPLEs and calculates the appropriate mortgage payment. Your code should look something like Listing 21.4.

On the CD

Listing 21.4 *2MORTGAGECALCULATOR.C* *CalculatePayment* Function for the Mortgage Calculator

```
/*-------------------------------------------------------------------
 *--
 *--     CalculatePayment
 *--
 *----------------------------------------------------------------*/
float CalculatePayment(CGI_TUPLE *cgi) {

    int iNumPayments;
    float fInterestRate;
    float fPrincipalAmount;

    int indx;
    float fConversionFactor = 1.0F;

    iNumPayments = atoi(cgi[0].szVal);
    fInterestRate = atof(cgi[1].szVal);
    fPrincipalAmount = atof(cgi[2].szVal);


    if ( fInterestRate > 1.0 ) {

     fInterestRate /= 100;

    }
      fInterestRate /= 12;


    for ( indx = 0; indx < iNumPayments ; indx++ ) {

     fConversionFactor *= ( 1 + fInterestRate );

    }

    return (fPrincipalAmount * fConversionFactor * fInterestRate) /
    (fConversionFactor - 1);
}
```

This example does not do any of the data validation that the VBScript version you built in a previous chapter completes. This data checking could easily be implemented, but has been omitted to keep our exploration of the CGI interface clear and concise.

4. Now code main. The first step is to declare main and any required variables that are local to main. Your code should look something like Listing 21.5.

Listing 21.5 *3MORTGAGECALCULATOR.C* **Variables That Are Local to** *main*

```
/*-------------------------------------------------------------------
 *--
 *--      Start of Main
 *--
 *------------------------------------------------------------------*/

void main(int argc, char *argv[]) {

    CGI_TUPLE cgiEntry[3];

    int indx = 0;
    char *pstrRawQueryString;
    float fPaymentAmount;
```

The form passes the names and values of three form text fields, so declare an array of CGI_TUPLEs to store them. Declare an indx variable to be used in the for loop that sets each of the entries in the cgiEntry array. The pstrRawQueryString points to the raw and encoded QUERY_STRING environment variable. Finally, declare a variable to store the calculated mortgage payment amount.

5. Next, send the Content-Type header. This header is the minimum required header information from the HTTP standard. Your code should look something like Listing 21.6.

Listing 21.6 *4MORTGAGECALCULATOR.C* **Sending the Content-Type Header**

```
printf("Content-type: text/html\n\n");
```

Notice the two new line characters at the end of the Content-Type header. The HTTP standard requires that the Content-Type header is followed by a blank line. The reason this step is completed first is to permit reporting of error events via an HTML document, as well as returning calculated results on success.

6. Now you'll need to verify that the application was properly called via the GET method. Your code should look something like Listing 21.7.

Listing 21.7 *5MORTGAGECALCULATOR.C* **Checking to Ensure That the** *GET* **Method is Used**

```
/*-----------------------------------------------
 *-- Make sure the FORM tag included the
 *-- GET method
 *-----------------------------------------*/
if(strcmp(getenv("REQUEST_METHOD"),"GET")) {

    printf("You must use the GET in your HTML document\n");
    exit(1);
}
```

Since you've already sent the Content-Type header, you can simply use `printf` statements with valid HTML to report any errors that occur.

7. Check to make sure that QUERY_STRING contains some data. Your code should look like Listing 21.8.

On the CD

Listing 21.8 6MORTGAGECALCULATOR.C Verify That QUERY_STRING Contains Data

```
/*-------------------------------------------------
*-- Make sure the QUERY_STRING has some data
*------------------------------------------------*/
pstrRawQueryString = getenv("QUERY_STRING");
if(pstrRawQueryString == NULL) {

        printf("Empty QUERY_STRING.\n");
          exit(1);

}
```

Now the `pstrRawQueryString` references the QUERY_STRING.

8. Parse `pstrRawQueryString` into useful CGI_TUPLE entries. Your code will resemble Listing 21.9.

On the CD

Listing 21.9 7MORTGAGECALCULATOR.C for Loop to Parse pstrRawQueryString

```
/*-------------------------------------------------
*-- Parse the QUERY_STRING and save the
*-- name/value pairs.
*------------------------------------------------*/
for(indx = 0; pstrRawQueryString[0] != '\0'; indx++) {

    // Get the name value pair into the szVal field
    getword(cgiEntry[indx].szVal, pstrRawQueryString,'&');

    // Change the '+' signs to spaces
    plustospace(cgiEntry[indx].szVal);

       //Convert escaped characters
    unescape_url(cgiEntry[indx].szVal);

    //Get the name part of the pair into the szName field
    getword(cgiEntry[indx].szName, cgiEntry[indx].szVal, '=');
}
```

This step employs the freely available functions from **http://hoohoo.ncsa.uiuc.edu/ cgi/**. You'll also find these functions on the CD in the `util.c` file (you'll need to add this `util.c` file to your project, as well).

9. Finally, you'll call `CalculatePayment` and print out the results in HTML format. Your code should look like Listing 21.10.

On the CD

Listing 21.10 *8MORTGAGECALCULATOR.C* **Calculate the Payment and Print Out HTML Results**

```c
// Calculate the payment amount
fPaymentAmount = CalculatePayment(cgiEntry);

// Print the results
printf("<H1>Mortgage Payment</H1>");
printf("<HR>");
printf("Payment Amount = %.2f", fPaymentAmount);
}
```

The final curly brace closes off `main`.

10. Save your work and compile the executable.

Now that you've completed the HTML document and the CGI application, you can test your work using Microsoft Internet Explorer 3.0. The procedures for placing the CGI application and the HTML document on the Web server vary widely from Web server to Web server. However, when the application is run with the text fields filled out as shown in figure 21.1, the result should look something like figure 21.2.

FIG. 21.2

The results of the MortgageCalculator.exe CGI application.

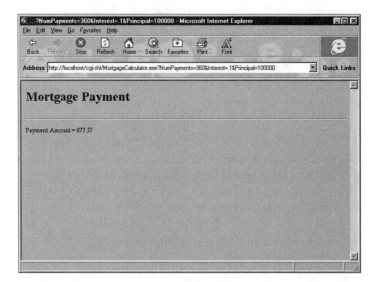

Customer Survey

Recall from Chapter 8 that the Customer Survey was as easy to implement as a VBScript application. However, storing the results of the survey to a file on the server was not possible. Such a requirement makes the application perfect for a CGI program. In this section, you'll construct the skeleton of a server-side Customer Survey application.

Laying Out the Form

Since you'll have several objects on-screen, let's start by taking a look at the basic layout of the objects on the page (see fig. 21.3).

FIG. 21.3
CGI Customer Survey example.

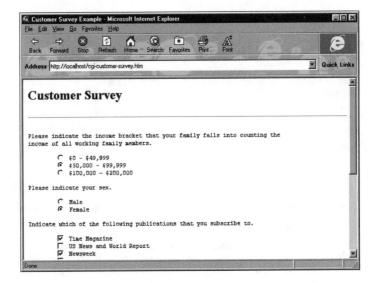

The form contains three different types of input:

- **Checkboxes**—Any number of these may be checked, making predicting the number of CGI_TUPLE entries you'll need impossible.
- **Radio buttons**—Return one CGI_TUPLE per radio button set.
- **Text boxes**—These return one CGI_TUPLE as well.

To build this Customer Survey example, follow these steps:

1. Using the ActiveX Control Pad or your favorite text editor, open your HTML template file.
2. Update the comment header, TITLE value, and H1 tag pair to reflect the name of the example.

Part
III

Ch
21

3. Save the file as CGI-CUSTOMER-SURVEY.HTM to a convenient working directory.

4. Now, add the FORM to the body of the HTML document. Go ahead and add the three form fields, and the Submit and Reset buttons. When you're finished, your code should look like Listing 21.11.

On the CD

Listing 21.11 *CGI-CUSTOMER-SURVEY.HTM* **Customer Survey Form Insertion**

```
<! ------------------------------------------------------->
<! --            >
<! -- Description: Customer Survey Example            >
<! --            >
<! -- Author:  Brian Farrar                          >
<! --            >
<! -- Date:   7/14/96                               >
<! ------------------------------------------------------->
<HTML>
<HEAD><TITLE>Customer Survey Example</TITLE>
</HEAD>
<BODY BGCOLOR=#FFFFFF>
<H1>Customer Survey</H1>
<HR>
<! ------------------------------------------------------->
<! -- Form to collect customer survey data            >
<! ------------------------------------------------------->
<FORM METHOD="POST" ACTION="/cgi-shl/CustomerSurvey.exe" NAME="CustomerSurvey">
<PRE>
Please indicate the income bracket that your family falls into counting the
income of all working family members.

    <INPUT TYPE=radio NAME=incomeBracket VALUE="IncomeBracket1" > $0 - $49,999
    <INPUT TYPE=radio NAME=incomeBracket VALUE="IncomeBracket2" > $50,000 - $99,999
    <INPUT TYPE=radio NAME=incomeBracket VALUE="IncomeBracket3" > $100,000 - $200,000

Please indicate your sex.

    <INPUT TYPE=radio NAME=Sex VALUE="Male" > Male
    <INPUT TYPE=radio NAME=Sex VALUE="Female" > Female

Indicate which of the following publications that you subscribe to.

    <INPUT TYPE=checkbox NAME=Publications VALUE="Time, " > Time Magazine
    <INPUT TYPE=checkbox NAME=Publications VALUE="USNews" > US News and World Report
    <INPUT TYPE=checkbox NAME=Publications VALUE="Newsweek" > Newsweek
    <INPUT TYPE=checkbox NAME=Publications VALUE="Atlantic" > Atlantic Monthly
    <INPUT TYPE=checkbox NAME=Publications VALUE="TVGuide" > TV Guide

How much would you be willing to pay for our EnhancedPlus service?

    <INPUT TYPE=text NAME=ServiceCost >

Please rate the service you've received from our company.

    <INPUT TYPE=radio NAME=RateUs VALUE="excellent" > Excellent
```

```
      <INPUT TYPE=radio NAME=RateUs VALUE="good" > Good
      <INPUT TYPE=radio NAME=RateUs VALUE="fair" > Fair
      <INPUT TYPE=radio NAME=RateUs VALUE="poor" > Poor


</PRE>
<BR>
<BR>
<INPUT TYPE="submit" VALUE="Tell Us">
<INPUT TYPE="reset"  VALUE="Reset">

</FORM>

</CENTER>

</BODY>
</HTML>
```

Use <PRE> (for preformatted) again so it's easy to lay out the form without messing with fancy formatting. The method for this application is POST instead of GET.

Coding the Script

Now that the HTML portion of this application is complete, let's turn to the server side of the equation; again, we'll use Microsoft Visual C++ 4.1. Follow these steps:

1. Open your C compiler and start a new project, the first thing you'll need is a small header (.h) file that defines the CGI_TUPLE structure. CGI_TUPLE will store the name/value pairs that arrive via the stdin when the application is started by the Web server. Your code should look like Listing 21.12.

Listing 21.12   *UTIL.H*   Header File to Define *CGI_TUPLE* Structure

On the CD

```
/*--------------------------------------------
 *-- Header file for util.c
 *--------------------------------------*/
typedef struct {
    char szName[128];
    char szVal[128];
} CGI_TUPLE;


void getword(char *word, char *line, char stop);
char x2c(char *what);
void unescape_url(char *url);
void plustospace(char *str);
```

Part
III

Ch
21

Note that you can use the util.h you created in the MortgageCalculator example.

2. Save the file as `util.h`, and start a new file in the project. This file (called `CustomerSurvey.c`) contains `main` for the CGI application, as well as any functions needed to calculate the mortgage payment. The first thing to do in `CustomerSurvey.c` is to declare the header files required. Your code should look like Listing 21.13.

On the CD

Listing 21.13   CUSTOMERSURVEY.C   Declare Required Header Files

```
/*------------------------------------------------------------------
 *--
 *--      Include required header files
 *--
 *----------------------------------------------------------------*/
#include <stdio.h>
#include <stdlib.h>
#include <string.h>
#include "util.h"
```

3. Code the `CalculatePayment` function. This function takes an array of `CGI_TUPLE`s and a count of the entries, and processes the survey information. Your code should look something like Listing 21.14.

On the CD

Listing 21.14   2CUSTOMERSURVEY.C   ProcessSurvey Function

```
/*------------------------------------------------------------------
 *--
 *--      Process the Customer Survey
 *--
 *----------------------------------------------------------------*/
void ProcessSurvey(CGI_TUPLE *cgi, int iTCount) {

    int indx;

    // Print the results
    printf("Content-type: text/html\n\n");
      printf("<H1>Customer Survey</H1>");
    printf("<HR>");
    printf("The survey responses were:<BR>\n");

    printf("<UL>\n");
    for ( indx = 0; indx < iTCount; indx++ ) {

      printf("%s = %s<BR>\n", cgi[indx].szName, cgi[indx].szVal);

    }
    printf("</UL>\n");
```

This example does not actually do anything with the survey data. However, you need only program the custom operations you'd like to perform on the data, such as storing it to a file, sending it in an e-mail address, or posting it to a relational database.

Programming these sorts of functions is no different than as if the data had been entered through the console in a traditional programming environment.

4. Now code main. The first step is to declare main, and any required variables that are local to main. Your code should look something like Listing 21.15.

On the CD

Listing 21.15   3CUSTOMERSURVEY.C   Variables That Are Local to *main*

```
/*-----------------------------------------------------------------
 *--
 *--     Start of Main
 *--
 *-------------------------------------------------------------*/

void main(int argc, char *argv[]) {

        CGI_TUPLE cgiEntry[255];

    int indx, iTupleCount;
char *pstrRawQueryString;
    unsigned int iContentLength;
```

The form passes the names and values of three form text fields, so declare an array of CGI_TUPLEs to store them. Declare an indx variable to be used in the for loop that sets each of the entries in the cgiEntry array. The iTupleCount variable stores the number of name/value pairs passed to the CGI application (i.e., read from stdin). The pstrRawQueryString points to the raw and encoded POST data once it's read from stdin. Finally, declare a variable, iContentLength, to store the size of the data to be read from stdin.

5. Send the Content-Type header. This header is the minimum required header information from the HTTP standard. Your code should look something like Listing 21.16.

On the CD

Listing 21.16   4CUSTOMERSURVEY.C   Sending the Content-Type Header

```
// Send the required Content-type header
printf("Content-type: text/html\n\n");
```

Don't forget the two new line characters at the end of the Content-Type header required by the HTTP standard.

6. Verify that the application was properly called via the POST method. Your code should look something like Listing 21.17.

Part III

Ch 21

Listing 21.17   _5CUSTOMERSURVEY.C_   Checking to Ensure That the _POST_ Method is Used

```
/*-----------------------------------------------
 *-- Make sure the FORM tag included the
 *-- POST method
 *-----------------------------------------*/
if(strcmp(getenv("REQUEST_METHOD"),"POST")) {

    printf("You must use the POST in your HTML document\n");
        exit(1);
}
```

Since you've already sent the Content-Type header, you can simply use `printf` statements with valid HTML to report any errors that occur.

7. Get the POST data from `stdin`. The best way to accomplish this task is to first obtain the size of the POST data block by reading the `CONTENT_LENGTH` environment variable. Then, get a buffer to store the POST data in and read it from `stdin`. Your code should look like Listing 21.18.

On the CD

Listing 21.18   _6CUSTOMERSURVEY.C_   Read the _POST_ Data From _stdin_

```
/*-----------------------------------------------
 *-- Ready the POST data for use
 *-----------------------------------------*/

// Get the size of the POST data
iContentLength = atoi(getenv("CONTENT_LENGTH"));

// Allocate enough memory for the POST data
if ( ( pstrRawQueryString = (char *) malloc(iContentLength) ) == NULL ) {

    printf("Internal CGI Error\n");
    exit(1);
}

// Read the POST data from stdin
if ( fread(pstrRawQueryString, 1, iContentLength, stdin) != iContentLength ) {

    printf("Error reading POST data<BR>\n");

}

// Terminate the pstrRawQueryString
pstrRawQueryString[iContentLength] = '\0';
```

You must add your own null terminator to the `pstrRawQueryString` before using it.

8. Now, parse `pstrRawQueryString` into useful `CGI_TUPLE` entries. The process is the same as in `CustomerSurvey.c`. However, this time you'll keep a count of the name/value pairs. Your code will resemble Listing 21.19.

On the CD

Listing 21.19 7CUSTOMERSURVEY.C for Loop to Parse *pstrRawQueryString*

```
//Initialize iTupleCount
iTupleCount = 0;

/*---------------------------------------------
 *-- Parse the QUERY_STRING and save the
 *-- name/value pairs.
 *---------------------------------------------*/
for(indx = 0; pstrRawQueryString[0] != '\0'; indx++) {

// Get the name value pair into the szVal filed
    getword(cgiEntry[indx].szVal, pstrRawQueryString,'&');

    // Change the '+' signs to spaces
     plustospace(cgiEntry[indx].szVal);

       //Convert escaped characters
    unescape_url(cgiEntry[indx].szVal);

    //Get the name part of the pair into the szName field
    getword(cgiEntry[indx].szName, cgiEntry[indx].szVal, '=');

    //Incremennt the iTupleCount
    iTupleCount++;
    }
}
```

9. Finally, you'll call ProcessSurvey and print out the results in HTML format. Your code should look like Listing 21.20.

On the CD

Listing 21.20 8CUSTOMERSURVEY.C Process the Survey

```
    ProcessSurvey(cgiEntry, iTupleCount);

}
```

The final curly brace closes off main.

10. Save your work, and compile the executable.

Now that you've completed the HTML document and the CGI application, you can test your work using Microsoft Internet Explorer 3.0. The procedures for placing the CGI application and the HTML document on the Web server will vary widely from Web server to Web server. However, when the application is run with the text fields filled out as shown in figure 21.3, the result should look something like figure 21.4.

Part
III

Ch
21

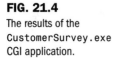

FIG. 21.4
The results of the
CustomerSurvey.exe
CGI application.

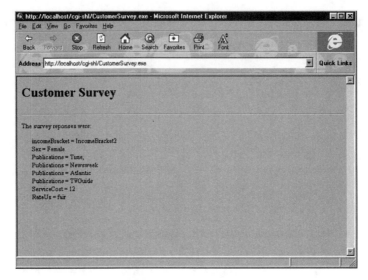

Drawbacks of the CGI Architecture

For most Internet applications, the CGI provides an excellent platform for developing custom development. However, there are two major drawbacks to the CGI architecture. These drawbacks can significantly affect the performance and functionality of Web-based applications. These two weaknesses are as follows:

- No persistent context information is available.
- It is system process intensive.

Recall that the HTTP protocol is *stateless*. That is, no contextual information between session connections is retained. So, for example, once the Web server has responded to a request to run a CGI application, the CGI completes it, and the connection between the client and the server is broken. Thus, no information about the status of the applications can easily be obtained. This presents a problem in some cases.

Say, for example, your CGI application takes a few parameters, and then executes a query against a large relational database. Some queries may return a large number of rows as a result set. Of course, you wouldn't want to return 1,000 rows in a single page. Instead, you need to show the rows ten or so at a time to the user. When the user asks for the first ten rows, the application executes the query and collects all 1,000 rows, but only the first ten are returned. The application finishes after sending these rows. Now the user requests the next ten rows. Unfortunately, using the standard CGI, the query for the 1,000 rows has to be executed all over again. In fact, each time the user requests an additional set of rows from the 1,000-row result set, the query must be executed. Unfortunately, the ISAPI interface does not offer much help with this weakness.

ISAPI does, however, address the second weakness. Web servers handle CGI execution requests by creating a new process and passing the data received from the browser through the environment variables and `stdin`. The CGI produces HTML-formatted output and writes it to the `stdout` of the newly created process. As shown in figure 21.5, for every request presented to the Web server, a new process is created.

FIG. 21.5
The CGI architecture.

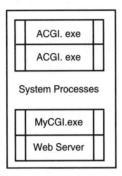

The more concurrent requests the Web server receives, the more concurrent processes run in memory on the server machine. Unfortunately, creating a process for every request requires significant overhead, and can chew up system resources.

Instead, the ISAPI approach uses Dynamic Link Libraries to avoid some of the overhead involved in spawning concurrent processes. A DLL can be loaded by the server the first time a request is received for that DLL, and then remain in memory ready to service additional requests. Unlike the CGI process model, ISAPI DLLs are loaded in the same address space as the HTTP server (see fig. 21.6).

FIG. 21.6
The ISAPI architecture.

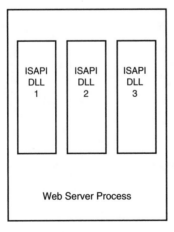

Since the DLLs can persist in memory, and the server knows that the DLLs are lying around waiting to service a request, there is virtually no overhead associated with servicing the next request. Of course, this higher performance comes at a cost. All ISAPI applications must be multithread safe. ●

Part

III

Ch

21

CHAPTER 22

Internet Server Application Program Interface (ISAPI)

Now that you've had the opportunity to review the elements of the CGI as well as build some simple examples, this chapter turns to the details of the ISAPI architecture. The ActiveX server framework ISAPI standard offers some distinct advantages over CGI for certain types of applications. So, in this chapter you'll be introduced to the details of ISAPI architecture. ■

Understand the required ISAPI DLL server entry points

ISAPI DLLs have two required entry points. Although you'll probably use the ISAPI wizard and ISAPI MFCs to build your ISAPI apps, you should understand these underlying functions.

Learn the `ReadClient`, `WriteClient`, and `ServerSupportFunction` functions

Communicating with the Web browser is the ultimate objective of most Web-based applications. When you build ISAPI applications, you'll use all three of these functions to accomplish that goal.

Study the details of the `EXTENSION_CONTROL_BLOCK`

ISAPI provides a mechanism for passing information from the Web browser much like the environment variables from the CGI interface. You'll learn the details of this important structure in this chapter.

Build an ISAPI DLL

The best way to learn about a programming topic is to build an example. The example you'll construct in this chapter will demonstrate the use of all the various data members of the `EXTENSION_CONTROL_BLOCK`.

The ISAPI Architecture

The ISAPI approach uses Dynamic Link Libraries (DLLs) to avoid some of the overhead involved in spawning concurrent processes in the CGI standard. Note that a DLL can be loaded by the server the first time a request is received for that DLL and then remain in memory ready to service additional requests. Unlike the CGI process model, ISAPI DLLs are loaded in the same address space as the HTTP server (see fig. 22.1).

FIG. 22.1
The ISAPI architecture employs dynamic linking to improve performance.

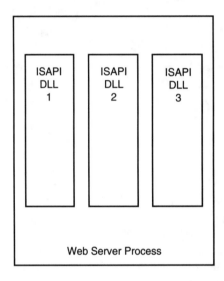

The DLLs can persist in memory, and the server knows that the DLLs are lying around waiting to service a request. Thus, there is virtually no overhead associated with servicing the next request. Of course, this higher performance comes at a cost. All ISAPI applications must be multithread safe. But before we immerse in the details of multithreaded and re-entrant code development (a subject beyond the scope of this book), let's take a look under the hood of ISAPI application development.

Required Server Entry Points

An ISAPI application is really just a Dynamic Link Library that conforms to a few simple rules. Every ISAPI application is required to provide two entry points:

- `GetExtensionVersion`
- `HttpExtensionProc`

When the Web server loads an ISAPI application for the first time, it calls the `GetExtensionVersion` function. Failure to make this function available will cause the ISAPI application to fail. A typical implementation of the `GetExtensionVersion` function (the one recommended by Microsoft) is shown in Listing 22.1.

Listing 22.1 Recommended Implementation of *GetExtensionVersion*

```
BOOL WINAPI GetExtensionVersion( HSE_VERSION_INFO  *pVer ) {
    pVer->dwExtensionVersion = MAKELONG( HSE_VERSION_MINOR, HSE_VERSION_MAJOR );

    lstrcpyn( pVer->lpszExtensionDesc,
              "This is a sample Web Server Application",
              HSE_MAX_EXT_DLL_NAME_LEN );

    return TRUE;

}
```

The GetExtensionVersion function is called by the Web server when it loads the ISAPI DLL. The purpose of this step is to permit the ISAPI application to identify the version of the ISAPI on which the application is based.

The server also depends upon a second entry point into your ISAPI application called the HttpExtensionProc. The HttpExtensionProc is basically the main function for your application. The prototype for the HttpExtensionProc function is shown in Listing 22.2.

Listing 22.2 *HttpExtensionProc* Function Prototype

```
DWORD  HttpExtensionProc( LPEXTENSION_CONTROL_BLOCK  *lpEcb );
```

The HttpExtensionProc is responsible for returning a status value. Possible return values are the following:

- HSE_STATUS_SUCCESS
- HSE_STATUS_SUCCESS_AND_KEEP_CONN
- HSE_STATUS_PENDING
- HSE_STATUS_ERROR

Notice that the HttpExtensionProc receives a long pointer to a structure called an EXTENSION_CONTROL_BLOCK. The EXTENSION_CONTROL_BLOCK is used to supply any context information or data relating to the Web browser request. You'll be exposed to this important structure in detail in just a moment. But first take a look at each of the various status values that HttpExtensionProc can return.

You'll report HSE_STATUS_SUCCESS when the ISAPI application has come to a happy conclusion. The server then shuts down the session with the client and frees up allocated resources.

Sometimes, you'll want to report success without causing the server to close the client connection. After sending an HTTP keep alive header, return HSE_STATUS_SUCCESS_AND_KEEP_CONN to request that the server keep the client connection open. In this case, the server may wait for the next HTTP request (assuming that the client supports persistent connections). Note that the server is not required to keep the session open.

Some ISAPI applications may need extended processing time so the HSE_STATUS_PENDING status is provided. This status is used in conjunction with the ServerSupportFunction function.

If the ISAPI DLL has encountered an error during processing, it returns HSE_STATUS_ERROR. When the server catches this status, it closes the client session free allocated resources.

Using Extension Control Blocks

Recall in the Common Gateway Interface that information about the client request is passed through a series of environment variables. These environment variables are set by the server based upon the request from the client when the application process is instantiated. ISAPI has a similar concept called the EXTENSION_CONTROL_BLOCK. As in the CGI, most of the information your ISAPI applications will need to get started are found in the EXTENSION_CONTROL_BLOCK. As you saw in Listing 22.2, HttpExtensionProc is passed a pointer to a filled out EXTENSION_CONTROL_BLOCK structure. The members of an EXTENSION_CONTROL_BLOCK structure are shown in Table 22.1.

Table 22.1   Members of the *EXTENSION_CONTROL_BLOCK* Structure

Name	Description
cbSize	Indicates the size of the current EXTENSION_CONTROL_BLOCK structure.
dwVersion	The HIWORD of this value holds the Major version number and the LOWORD stores the Minor version number.
ConnID	Uniquely identifies the connection. Used in calls to ServerSupportFunction.
dwHttpStatusCode	Set this value to indicate the status of the transaction when the request is completed.
lpszLogData	Indicates the string to enter into the log file.
lpszMethod	Contains an HTTP request method like GET or POST. Use this field just like the REQUEST_METHOD environment variable in the CGI.
lpszQueryString	This is the equivalent of the CGI variable QUERY_STRING.
lpszPathInfo	This is the equivalent to the CGI variable PATH_INFO.
lpszPathTranslated	This is the equivalent to the CGI variable PATH_TRANSLATED.
cbTotalBytes	Indicates the total number of bytes to be received from the client. Is the same as the CGI variable CONTENT_LENGTH.
cbAvailable	Indicates the available number of bytes (out of a total of cbTotalBytes) in the buffer pointed to by lpbData.
lpbData	Indicates the data sent by the client.
lpszContentType	Indicates the content type of the data sent by the client. Is the equivalent to the CGI variable CONTENT_TYPE.

Many of these items are simply passing along the information from the Common Gateway Interface. However, there are a couple of these that bear further discussion.

The `lpszLogData` member offers a capability not available to CGI applications directly. ISAPI applications are permitted to supply (or not supply) a text string for entry into the Web server's transaction log. CGI applications have always been free to keep private logs. However, the Extension Control Block approach in ISAPI permits simple integrated transaction logging.

The `cbTotalBytes` member indicates the total number of bytes to be received from the client. As mentioned in Table 22.1, this is equivalent to the CGI variable CONTENT_LENGTH. You'll use the `ReadClient` function in conjunction with the `cbAvailable` member to obtain the information passed by the Web browser through the `lpbData` member.

The `cbAvailable` variable shows the available number of bytes (out of a total of `cbTotalBytes`) in the buffer pointed to by `lpbData`. If `cbTotalBytes` is the same as `cbAvailable`, `lpbData` will point to all the data as sent by the client.

The `EXTENSION_CONTROL_BLOCK` has several member functions as well. These functions are briefly summarized in Table 22.2 and then discussed in detail as necessary.

Table 22.2   *EXTENSION_CONTROL_BLOCK* Member Functions

Name	Description
GetServerVariable	Used to retrieve server variables not passed as data members in the EXTENSION_CONTROL_BLOCK.
WriteClient	Sends information to the client.
ReadClient	Reads information from the client.
ServerSupportFunction	Used to execute certain server and HTTP specific transactions.

Using *GetServerVariable* The `GetServerVariable` function is handy for retrieving other information relating to the application's session with the Web browser that is not passed through the `EXTENSION_CONTROL_BLOCK`. All of these items originate in the CGI specification. Listing 22.3 shows the function prototype for the `GetServerVariable` function.

Listing 22.3   *GetServerVariable* Function Prototype

```
BOOL WINAPI GetServerVariable(HCONN hConn, LPSTR lpszVariableName,
LPVOID lpvBuffer, LPDWORD lpdwSize);
```

Using this function is fairly straightforward. You'll be passed the appropriate value for hConn in the lpECB parameter from HttpExtensionProc. You'll supply a buffer and its size which the server will pass back filled out with the appropriate data. The lpszVariableName can take on a number of values as shown in Table 22.3.

Table 22.3 Possible Values for *lpszVariableName*

Value	Description
ALL_HTTP	Use this value to obtain all of the variables that are not passed through an EXTENSION_CONTROL_BLOCK.
AUTH_PASS	Holds the password.
AUTH_TYPE	Contains the type of authentication used.
CONTENT_LENGTH	Indicates the size of the data in bytes received from the client.
CONTENT_TYPE	Indicates the content type of POST data sent from the client.
GATEWAY_INTERFACE	Indicates the version of the CGI spec that the server supports.
HTTP_ACCEPT	Indicates a special case HTTP header.
PATH_INFO	Indicates the part of the URL that appears following the domain name.
PATH_TRANSLATED	Stores the PATH_INFO with any virtual path name replaced with the fully qualified path.
QUERY_STRING	Contains the field value pairs supplied from a GET request.
REMOTE_ADDR	Indicates the IP address of the client.
REMOTE_HOST	Indicates the hostname of the client.
REMOTE_USER	Contains the user name supplied during authentication.
REQUEST_METHOD	Contains the HTTP request method. Usually, this is either GET or POST.
SCRIPT_NAME	Indicates the name of the application being executed.
SERVER_NAME	Indicates the host name or IP address of the server.
SERVER_PORT	Contains the TCP/IP port on which the request was received.
SERVER_PROTOCOL	Contains the protocol supported by the server.
SERVER_SOFTWARE	Indicates the name of the server software processing the application.

A call to GetServerVariable is really quite straightforward. Take a look at Listing 22.4.

Listing 22.4 Calling *GetServerVariable*

```
...
...
char szBuffer[BUFSIZE];
```

Listing 22.4 Calling *GetServerVariable*

```
if ( lpECB->GetServerVariable(lpECB->ConnID, AUTH_TYPE, (LPVOID) szBuffer,
BUFSIZE) )
{
    if ( strcmp(szBuffer, "NTLM") )
    {
        //Do something for NT security authenticated users only
    }
}
...
...
```

Using *ReadClient* ReadClient is used for POST operations. Rather than reading data from stdin as you would in a CGI application, you'll use the ReadClient function. The prototype for ReadClient is displayed in Listing 22.5.

Listing 22.5 *ReadClient* Function Prototype

```
BOOL WINAPI ReadClient( HCONN ConnID, LPVOID lpvBuffer, LPDWORD lpdwSize );
```

As with GetServerVariable, you'll have the appropriate value for hConn in the lpECB parameter from HttpExtensionProc. You'll supply a buffer and its size which the server will pass back filled out with the appropriate data.

Calling ReadClient is simple. Take a look at Listing 22.6.

Listing 22.6 Calling *ReadClient*

```
...
...
char szBuffer[BUFSIZE];
DWORD dwErrorCode;


if ( lpECB->ReadClient(lpECB->ConnID, (LPVOID) szBuffer, BUFSIZE) )
{
    //Process the data
}
else
{
    dwErrorCode = GetLastError();

    //Handle Error
    ...
}
...
...
```

Using *WriteClient*   WriteClient is used to send data to the client. Rather than writing your responses to stdout as you would in a CGI application, you'll use the WriteClient function. The prototype for WriteClient is displayed in Listing 22.7.

Listing 22.7   *WriteClient* Function Prototype

```
BOOL WINAPI WriteClient( HCONN ConnID, LPVOID Buffer, LPDWORD lpdwBytes,
DWORD dwReserved );
```

Calling WriteClient is simple. Take a look at Listing 22.8.

Listing 22.8   Calling *WriteClient*

```
...
DWORD dwSize;
char szBuffer[255];

wsprintf(szBuffer, "The ConnID is %u<BR>", lpECB->ConnID);
dwSize = strlen(szBuffer);

if ( lpECB->WriteClient(lpECB->ConnID, szBuffer, &dwSize, 0L) )
{
     //Do something on success
}
```

Using *ServerSupportFunction*

The ServerSupportFunction is used to send various HTTP headers to the Web browser. The prototype for the ServerSupportFunction is shown in Listing 22.9.

Listing 22.9   *ServerSupportFunction* Function Prototype

```
BOOL WINAPI ServerSupportFunction( HCONN hConn,
                          DWORD dwHSERRequest,
                          LPVOID lpvBuffer,
                          LPDWORD lpdwSize,
                          LPDWORD lpdwDataType );
```

You can use ServerSupportFunction to pass various constants to the server. These constants typically provide status and request action from the server (see Table 22.4).

Table 22.4 *dwHSERRequest* **Constants to Send Via** *ServerSupportFunction*

Constant	Meaning
HSE_REQ_SEND_URL_REDIRECT_RESP	Used to send Redirect (302) message to the client. Use lpvBuffer to points at the URL to which the client should be redirected.
HSE_REQ_SEND_URL	Sends a local URL (pointed to by lbvBuffer) to the client as if the client had requested that URL. The URL must be on this server.
HSE_REQ_SEND_RESPONSE_HEADER	Sends a complete HTTP server response header. Your ISAPI application must append other HTTP headers such as the Content-Type.
HSE_REQ_DONE_WITH_SESSION	ISAPI apps that require significant processing time may want to hold on to the connection. Use this constant to signal the server that the session can be closed.
HSE_REQ_END_RESERVED	Used to mark the end of space reserved for requests. Special server specific requests are above this number.
HSE_REQ_MAP_URL_TO_PATH	Used to map URLs to physical path on the server.

Take a look at the code snippet in Listing 22.10 for an example of using
ServerSupportFunction.

Listing 22.10   Using *ServerSupportFunction*

```
strcpy(szBuffer,"Content-Length: 1023");
lpECB->ServerSupportFunction ( pECB->ConnID,
                               HSE_REQ_SEND_RESPONSE_HEADER,
                               "200 OK",
                               NULL,
                               (LPDWORD) szBuffer);
//Send other headers and HTML
...
```

Building a Simple ISAPI Application

To demonstrate the use of some of the methods and data members of the EXTENSION_CONTROL_BLOCK, you'll build a simple ISAPI DLL to display the values stored in the EXTENSION_CONTROL_BLOCK. This example ISAPI application was compiled and constructed using Microsoft Visual C++ 4.1. This application is called GetECBNoMFC. The NoMFC part of the name is included because you'll repeat this exercise again using the ISAPI Wizard and Microsoft Foundation Classes. However, it is quite educational to try it without MFCs first so that you clearly understand what's going on under the covers. To build this simple ISAPI application, follow these steps:

1. Start Microsoft Visual C++ 4.1 (or higher) and begin a new project. Select File, New and choose Project Workspace. ISAPI applications are DLLs so choose Dynamic Link Library from the list of project types (see fig. 22.2). Now, press the Create button.

FIG. 22.2
Starting the ISAPI project.

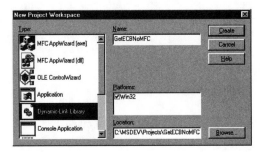

2. The first thing you'll need is definition (.def) file that indicates the functions that will be exported by this DLL. So create a GetECBNoMFC.def file and add exports for GetExtensionVersion and HttpExtensionProc. Your definition file should look like Listing 22.11.

On the CD

Listing 22.11   *GETECBNOMFC.DEF*   Definition File for the ISAPI Application

```
LIBRARY            "GETECBNOMFC"

EXPORTS
    HttpExtensionProc
    GetExtensionVersion
```

3. Go ahead and build a small header file for the application. You'll be constructing four functions: SendHTML, SendECB, GetExtensionVersion, and HttpExtensionProc. Your code should look like Listing 22.12.

On the CD

Listing 22.12 *GETECBNOMFC.H* Header File for the ISAPI Application

```
//
//      Function Prototypes
//
BOOL SendHTML(EXTENSION_CONTROL_BLOCK *pECB, LPSTR lpData);
BOOL SendECB(EXTENSION_CONTROL_BLOCK *pECB);
BOOL WINAPI GetExtensionVersion(HSE_VERSION_INFO *pVer);
DWORD WINAPI HttpExtensionProc(EXTENSION_CONTROL_BLOCK *pECB);
```

Note that GetExtensionVersion and HttpExtensionProc are required interfaces for the DLL.

4. Now start the GetECBNoMFC.cpp file. The first function you'll want to build is SendHTML. This function uses WriteClient to send strings of HTML back to the Web browser. Your code should look like Listing 22.13.

On the CD

Listing 22.13 *GETECBNOMFC.C* *SendHTML* Function

```
#include "windows.h"
#include "windowsx.h"
#include "httpext.h"
#include "GetECBNoMFC.h"


/*------------------------------------------
 *--   Used to Send HTML to the browser
 *----------------------------------------*/
BOOL SendHTML(EXTENSION_CONTROL_BLOCK *pECB, LPSTR lpData)
{
    DWORD       dwSize;

    dwSize = strlen(lpData);
    return pECB->WriteClient(pECB->ConnID, lpData, &dwSize, 0L);
}
```

Remember to include required header files. Note that many of the constants applicable to an ISAPI application are included in HttpExt.h. The call to WriteClient is really quite simple.

5. The next function to build is SendECB. SendECB employs the SendHTML function you just wrote to display the values of each of the data members of the EXTENSION_CONTROL_BLOCK referenced by pECB. Your code should look like Listing 22.14.

Listing 22.14 *2GETECBNOMFC.C* *SendECB* Function

```
/*------------------------------------------
 *--   Used to Send the ECB values
 *----------------------------------------*/
BOOL SendECB(EXTENSION_CONTROL_BLOCK *pECB)
{
```

continues

Listing 22.14   *Continued*

```
    char szBuffer[4096];

    wsprintf(szBuffer, "cbSize              ---GT %u<BR>", pECB->cbSize);
    SendHTML(pECB, szBuffer);

    wsprintf(szBuffer, "dwVersion           ---&GT %ul<BR>", pECB->dwVersion);
    SendHTML(pECB, szBuffer);

    wsprintf(szBuffer, "ConnID              ---&GT %u<BR>", pECB->ConnID);
    SendHTML(pECB, szBuffer);

    wsprintf(szBuffer, "lpszMethod   ---&GT %s<BR>", pECB->lpszMethod);
    SendHTML(pECB, szBuffer);

    wsprintf(szBuffer, "lpszQueryString   ---&GT %s<BR>", pECB-
>lpszQueryString);
    SendHTML(pECB, szBuffer);

    wsprintf(szBuffer, "lpszPathInfo      ---&GT %s<BR>", pECB->lpszPathInfo);
    SendHTML(pECB, szBuffer);

    wsprintf(szBuffer, "lpszPathTranslated ---&GT %s<BR>", pECB-
>lpszPathTranslated);
    SendHTML(pECB, szBuffer);

    wsprintf(szBuffer, "cbTotalBytes      ---&GT %u<BR>", pECB->cbTotalBytes);
    SendHTML(pECB, szBuffer);

    wsprintf(szBuffer, "cbAvailable       ---&GT %u<BR>", pECB->cbAvailable);
    SendHTML(pECB, szBuffer);

    if (pECB->lpbData == NULL)
    {
        SendHTML(pECB, "lpbData ---&GT (null)<BR>");
    }
    else
    {
        wsprintf(szBuffer, "lpbData             ---&GT %s<BR>", pECB->lpbData);
        SendHTML(pECB, szBuffer);
    }

    wsprintf(szBuffer, "lpszContentType   ---&GT %s<BR>", pECB-
>lpszContentType);
    SendHTML(pECB, szBuffer);

    return TRUE;

}
```

6. The `GetExtensionVersion` function is a required interface with a straightforward implementation. Your code should look like Listing 22.15.

On the CD

**Listing 22.15 *3GETECBNOMFC.C* Implementation of the
GetExtensionVersion Interface**

```c
/*---------------------------------------------
 *--    Required interface
 *-------------------------------------------*/
BOOL WINAPI GetExtensionVersion(HSE_VERSION_INFO *pVer)
{
    // Set the version number
    pVer->dwExtensionVersion = MAKELONG(1,0);

    // Set the description field
    strcpy(pVer->lpszExtensionDesc,"Get Extension Control Block");

    return TRUE;
}
```

Recall that the dwExtensionVersion member is a HIWORD/LOWORD style variable representing the major and minor version of ISAPI for which this application was written. A short, simple description is customary for the lpszExtensionDesc member.

7. The HttpExtensionProc function is the main for an ISAPI DLL. For this simple application, you'll print out the values of each of the relevant EXTENSION_CONTROL_BLOCK data members. Your code should look like Listing 22.16.

On the CD

**Listing 22.16 *4GETECBNOMFC.C* Implementation of the *HttpExtensionProc*
Interface**

```c
/*-----------------------------------------------
 *--    The Main of this ISAPI (required function)
 *---------------------------------------------*/
DWORD WINAPI HttpExtensionProc(EXTENSION_CONTROL_BLOCK *pECB)
{
    char    szBuffer[4096]; //Buffer size is arbitrary

    // Set the return code to success
    pECB->dwHttpStatusCode = HSE_STATUS_SUCCESS;

    // Send HTTP Headers
    strcpy(szBuffer,"Content-Type: text/html\r\n\r\n");
    pECB->ServerSupportFunction ( pECB->ConnID,
                                  HSE_REQ_SEND_RESPONSE_HEADER,
                                  "200 OK",
                                  NULL,
                                  (LPDWORD) szBuffer);

    // Send HTML Document
    SendHTML(pECB,"<HTML><HEAD>\n");
    SendHTML(pECB,"<HEAD><TITLE>Extension Control Block</TITLE>\n");
    SendHTML(pECB,"</HEAD><BODY>\n");
    SendHTML(pECB,"<H1>Extension Control Block</H1>\n");
```

continues

Listing 22.16 *Continued*

```
        SendECB(pECB);
        SendHTML(pECB,"</BODY></HTML>");


        return HSE_STATUS_SUCCESS;
}
```

You are required to append application-specific HTTP headers (such as the Content-Type directive followed by a pair of carriage returns and linefeeds) to an HSE_REQ_SEND_RESPONSE_HEADER. Next, you'll send out the HTML for your document and finally return an HSE_STATUS_SUCCESS to the caller.

Now you're ready to test the application. You'll need access to a Windows NT server running Microsoft's IIS or another ISAPI-compatible Web server. Follow these steps to test your ISAPI application:

1. Place the compiled version of your ISAPI DLL in the appropriate "scripts" directory on the Web server.

2. You can make a simple form to execute the DLL as a GET from a form. You'll find a simple form on the enclosed CD for this purpose, but you can use any form you choose. The example form on the disk looks like figure 22.3.

FIG. 22.3
Use a form like this to execute GetECBNoMFC.

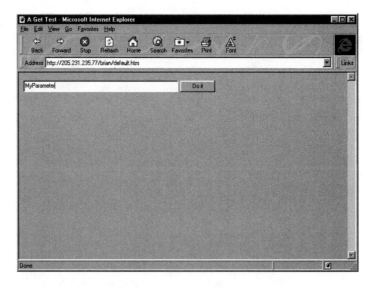

3. Enter some information into the form and then press the Submit button. When executed as the action of a simple form, the output should look like figure 22.4.

FIG. 22.4

Execute
`GetECBNoMFC.dll` as
a GET from a form.

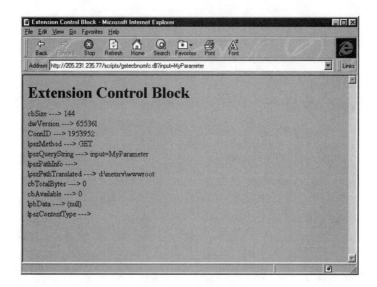

4. You can use `GetECBNoMFC.dll` with a POST form as well. When executed as the action of a simple form using POST, the output should look like figure 22.5.

FIG. 22.5

Execute
`GetECBNoMFC.dll` as
a POST from a form.

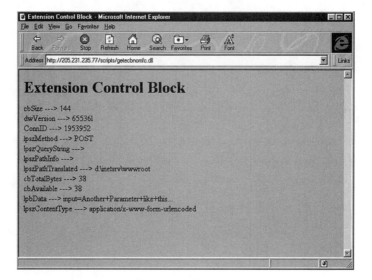

CHAPTER 23

Using ISAPI MFCs and the ISAPI Extension Wizard

In the last chapter, you learned the nitty gritty of an ISAPI application. Of course, if you're planning to build lots of ISAPI applications, you'll want to check out the Microsoft Foundation Classes for constructing ISAPI applications. These MFCs make building ISAPI applications easier. In this chapter, we'll turn to the business of using MFCs to create ISAPI applications. First, you'll be introduced to the relevant classes and methods. Then you'll use what you've learned in a step-by-step example. ■

Learn the MFCs required to build an ISAPI application

Building ISAPI extensions is made easier by use of the ISAPI MFCs in Visual C++ 4.1 or higher. You'll learn the details of these important objects.

Use PARSE_MAPS

PARSE_MAPS make mapping actions to functions in your ISAPI application easy. You'll use PARSE_MAPS extensively when building ISAPI applications using Microsoft Foundation Classes.

Use the ISAPI Extension Wizard

Beginning with MS-Visual C++ 4.1, Microsoft includes a wizard for developing ISAPI DLLs. This chapter will expose you to using this tool.

Build a simple ISAPI application using MFCs

Using the Microsoft Foundation Classes and the ISAPI Extension Wizard, you'll recreate the application from the previous chapter. Recall that this application demonstrates the use of all the various data members of the EXTENSION_CONTROL_BLOCK..

The ISAPI Classes

The ISAPI specification is implemented in Microsoft Foundation Classes as five distinct classes as shown in Table 23.1. These classes provide the basis for any application. For example, you'll use these classes to obtain information about the request information received from the Web browser.

Table 23.1   ISAPI MFCs

Class	Description
CHttpServer	This object manages the application's interaction with the server through the EXTENSION_CONTROL_BLOCK.
CHttpServerContext	CHttpServer creates CHttpServerContext objects to respond to requests. A CHttpServer can have many CHttpServerContext objects.
CHtmlStream	This class is used to manage HTML data prior to transmission to the client.
CHttpFilter	This is the managing class for an ISAPI filter (this class will be the subject of discussion in the next chapter on ISAPI filters).
CHttpFilterContext	CHttpFilter creates CHttpFilterContext objects for handling requests. More on this in the next chapter on ISAPI filters.

In this section, you'll learn the details about CHttpServer, CHttpServerContext, and CHtmlStreams. The CHttpFilter and CHttpFilterContext classes will be covered in detail in the next chapter.

Using the *CHttpServer* Class

The CHttpServer class offers a number of methods as shown in Table 23.2. Most of the time, you'll use the default implementation for these functions.

Table 23.2   Key Methods for the *CHttpServer* Class

Method	Description
CallFunction	Executes the function indicated by the URL.
OnParseError	Constructs a description of the error to be returned to the client.
HttpExtensionProc	This is the main function for your application.
GetExtensionVersion	Gets the version number that the DLL extension is based on.
ConstructStream	Constructs a CHtmlStream object.

However, there is one exception. This exception is the `GetExtensionVersion` function. In most of your ISAPI applications, you'll want to override the `GetExtensionVersion` method. (Recall that in the ISAPI architecture the `GetExtensionVersion` is one of two required entry points for a native ISAPI application. As pointed out earlier, `GetExtensionVersion` is called by the server framework when the ISAPI application is loaded.)

Since the MFCs supply a default implementation in the `CHttpServer` class, you aren't required to override this function. However, your applications will typically call the default implementation in order to set the DLL version number. Usually, your implementation will supply a default text string with your own short description of the ISAPI application. See Listing 23.1 for an example of this technique.

Listing 23.1 Overriding the *GetExtensionVersion* Method

```
BOOL CGetECBExtension::GetExtensionVersion(HSE_VERSION_INFO* pVer)
{
     // Call default implementation for initialization
     CHttpServer::GetExtensionVersion(pVer);

     // Load description string
     TCHAR sz[HSE_MAX_EXT_DLL_NAME_LEN+1];
     ISAPIVERIFY(::LoadString(AfxGetResourceHandle(),
              IDS_SERVER, sz, HSE_MAX_EXT_DLL_NAME_LEN));
     _tcscpy(pVer->lpszExtensionDesc, sz);
     return TRUE;
}
```

In fact, this is the default implementation generated by the ISAPI Wizard. Obviously, you could fill out the `HSE_VERSION_INFO` structure using any string you choose rather than reading it from the string table as done here. Note also that the `HSE_VERSION_INFO` is a simple structure that contains two members—the `DWORD` value `dwExtensionVersion`, and the character string `lpszExtensionDescription`.

There are a number of additional methods you'll find useful in building your ISAPI applications. A list of these methods is shown in Table 23.3. You'll probably use `StartContent`, `EndContent`, and `WriteTitle` in every ISAPI application you ever build with the ISAPI MFC framework.

Table 23.3 Other *CHttpServer* Methods

Method	Description
StartContent	Writes the initial HTML tags required to be returned to the client.
EndContent	Writes the HTML tags required to mark the end of a document.
WriteTitle	Sends the <TITLE> tag pair wrapped around the supplied string.
GetTitle	Returns a pointer to the document's title.

continues

Table 23.3   Continued

Method	Description
AddHeader	Adds headers to the top of a response to the server.
InitInstance	Initializes the CHttpServer object.

Take a look at Listing 23.2. For the moment, don't worry about the CHttpServerContext object used in this example. Just assume it refers to the place where HTML content is written for return to the Web browser.

Listing 23.2   Using *StartContent*, *WriteTitle*, and *EndContent*

```
void CMyExtension::Default(CHttpServerContext* pCtxt)
{

    StartContent(pCtxt);
    WriteTitle(pCtxt);
    ...
    ...
    // Place your own HTML and processing here
    ...
    ...

    EndContent(pCtxt);
}
```

As you can see, the StartContent and WriteTitle functions initiate the HTML document. EndContent is executed after the body of the HTML document has been written out. In the middle, you would add the body of the HTML document.

Using the *CHttpServerExtension* Class

The CHttpServer class creates CHttpServerExtension objects to service the individual requests coming from Web browsers over the Internet. The CHttpServerExtension class provides members that contain all the information needed to execute your ISAPI application in terms of server context information. As shown in Table 23.4, CHttpServerExtension class provides a wealth of information and functionality.

Table 23.4   Data Members

Method	Description
m_pECB	Points to the EXTENSION_CONTROL_BLOCK to be used in processing.
m_pStream	Points to the CHtmlStream that will manage the output from your ISAPI application.

In the ISAPI architecture, the EXTENSION_CONTROL_BLOCK is the primary data structure serving as an interface between your ISAPI application and the Web browser. The m_pECB member of the CHttpServerExtension provides a pointer to this information in your applications.

The CHttpServerExtension class offers a number of methods as shown in Table 23.5. Most of the time, you'll use the default implementation for all of these functions.

Table 23.5   Key Methods for the *CHttpServerExtension* Class

Method	Description
GetServerVariable	Used to retrieve server variables not passed as data members in the EXTENSION_CONTROL_BLOCK.
WriteClient	Sends information to the client.
ReadClient	Reads information from the client.
ServerSupportFunction	Used to execute certain server and HTTP specific transactions.

These functions should seem very familiar. The basic ISAPI spec includes these functions to provide the means for communicating between the client and server. Rather than go over each of these in detail again, take a look at the main difference between the MFC version of these methods and the native functions discussed in Chapter 22, "Internet Server Application Program Interface (ISAPI)" (see Listing 23.3).

Listing 23.3   Comparing Function Prototypes

```
//
//      Review of the ISAPI definition of these functions
//
BOOL WINAPI GetServerVariable(HCONN hConn, LPSTR lpszVariableName,
LPVOID lpvBuffer, LPDWORD lpdwSize);
BOOL WINAPI ReadClient( HCONN ConnID, LPVOID lpvBuffer, LPDWORD lpdwSize );
BOOL WINAPI WriteClient( HCONN ConnID, LPVOID Buffer, LPDWORD lpdwBytes,
DWORD dwReserved );
BOOL WINAPI ServerSupportFunction( HCONN hConn,
                        DWORD dwHSERRequest,
                        LPVOID lpvBuffer,
                        LPDWORD lpdwSize,
                            LPDWORD lpdwDataType );

//
//      MFC implementation in CHttpServerExtension
//

BOOL GetServerVariable( LPTSTR lpszVariableName, LPVOID lpvBuffer, LPDWORD
lpdwSize );
BOOL ReadClient( LPVOID lpvBuffer, LPDWORD lpdwSize );
```

continues

Listing 23.3   Continued

```
BOOL WriteClient( LPVOID Buffer, LPDWORD lpdwBytes, DWORD dwReserved );
BOOL ServerSupportFunction(     DWORD dwHSERRequest,
                            LPVOID lpvBuffer,
                       LPDWORD lpdwSize,
                       LPDWORD lpdwDataType );
```

Note that the MFC versions do not require an HCONN variable; the framework takes care of it for you.

The MFCs framework also provides a << operator for writing HTML data to the CHttpServerContext. You'll be using this operator all the time, so let's take a moment and discuss how to use it. Listing 23.4 shows how to output a simple HTML string using the << operator.

Listing 23.4   Using the << Operator

```
void CMyExtension::Default(CHttpServerContext* pCtxt)
{

    StartContent(pCtxt);
    WriteTitle(pCtxt);
    ...
    ...
    *pCtxt << "<H3>Using the &LT&LT operator is easy</H1><BR>"
    ...
    ...

    EndContent(pCtxt);
}
```

Using Parse Maps

The Microsoft Foundation Classes implementation of ISAPI includes the concept of a *parse map*. Parse maps permit you to map the requests coming from the Web browser to specific methods in your CHttpServer object. A parse map consists of up to five different elements (actually macros). These elements are shown in Table 23.6 and described briefly.

Table 23.6   Elements of a Parse Map

Element	Description
BEGIN_PARSE_MAP	Defines the beginning of a parse map.
ON_PARSE_COMMAND	Sets up a client side command to be processed.
ON_PARSE_COMMAND_PARAMS	Must follow an ON_PARSE_COMMAND and identifies the parameters for the the command identified by the ON_PARSE_COMMAND.

Element	Description
`DEFAULT_PARSE_COMMAND`	Sets the default command to be used when no command is specified.
`END_PARSE_MAP`	Ends the definition of a parse map.

Take a look at the simple parse map shown in Listing 23.5.

Listing 23.5 A Simple Parse Map

```
BEGIN_PARSE_MAP(CMyExtension, CHttpServer)

    ON_PARSE_COMMAND(MyCmd, CMyExtension, ITS_PSTR)
    ON_PARSE_COMMAND_PARAMS("input=~")
    DEFAULT_PARSE_COMMAND(MyCmd, CMyExtension)

END_PARSE_MAP(CMyExtension)
...
...
void CMyExtension::MyCmd(CHttpServerContext* pCtxt, LPTSTR sz);
...
...
```

The call to `BEGIN_PARSE_MAP` requires two parameters. The first parameter identifies the class that owns this parse map. So if you're building `CMyExtension` which descends from `CHttpServer`, `CMyExtension` would own the parse map. The second parameter must identify the base class of the first parameter. In this example, that would be `CHttpServer`. Note that the second parameter must be `CHttpServer` or descended from `CHttpServer`.

The next call is to `ON_PARSE_COMMAND`. `ON_PARSE_COMMAND` requires three parameters. The first parameter identifies the name of the command to be received from the Web client. This name must also be the name of the method that will be called via the parse map. In this case, the method to execute will be `MyCmd`. The second parameter requires the name of the class that contains `MyCmd`. The third parameter is a constant identifying the data type of the parameter list for the method named in the first argument to `ON_PARSE_COMMAND`. In Listing 23.5, the function `MyCmd` requires one parameter of type `PSTR`. You may have multiple parameters by simply appending them as shown in Listing 23.6.

Listing 23.6 Another Simple Parse Map

```
BEGIN_PARSE_MAP(CMyExtension, CHttpServer)

    ON_PARSE_COMMAND(MyCmd, CMyExtension, ITS_PSTR ITS_I2)
    ON_PARSE_COMMAND_PARAMS(lpszAnInput, iAnotherInput )
    DEFAULT_PARSE_COMMAND(MyCmd, CMyExtension)

END_PARSE_MAP(CMyExtension)
```

continues

Listing 23.6 Continued

```
...
...
void CMyExtension::MyCmd(CHttpServerContext* pCtxt, LPTSTR lpszAnInput,
int iAnotherInput);
...
...
```

Note that the order of the variables is important. The `ON_PARSE_COMMAND` indicates that the first parameter after the `CHttpServerContext` pointer will be a `PSTR` of some sort. The second parameter is an integer. In both the `ON_PARSE_COMMAND_PARAMS` and in the implementation of the method itself, the parameters must appear in the same order.

Using the ISAPI Wizard

By adding the ISAPI Wizard to Visual C++, Microsoft has made your life easier. Using the ISAPI Wizard, the basic template of an ISAPI application is generated for you. In this section, you'll step through the use of the ISAPI Wizard. You'll also use the ISAPI Wizard to rebuild the Extension Control Block example that you built without the ISAPI MFCs. This example ISAPI application was compiled and constructed using Microsoft Visual C++ 4.1. This application is called `GetECB`. Recall from Chapter 22, "Internet Server Application Program Interface (ISAPI)," that you built `GetECBNoMFC`. To build this simple ISAPI application, follow these steps:

1. Start Microsoft Visual C++ 4.1 (or higher) and begin a new project. Select File, New and select Project Workspace from the list of new file types. Select ISAPI Extension Wizard from the list of project types in the New Project Workspace dialog box (see fig. 23.1). Now press the <u>C</u>reate button.

FIG. 23.1

Start the ISAPI project from this dialog box.

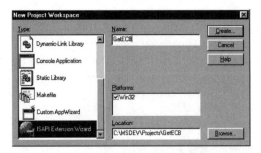

2. The ISAPI Wizard will next prompt you with the screen shown in figure 23.2. Select Generate a Server <u>E</u>xtension object. By default, the extension's class name and description will be set to the same name as the project file. You can also choose to have the MFCs statically linked or available as a shared DLL. In most cases, you'll want to accept the default choice of shared DLL.

FIG. 23.2

The ISAPI Wizard dialog box should be filled out as shown.

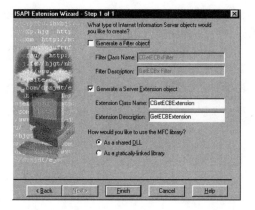

3. The ISAPI Wizard is then kind enough to generate the following files for you: GetECB.cpp, GetECB.def, GetECB.rc, and GetECB.h. Leave the .def and the .rc files for last. The first place to start is the parse map. Since this is a simple application that will just report the values in the Extension Control Block, we'll treat whatever comes in as a command parameter as a string. The parse map is declared in the GetECB.h file (which we'll address in a moment), but the body of the parse map is placed by the ISAPI Wizard at the top of the GetECB.cpp file. Listing 23.7 shows the code generated by the ISAPI Wizard.

On the CD

Listing 23.7 *GETECB.CPP* Body of the Parse Map Before Alteration

```
// GETECB.CPP - Implementation file for your Internet Server
//     GetECBxExtension

#include <afx.h>
#include <afxwin.h>
#include <afxisapi.h>
#include "resource.h"
#include "GetECB.h"

/////////////////////////////////////////////////////////////////////////
// command-parsing map

BEGIN_PARSE_MAP(CGetECBExtension, CHttpServer)
    // TODO: insert your ON_PARSE_COMMAND() and
    // ON_PARSE_COMMAND_PARAMS() here to hook up your commands.
    // For example:

    ON_PARSE_COMMAND(Default, CGetECBExtension, ITS_EMPTY)
    DEFAULT_PARSE_COMMAND(Default, CGetECBExtension)
END_PARSE_MAP(CGetECBExtension)
```

Notice that the ISAPI wizard generates the Default command in the parse map for you. Remember that the parameter list in the ON_PARSE_COMMAND is required. That's the reason for the ITS_EMPTY. Even when no parameters are expected, you must declare that the parameter list will be empty. For the GetECB application, we want to show a command line parameter if it exists. So we'll alter the generated parse map to treat anything in the command part of the URL as a string. Your code should look something like Listing 23.8.

On the CD

Listing 23.8 *2GETECB.CPP* The Altered Parse Map

```
// GETECB.CPP - Implementation file for your Internet Server
//    GetECB Extension

#include <afx.h>
#include <afxwin.h>
#include <afxisapi.h>
#include "resource.h"
#include "GetECB.h"

///////////////////////////////////////////////////////////////////
// command-parsing map

BEGIN_PARSE_MAP(CGetECBExtension, CHttpServer)
    // TODO: insert your ON_PARSE_COMMAND() and
    // ON_PARSE_COMMAND_PARAMS() here to hook up your commands.
    // For example:

    ON_PARSE_COMMAND(Default, CGetECBExtension, ITS_PSTR)
    ON_PARSE_COMMAND_PARAMS("input=~")
    DEFAULT_PARSE_COMMAND(Default, CGetECBExtension)

END_PARSE_MAP(CGetECBExtension)
```

4. Next switch to the GetECB.h file. This is the file where you'll add method prototypes for your ISAPI application. Listing 23.9 shows the code as generated by the ISAPI wizard.

On the CD

Listing 23.9 *GETECB.H* The *GetECB.h* File Before Alteration

```
// GETECB.CPP - Implementation file for your Internet Server
//    GetECBExtension

class CGetECBExtension : public CHttpServer
{
public:
    CGetECBExtension();
    ~CGetECBExtension();

    BOOL GetExtensionVersion(HSE_VERSION_INFO* pVer);

    // TODO: Add handlers for your commands here.
    // For example:

    void Default(CHttpServerContext* pCtxt);

    DECLARE_PARSE_MAP()
};
```

The only customization you'll need to do is to add the LPTSTR parameter to the Default function. Default's prototype should look like Listing 23.10.

Listing 23.10 *3GETECB.CPP* The *Default* Method Protoype

```
void Default(CHttpServerContext* pCtxt, LPTSTR sz);
```

Part
III

Ch
23

5. There's really no reason to modify the GetExtensionVersion function generated by the ISAPI Wizard. You may, however, want to change the description text. To change this text, you'll need to select the GetECB.rc file. When you open the string table for GetECB.rc, you'll see a single entry for the IDS_SERVER constant. You can make this text any short description you choose.

6. The next thing to work on is the Default method. You'll be doing major overhaul on this sucker, so hold on to your hat. The ISAPI wizard generates the default listing shown in Listing 23.11.

Listing 23.11 *4GETECB.CPP* The *Default* Function Before Alteration

```
/////////////////////////////////////////////////////////////////////
// CGetECBExtension command handlers

void CGetECBExtension::Default(CHttpServerContext* pCtxt)
{
    StartContent(pCtxt);
    WriteTitle(pCtxt);

    *pCtxt << _T("This default message was produced by the Internet");
    *pCtxt << _T(" Server DLL Wizard. Edit your CGetECBExtension::Default()");
    *pCtxt << _T(" implementation to change it.\r\n");

    EndContent(pCtxt);
}
```

The generated code is thoughtful enough to use generic text macros like _T. Rather than get into an explanation of why you should or shouldn't worry about using generic text routines, the altered Default method ignores these issues. This is so you can focus on the ISAPI issues. Listing 23.12 shows the process of reporting each of the items available in the Extension Control Block.

Listing 23.12 *5GETECB.CPP* The Altered *Default* Method

```
/////////////////////////////////////////////////////////////////////
// CGetECBExtension command handlers

void CGetECBExtension::Default(CHttpServerContext* pCtxt, LPTSTR sz)
{
```

continues

Listing 23.12   Continued

```
    StartContent(pCtxt);
    WriteTitle(pCtxt);
    *pCtxt << "<H1>EXTENSION_CONTROL_BLOCK</H1>\n";

/*---------------------------------------------
 *    Show all the members of an ECB structure
 *
     DWORD      cbSize;
     DWORD      dwVersion
     HCONN      ConnID;
     LPSTR      lpszMethod;
     LPSTR      lpszQueryString;
     LPSTR      lpszPathInfo;
     LPSTR      lpszPathTranslated;
     DWORD      cbTotalBytes;
     DWORD      cbAvailable;
     LPBYTE     lpbData;
     LPSTR      lpszContentType;
 *
 *
 *---------------------------------------------*/

    wsprintf(sz, "cbSize              ---&GT %ul<BR>", pCtxt->m_pECB->cbSize);
    *pCtxt << sz;
    wsprintf(sz, "dwVersion            ---&GT %ul<BR>", pCtxt->m_pECB-
>dwVersion);
    *pCtxt << sz;
    wsprintf(sz, "ConnID               ---&GT %ul<BR>", pCtxt->m_pECB->ConnID);
    *pCtxt << sz;
    wsprintf(sz, "lpszMethod          ---&GT %s<BR>", pCtxt->m_pECB-
>lpszMethod);
    *pCtxt << sz;
    wsprintf(sz, "lpszQueryString     ---&GT %s<BR>", pCtxt->m_pECB-
>lpszQueryString);
    *pCtxt << sz;
    wsprintf(sz, "lpszPathInfo        ---&GT %s<BR>", pCtxt->m_pECB-
>lpszPathInfo);
    *pCtxt << sz;
    wsprintf(sz, "lpszPathTranslated ---&GT %s<BR>", pCtxt->m_pECB-
>lpszPathTranslated);
    *pCtxt << sz;
    wsprintf(sz, "cbTotalBytes        ---&GT %ul<BR>", pCtxt->m_pECB-
>cbTotalBytes);
    *pCtxt << sz;
    wsprintf(sz, "cbAvailable         ---&GT %ul<BR>", pCtxt->m_pECB-
>cbAvailable);
    *pCtxt << sz;
    if (pCtxt->m_pECB->lpbData == NULL)
    {
         *pCtxt << "lpbData ---&GT (null)<BR>";
    }
    else
    {
```

```
        wsprintf(sz, "lpbData                ---&GT %s<BR>", pCtxt->m_pECB-
    >lpbData);
        *pCtxt << sz;
    }
    wsprintf(sz, "lpszContentType    ---&GT %s<BR>", pCtxt->m_pECB-
    >lpszContentType);
        *pCtxt << sz;


    EndContent(pCtxt);
}
```

Notice that `Default` checks to see if `lpbData` is null before using it. This is because the ISAPI MFCs do not allocate memory for this item unless there is data from the client to pass.

Now you're ready to test the application. You'll need access to a Windows NT server running Microsoft's IIS or another ISAPI compatible Web server. Follow these steps to test your ISAPI application:

1. Place the compiled version of your ISAPI DLL in the appropriate "scripts" directory on the Web server. (Make sure to compile your script for release and not debug.)

2. Run the `GetECB.dll` by typing the URL into MSIE 3.0. If the DLL exists on a Web server at `foo.com`, the URL would be **http://foo.com/scripts/GetECB.dll**. The results of this execution should look something like figure 23.3.

FIG. 23.3
Execute `GetECB.dll` as a GET form.

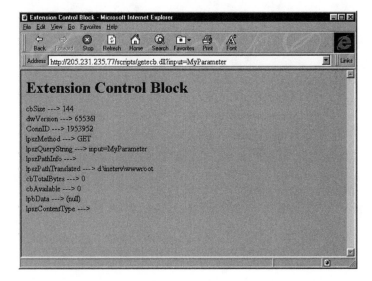

CHAPTER 24

Building ISAPI Filters

I SAPI applications enable you to add functionality to your Web site. Performing database lookups, building HTML files on-the-fly, and the like are important aspects of providing a dynamic and interesting Web site. Obviously, the ISAPI applications we've discussed support this mission quite well. But the ISAPI applications you've worked with so far don't really have any effect on how the Web server responds to client requests. To modify the behavior of the Web server itself, the ISAPI spec provides for an ISAPI filter. ▪

Understand the use of ISAPI filters

ISAPI filters allow you to modify the behavior of your Web server in a number of ways.

Learn the MFCs required to build an ISAPI filter

Building ISAPI filters with the ISAPI Extension Wizard and MFCs allows you to add high-end functionality to your Web server. You'll learn the details of these important objects.

Use the ISAPI Extension Wizard

Beginning with MS-Visual C++ 4.1, Microsoft includes a wizard for developing ISAPI filters. This chapter will expose you to using this tool.

Build a simple ISAPI filter using MFCs

Using the Microsoft Foundation Classes and the ISAPI Extension Wizard, you'll build your own ISAPI filter to add custom authentication procedures to your Web server.

ISAPI Filter Architecture

An ISAPI filter is a customized dynamic link library that the Web server calls on every HTTP request. The filter is responsible for telling the server the kinds of server activities it wants to handle. Once the server loads the filter, the server will give the ISAPI filter an opportunity to process each request at the various points in the process the filter has asked to handle. ISAPI filters can be implemented for any of the following server functions:

- **Pre-processing HTTP headers**—Your filters can alter the way that the server processes the HTTP headers in a client request.

- **Authentication request**—Supply your own custom authentication scheme using an ISAPI filter.

- **Logical to physical URL mapping**—A filter can be used to modify the way that the server maps logical paths to physical disk for an URL.

- **Sending data**—Writing the raw response data back to the client can be accomplished using ISAPI filters.

- **Constructing and entering information in the log**—Use filters to replace the server's standard logging in order to do customized logging.

- **Closing the HTTP connection**—Your ISAPI filters can also do any clean-up or other end-of-session activities.

In fact, you can supply filters for any number of the various server functions for which filters can be implemented. Filters are notified to handle a request irrespective of the type of document the client requests. For instance, the client could have asked for a static page, the execution of a CGI, or even an ISAPI application.

The ISAPI Filter Classes

The ISAPI specification is implemented in Microsoft Foundation Classes as two distinct classes as shown in Table 24.1.

Table 24.1   ISAPI Filter MFCs

Class	Description
CHttpFilter	Each instance of CHttpFilterContext is managed by the CHttpFilter.
CHttpFilterContext	CHttpFilter creates CHttpFilterContext objects for handling requests.

In this section, you'll learn the details about the CHttpFilter and CHttpFilterContext classes.

Using the *CHttpFilter* Class

The CHttpFilter class offers a number of methods as shown in Table 24.2. Most of the time, you'll select one or two of these to be the focus of your ISAPI filter and rely on the default implementations for the rest.

Table 24.2 Key Methods

Method	Description
GetFilterVersion	Gets the version of the filter
OnReadRawData	Called so that a filter can inspect incoming data and headers
OnPreprocHeaders	Used to react to preprocessed headers
OnAuthentication	Called so that filters can authenticate the client
OnUrlMap	Permits the filter to map the logical URL to the physical URL
OnSendRawData	Called so that a filter can write outgoing data and headers
OnLog	Used so that filters can write to the server log
OnEndOfNetSession	Used by filters to clean up before the connect session is closed
HttpFilterProc	The main function of an ISAPI filter application

Working with *GetFilterVersion* Much like the GetExtensionVersion function in an ISAPI application, the GetFilterVersion is used to obtain the version number of the ISAPI filter. Take a look at the default GetFilterVersion generated by the ISAPI filter wizard as shown in Listing 24.1. The first step is to call the default implementation carried down from CHttpFilter. This default implementation sets dwFlags equal to SF_NOTIFY_ORDER_DEFAULT, dwFilterVersion equal to HTTP_FILTER_REVISION, and lpszFilterDesc equal to an empty, null terminated string.

Listing 24.1 The Default *GetFilterVersion* Method

```
BOOL CMyFilter::GetFilterVersion(PHTTP_FILTER_VERSION pVer)
{
    // Call default implementation for initialization
    CHttpFilter::GetFilterVersion(pVer);

    // Clear the flags set by base class
    pVer->dwFlags &= ~SF_NOTIFY_ORDER_MASK;

    // Set the flags we are interested in
    pVer->dwFlags |= SF_NOTIFY_ORDER_LOW | SF_NOTIFY_SECURE_PORT |
```

continues

Part
III

Ch
24

Listing 24.1 Continued

```
SF_NOTIFY_NONSECURE_PORT
                    | SF_NOTIFY_AUTHENTICATION | SF_NOTIFY_END_OF_NET_SESSION;

    // Load description string
    TCHAR sz[SF_MAX_FILTER_DESC_LEN+1];
    ISAPIVERIFY(::LoadString(AfxGetResourceHandle(),
                IDS_FILTER, sz, SF_MAX_FILTER_DESC_LEN));
    _tcscpy(pVer->lpszFilterDesc, sz);
    return TRUE;
}
```

This function takes a pointer to an HTTP_FILTER_VERSION structure called pVer. The HTTP_FILTER_VERSION structure contains a number of data members. The declaration for HTTP_FILTER_VERSION is shown in Listing 24.2.

On the CD

Listing 24.2 *HTTPFILT.H* Declaration of *HTTP_FILTER_VERSION*

```
typedef struct _HTTP_FILTER_VERSION

{
    DWORD   dwServerFilterVersion;
    DWORD   dwFilterVersion;
    CHAR    lpszFilterDesc[SF_MAX_FILTER_DESC_LEN+1];
    DWORD   dwFlags;

} HTTP_FILTER_VERSION, *PHTTP_FILTER_VERSION;
```

The dwServerFilterVersion member is set by the Web server. When the GetFilterVersion method is called by the server, dwServerFilterVersion is passed with a valid value. The version number refers to the version of the header file used to create the filter, more specifically, the value of HTTP_FILTER_VERSION.

The most important element in this structure, however, is the dwFlags member. The dwFlags property is used to set the types of events the filter wants to be notified about as well as the priority at which the filter should be run. The various values that can be specified in this field are listed in Table 24.3.

Table 24.3 Possible Settings for *dwFlags*

Name	Description
SF_NOTIFY_ORDER_DEFAULT	This is the priority you'll use unless you have a good reason to change it.
SF_NOTIFY_ORDER_LOW	Loads the filter at low priority.
SF_NOTIFY_ORDER_MEDIUM	Loads the filter at medium priority.
SF_NOTIFY_ORDER_HIGH	Loads the filter at high priority.

Name	Description
SF_NOTIFY_SECURE_PORT	Notifies the application that it is passing data through a secure port.
SF_NOTIFY_NONSECURE_PORT	Notifies the application that it is passing data through a nonsecure port.
SF_NOTIFY_READ_RAW_DATA	Allows the application to see the raw data. The data returned to the client will contain both headers and data.
SF_NOTIFY_PREPROC_HEADERS	The server has pre-processed the headers.
SF_NOTIFY_AUTHENTICATION	The server is authenticating the client.
SF_NOTIFY_URL_MAP	The server is mapping a logical URL to a physical path.
SF_NOTIFY_SEND_RAW_DATA	The server is sending raw data back to the client.
SF_NOTIFY_LOG	The server is writing information to the server log.
SF_NOTIFY_END_OF_NET_SESSION	The session with the client is ending.

Part
III

Ch
24

Notice that these fields must be constructed using a bit wise OR (in C++, this is accomplished using the vertical bar (|) as shown in Listing 24.1).

Working with *OnReadRawData* If you need to get at the HTTP requests being received from the Web browser before they are processed by the Web server, you'll need to override this virtual function. You'll need to make sure that dwFlags is set to SF_NOTIFY_READ_RAW_DATA. The default version of this function does nothing, so there is no point in calling it first in your own implementation. The function prototype for OnReadRawData is shown in Listing 24.3.

On the CD

Listing 24.3   *2HTTPFILT.H*   *OnReadRawData* Function Prototype

```
DWORD CMyHttpFilter::OnReadRawData(CHttpFilterContext* pCtxt,
PHTTP_FILTER_RAW_DATA pRawData)
```

We'll talk about CHttpFilterContext objects in a moment. However, the HTTP_FILTER_RAW_DATA structure deserves a bit of examination (see Listing 24.4).

On the CD

Listing 24.4   *3HTTPFILT.H*   *HTTP_FILTER_RAW_DATA* Declaration

```
//
//   This structure is the notification info for the read and send raw data
//   notification types
//

typedef struct _HTTP_FILTER_RAW_DATA
```

continues

Listing 24.4 *Continued*

```
{

    PVOID          pvInData;
    DWORD          cbInData;        // Number of valid data bytes
     DWORD          cbInBuffer;      // Total size of buffer

    DWORD          dwReserved;

} HTTP_FILTER_RAW_DATA, *PHTTP_FILTER_RAW_DATA; //
```

The pvInData member holds a pointer to a block of data that represents the in-bound HTTP request from the Web client. The cbInData field stores the number of valid data bytes in the buffer block pointed to by pvInData. The cbInBuffer field stores the total size of the buffer.

Working with *OnPreProcessHeaders* If you need to process the HTTP headers being received from the client browser, rather than leaving them to be processed by the Web server, you'll need to override this virtual function. To make this happen, you set dwFlags to SF_NOTIFY_PREPROC_HEADERS. Of course, the default version of this function does nothing, so there is no point in calling it first in your own implementation. The function prototype for OnPreProcessHeaders is shown in Listing 24.5.

Listing 24.5 *4HTTPFILT.H OnPreprocHeaders* Function Prototype

```
virtual DWORD OnPreprocHeaders( CHttpFilterContext* pfc,
PHTTP_FILTER_PREPROC_HEADERS pHeaders );
```

Ignore the CHttpFilterContext objects for the moment. Instead, focus on the HTTP_FILTER_PREPROC_HEADERS structure (see Listing 24.6).

Listing 24.6 *5HTTPFILT.H HTTP_FILTER_PREPROC_HEADERS* Declaration

```
//
// This structure is the notification info for when the server is about to
// process the client headers
//

typedef struct _HTTP_FILTER_PREPROC_HEADERS
{
    //
    // Retrieves the specified header value.  Header names should include
    // the trailing ':'.  The special values 'method', 'url' and 'version'
    // can be used to retrieve the individual portions of the request line
    //

    BOOL (WINAPI * GetHeader) (
        struct _HTTP_FILTER_CONTEXT * pfc,
        LPSTR                         lpszName,
        LPVOID                        lpvBuffer,
```

```
        LPDWORD                         lpdwSize
    );

    //
    //  Replaces this header value to the specified value.  To delete a header,
    //  specified a value of '\0'.
    //

    BOOL (WINAPI * SetHeader) (
        struct _HTTP_FILTER_CONTEXT * pfc,
        LPSTR                           lpszName,
        LPSTR                           lpszValue
        );

    //
    //  Adds the specified header and value
    //

    BOOL (WINAPI * AddHeader) (
        struct _HTTP_FILTER_CONTEXT * pfc,
        LPSTR                           lpszName,
        LPSTR                           lpszValue
        );

    DWORD dwReserved;

} HTTP_FILTER_PREPROC_HEADERS, *PHTTP_FILTER_PREPROC_HEADERS;
```

This structure declares three methods for handling HTTP headers. Let's take a look at each of these briefly.

The GetHeader method is used to retrieve HTTP headers from the incoming HTTP requests. GetHeader requires that the lpszName field be set to the desired header. You'll need to include the trailing colon in the request. GetHeader also provides for three special header requests— url, method, and version. Set lpszName to one of these values when you want to obtain a piece of the request line itself.

The SetHeader method is used to change the value of an existing incoming header. If you want to delete a header from the HTTP request, simply set lpszName to the name of the header to be changed and set the lpszValue to a zero length, null terminated string.

Use the AddHeader method to include additional HTTP headers in the incoming HTTP requests. AddHeader uses the lpszName field for the header and the lpszValue field as the header value.

Working with _OnAuthentication_ Sometimes, you may want to provide your own custom authentication scheme. To do this, you'll need to override the OnAuthentication virtual function. First, you set dwFlags to SF_NOTIFY_PREPROC_HEADERS. You won't need to call the default version of this function in your own implementations because it does nothing. The function prototype for OnAuthentication is shown in Listing 24.7.

Part

III

Ch

24

Listing 24.7 *6HTTPFILT.H OnAuthentication* **Function Prototype**

```
virtual DWORD OnAuthentication( CHttpFilterContext* pfc,
PHTTP_FILTER_AUTHENT pAuthent );
```

Notice the pointer to an HTTP_FILTER_AUTHENT structure (refer to Listing 24.7). The information you need to do any custom authentication processing is passed in this structure. The declaration of HTTP_FILTER_AUTHENT is shown in Listing 24.8.

Listing 24.8 *7HTTPFILT.H HTTP_FILTER_AUTHENT* **Declaration**

```
typedef struct _HTTP_FILTER_AUTHENT
{
    //
    //  Pointer to username and password, empty strings for the anonymous user
    //
    //  Client's can overwrite these buffers which are guaranteed to be at
    //  least SF_MAX_USERNAME and SF_MAX_PASSWORD bytes large.
    //

    CHAR * pszUser;
    DWORD  cbUserBuff;

    CHAR * pszPassword;
    DWORD  cbPasswordBuff;

} HTTP_FILTER_AUTHENT, *PHTTP_FILTER_AUTHENT;
```

The pszUser and pszPassword fields contain the actual text of the user name and password entered by the user through the Web browser. Each of these two fields has an accompanying DWORD member that stores the size of the buffer.

Working with *OnUrlMap* Web servers employ the concept of a logical (or virtual) URL as a separate entity from the physical location of a document on a Web server. So one of the steps a Web server must take is to map the logical URL supplied by the user to the physical location of that file on the Web server's document space.

Sometimes you may want to provide your own custom mapping function. To do this, you need to override the OnUrlMap virtual function. Set dwFlags to SF_NOTIFY_URL_MAP. The default version of this function does nothing so you won't want to call it in your own implementations. The function prototype for OnUrlMap is shown in Listing 24.9.

Listing 24.9 *8HTTPFILT.H OnUrlMap* **Function Prototype**

```
virtual DWORD OnUrlMap( CHttpFilterContext* pfc,
PHTTP_FILTER_URL_MAP pUrlMap );
```

Let's take a look at the HTTP_FILTER_URL_MAP structure (refer to Listing 24.9). The server will pass you the pszURL value as well as the cbPathBuff data. The declaration of HTTP_FILTER_URL_MAP is shown in Listing 24.10.

Listing 24.10   9HTTPFILT.H   HTTP_FILTER_URL_MAP Declaration

```
//
//   Indicates the server is going to use the specific physical mapping for
//   the specified URL.  Filters can modify the physical path in place.
//

typedef struct _HTTP_FILTER_URL_MAP
{
    const CHAR * pszURL;

    CHAR *       pszPhysicalPath;
    DWORD        cbPathBuff;

} HTTP_FILTER_URL_MAP, *PHTTP_FILTER_URL_MAP;
```

You use this structure as a means of receiving the URL passed from the Web browser. After completing any custom processing of the URL, you pass back an appropriate physical path to the requested document.

Working with *OnSendRawData* If you need to get at the HTTP responses before they are returned to the Web browser, you need to override this virtual function. Make sure that dwFlags is set to SF_NOTIFY_SEND_RAW_DATA. The default version of this function does nothing, so there is no point in calling it first in your own implementation. The function prototype for OnSendRawData is shown in Listing 24.11.

Listing 24.11   10HTTPFILT.H   OnReadRawData Function Prototype

```
virtual DWORD OnSendRawData( CHttpFilterContext* pfc,
PHTTP_FILTER_RAW_DATA pRawData );
```

OnSendRawData uses the same data structure as OnReadRawData for passing the request data.

Working with *OnLog* One of the most useful things a Web server does is log the transactions it executes on behalf of Web browsers. The OnLog virtual function allows you to supply any custom logging features. To use the OnLog function, you set dwFlags to SF_NOTIFY_LOG. There is no reason to call the default version of this function in your own implementation; it does nothing. The function prototype for OnLog is shown in Listing 24.12.

Listing 24.12   11HTTPFILT.H   OnLog Function Prototype

```
virtual DWORD OnLog( CHttpFilterContext* pfc, PHTTP_FILTER_LOG pLog );
```

Defer your curiosity about the CHttpFilterContext objects for just another moment. Instead, check out the HTTP_FILTER_LOG structure (see Listing 24.13).

On the CD

Listing 24.13   *12HTTPFILT.H   HTTP_FILTER_LOG* Declaration

```
//
//  The log information about to be written to the server log file.  The
//  string pointers can be replaced but the memory must remain valid until
//  the next notification
//

typedef struct _HTTP_FILTER_LOG
{
    const CHAR * pszClientHostName;
    const CHAR * pszClientUserName;
    const CHAR * pszServerName;
    const CHAR * pszOperation;
    const CHAR * pszTarget;
    const CHAR * pszParameters;

    DWORD  dwHttpStatus;
    DWORD  dwWin32Status;

} HTTP_FILTER_LOG, *PHTTP_FILTER_LOG;
```

Each of these members is briefly described in Table 24.4.

Table 24.4   Members of the *HTTP_FILTER_LOG* Structure

Member	Description
pszClientHostName	Host name of the client resulting from a DNS lookup
pszClientUserName	User name (if supplied)
pszServerName	The server servicing this request
pszOperation	The HTTP command requested
pszTarget	Target of the HTTP command
pszParameters	Any parameters passed to the HTTP command
dwHttpStatus	HTTP return status
dwWin32Status	Win32 error code

Using the *CHttpFilterContext* Class

The CHttpFilter class creates CHttpFilterContext objects that handle processing the individual requests. The CHttpFilterContext class provides members that contain all the information and functionality needed to process an HTTP request. CHttpFilterContext contains a member called m_pFC that is of type HTTP_FILTER_CONTEXT. In the discussion of CHttpFilter, a pointer to this type of structure was passed in each of the virtual functions you could override (such as OnLog or OnAuthenticate). Listing 24.14 shows the declaration of the HTTP_FILTER_CONTEXT structure.

Listing 24.14 *13HTTPFILT.H* **Declaration of *HTTP_FILTER_CONTEXT***

```
typedef struct _HTTP_FILTER_CONTEXT
{
    DWORD           cbSize;

    //
    //  This is the structure revision level.
    //

    DWORD           Revision;

    //
    //  Private context information for the server.
    //

    PVOID           ServerContext;
    DWORD           ulReserved;

    //
    //  TRUE if this request is coming over a secure port
    //

    BOOL            fIsSecurePort;

    //
    //  A context that can be used by the filter
    //

    PVOID           pFilterContext;

    //
    //  Server callbacks
    //

    BOOL (WINAPI * GetServerVariable) (
        struct _HTTP_FILTER_CONTEXT * pfc,
        LPSTR                         lpszVariableName,
        LPVOID                        lpvBuffer,
        LPDWORD                       lpdwSize
        );

    BOOL (WINAPI * AddResponseHeaders) (
        struct _HTTP_FILTER_CONTEXT * pfc,
        LPSTR                         lpszHeaders,
        DWORD                         dwReserved
```

continues

Part
III

Ch
24

Listing 24.14   *Continued*

```
        );

    BOOL (WINAPI * WriteClient) (
        struct _HTTP_FILTER_CONTEXT * pfc,
        LPVOID                        Buffer,
        LPDWORD                       lpdwBytes,
        DWORD                         dwReserved
        );

    VOID * (WINAPI * AllocMem) (
        struct _HTTP_FILTER_CONTEXT * pfc,
        DWORD                         cbSize,
        DWORD                         dwReserved
        );

    BOOL (WINAPI * ServerSupportFunction) (
        struct _HTTP_FILTER_CONTEXT * pfc,
        enum SF_REQ_TYPE              sfReq,
        PVOID                         pData,
        DWORD                         ul1,
        DWORD                         ul2
        );

} HTTP_FILTER_CONTEXT, *PHTTP_FILTER_CONTEXT;
```

The data elements of HTTP_FILTER_CONTEXT are summarized briefly in Table 24.5.

Table 24.5   Data Members of *HTTP_FILTER_CONTEXT*

Method	Description
cbSize	Indicates the size of this structure.
Revision	Revision number of this structure. This number must be less than or equal to HTTP_FILTER_REVISION.
ServerContext	Reserved for use by the server.
ulReserved	Reserved for use by the server.
fIsSecurePort	When this event occurs over a secured port, this member is true.
pFilterContext	This pointer is used by the filter to point to context information to associate with this request. Any allocated memory pointed to by this variable can be freed during the OnEndOfNetSession execution.

HTTP_FILTER_CONTEXT also makes several methods available for use in your DLL. These functions should seem very familiar. A number of these functions have an analogous function in the CHttpServerExtension object. Table 24.6 describes each of these methods briefly.

Table 24.6 Methods in the *HTTP_FILTER_CONTEXT* Structure

Method	Description
GetServerVariable	Used to retrieve HTTP headers.
AddResponseHeaders	Adds an HTTP header to the response.
WriteClient	Sends information to the client.
AllocMem	Used to allocate memory that is automatically freed when the OnEndOfNetSession method is called.
ServerSupportFunction	Used to execute certain server and HTTP specific transactions.

Using the ISAPI Wizard

The ISAPI Wizard from Microsoft also supports generating ISAPI filters. Using the ISAPI Wizard, the basic template of an ISAPI filter is generated for you. In this section, you step through the use of the ISAPI Wizard for generating filters. You'll also use the ISAPI Wizard to build a filter that implements a simple custom authentication. This example ISAPI filter was compiled and constructed using Microsoft Visual C++ 4.1 and is called Auth. To build this simple ISAPI filter, follow these steps:

1. Start Microsoft Visual C++ 4.1 (or higher) and begin a new project. Select File, New and choose Project Workspace. Choose ISAPI Extension Wizard from the list of project types (see fig. 24.1). Now press the Create button.

FIG. 24.1
Start the ISAPI project.

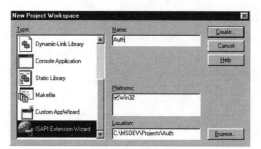

2. The ISAPI Wizard will next prompt you with the screen shown in figure 24.2. Select Generate a Filter object. By default, the extension's class name and description will be set to the same name as the project file. You can also choose to have the MFCs statically linked or available as a shared DLL. In most cases, you'll want to accept the default choice of shared DLL.

FIG. 24.2

Fill out the ISAPI Wizard dialog box.

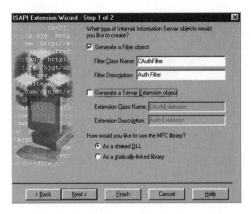

3. Press the Next button and the Wizard will present you with the screen shown in figure 24.3. You need to select the notification priority, connection types of interest, and the notifications that the filter should respond to. Notice that the notification priority is set to Low, which is the default. Changing this can have serious consequences on the performance of the server. Both Secured and Nonsecured port connections are selected by default. This will be fine for our authentication program. By default, the End of Connection notification is selected. Select the Client Authentication Requests checkbox, since this is an authentication filter. Now press Finish.

FIG. 24.3

Fill out the ISAPI filter configuration dialog box.

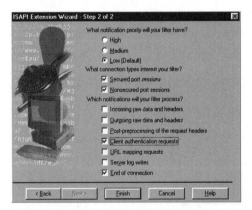

4. Before the ISAPI Wizard generates the template source files, you are prompted with a confirmation dialog box like the one shown in figure 24.4. Just press OK if everything looks correct.

FIG. 24.4

Check the filter wizard confirmation dialog box.

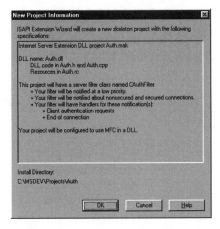

Part

III

Ch

24

5. The ISAPI Wizard is then kind enough to generate the following files for you: Auth.cpp, Auth.def, Auth.rc, and Auth.h. Start with the .h file. Listing 24.15 shows the code generated by the ISAPI Wizard.

Listing 24.15   AUTH.H   Header File Generated by the Wizard

```
// AUTH.CPP - Implementation file for your Internet Server
//     Auth Filter


class CAuthFilter : public CHttpFilter
{
public:
      CAuthFilter();
      ~CAuthFilter();

      BOOL GetFilterVersion(PHTTP_FILTER_VERSION pVer);

      DWORD OnAuthentication(CHttpFilterContext* pCtxt,
            PHTTP_FILTER_PREPROC_HEADERS pHeaderInfo);
      DWORD OnEndOfNetSession(CHttpFilterContext* pCtxt);

      // TODO: Add your own overrides here
};
```

Notice that the ISAPI Wizard generates method prototypes for the two notifications you requested in the configuration dialog. Of course, you could add another notification later simply by adding the correct prototype and properly setting dwFlags.

6. Next switch to the Auth.cpp file. This is the file where you'll customize your implementation of the OnAuthentication notification response method. Listing 24.16 shows the code as generated by the ISAPI Wizard before making any modifications to OnAuthentication.

On the CD

Listing 24.16 *AUTH.CPP* The *OnAuthentication* Method Implementation Before Alteration

```
DWORD CAuthFilter::OnAuthentication(CHttpFilterContext* pCtxt,
        PHTTP_FILTER_AUTHENT pAuthEnt)
{
    return SF_STATUS_REQ_NEXT_NOTIFICATION;

}
```

The authentication method implemented here (shown in Listing 24.17) is a simple string compared to a hard-coded name. Obviously, you could implement any method, simple or complicated, as required for your application.

On the CD

Listing 24.17 *2AUTH.CPP* The *OnAuthentication* Method Implementation After Alteration

```
DWORD CAuthFilter::OnAuthentication(CHttpFilterContext* pCtxt,
        PHTTP_FILTER_AUTHENT pAuthEnt)
{
    int iResult;
    BOOL bIsUser;
    BOOL bIsPassword;

    // set bIsUser
    iResult = strcmp(pAuthEnt->pszUser, "Brian");
    if (iResult == 0)
        bIsUser = TRUE;
    else
        bIsUser = FALSE;

    // set bIsPassword
    iResult = strcmp(pAuthEnt->pszPassword, "Farrar");
    if (iResult == 0)
        bIsPassword = TRUE;
    else
        bIsPassword = FALSE;

    // Permit or reject access to the web server
    if (bIsUser && bIsPassword)
        return SF_STATUS_REQ_NEXT_NOTIFICATION;
    else
        return SF_STATUS_REQ_ERROR;

}
```

Index

GET CONNECTED
to the ultimate source of computer information!

The MCP Forum on CompuServe

Go online with the world's leading computer book publisher! Macmillan Computer Publishing offers everything you need for computer success!

Find the books that are right for you!
A complete online catalog, plus sample chapters and tables of contents give you an in-depth look at all our books. The best way to shop or browse!

➤ Get fast answers and technical support for MCP books and software

➤ Join discussion groups on major computer subjects

➤ Interact with our expert authors via e-mail and conferences

➤ Download software from our immense library:

  ▷ Source code from books
  ▷ Demos of hot software
  ▷ The best shareware and freeware
  ▷ Graphics files

Join now and get a free CompuServe Starter Kit!

To receive your free CompuServe Introductory Membership, call **1-800-848-8199** and ask for representative #597.

The Starter Kit includes:
➤ Personal ID number and password
➤ $15 credit on the system
➤ Subscription to *CompuServe Magazine*

Once on the CompuServe System, type:

GO MACMILLAN

for the most computer information anywhere!

 MACMILLAN COMPUTER PUBLISHING

 CompuServe

Check out Que® Books on the World Wide Web
http://www.mcp.com/que

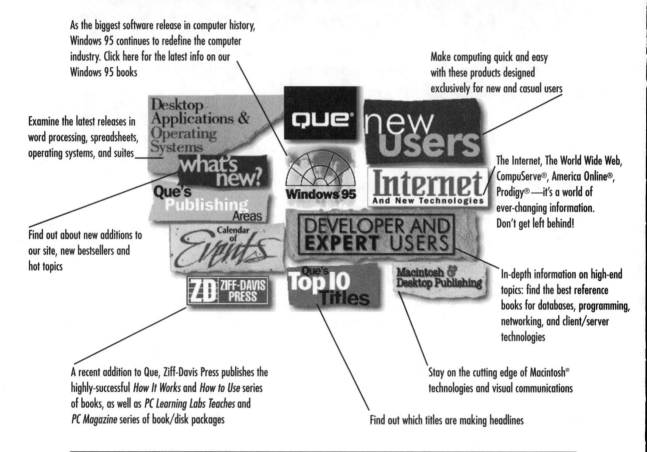

As the biggest software release in computer history, Windows 95 continues to redefine the computer industry. Click here for the latest info on our Windows 95 books

Make computing quick and easy with these products designed exclusively for new and casual users

Examine the latest releases in word processing, spreadsheets, operating systems, and suites

The Internet, The World Wide Web, CompuServe®, America Online®, Prodigy®—it's a world of ever-changing information. Don't get left behind!

Find out about new additions to our site, new bestsellers and hot topics

In-depth information on high-end topics: find the best reference books for databases, programming, networking, and client/server technologies

A recent addition to Que, Ziff-Davis Press publishes the highly-successful *How It Works* and *How to Use* series of books, as well as *PC Learning Labs Teaches* and *PC Magazine* series of book/disk packages

Stay on the cutting edge of Macintosh® technologies and visual communications

Find out which titles are making headlines

With 6 separate publishing groups, Que develops products for many specific market segments and areas of computer technology. Explore our Web Site and you'll find information on best-selling titles, newly published titles, upcoming products, authors, and much more.

- Stay informed on the latest industry trends and products available
- Visit our online bookstore for the latest information and editions
- Download software from Que's library of the best shareware and freeware

Copyright © 1996, Macmillan Computer Publishing-USA, A Viacom Company

QUE® has the right choice for every computer user

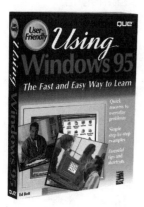

From the new computer user to the advanced programmer, we've got the right computer book for you. Our user-friendly *Using* series offers just the information you need to perform specific tasks quickly and move onto other things. And, for computer users ready to advance to new levels, QUE *Special Edition Using* books, the perfect all-in-one resource—and recognized authority on detailed reference information.

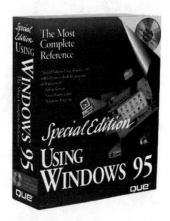

The *Using* series for casual users

Who should use this book?

Everyday users who:

- Work with computers in the office or at home
- Are familiar with computers but not in love with technology
- Just want to "get the job done"
- Don't want to read a lot of material

The user-friendly reference

- The fastest access to the one best way to get things done
- Bite-sized information for quick and easy reference
- Nontechnical approach in plain English
- Real-world analogies to explain new concepts
- Troubleshooting tips to help solve problems
- Visual elements and screen pictures that reinforce topics
- Expert authors who are experienced in training and instruction

Special Edition Using for accomplished users

Who should use this book?

Proficient computer users who:

- Have a more technical understanding of computers
- Are interested in technological trends
- Want in-depth reference information
- Prefer more detailed explanations and examples

The most complete reference

- Thorough explanations of various ways to perform tasks
- In-depth coverage of all topics
- Technical information cross-referenced for easy access
- Professional tips, tricks, and shortcuts for experienced users
- Advanced troubleshooting information with alternative approaches
- Visual elements and screen pictures that reinforce topics
- Technically qualified authors who are experts in their fields
- "Techniques from the Pros" sections with advice from well-known computer professionals

Copyright © 1996, Macmillan Computer Publishing-USA, A Viacom Company

Your Source for Quality CD ROMs

- Development - Entertainment - Productivity -

If you Like it Hot and Spicy . . . . . **BLACK COFFEE**.

Just about anything and everything someone interested in Java and web programming would find interesting.
Hundreds of Applets *(many with full source)*covering such topics as Art, Business, Education, Programming, Graphics, Special Effects, Communications, etc.

A Computer Language MUST . . . Dragon Fodder

Create your own computer language! Learn how Basic, Pascal, Forth, are written. Source code to 100 of the latest and greatest computer languages. Accompanied book covers each language and its files. Ideal companion to the "Dragon Book" on compilers.

Everything you need. . . Web Weaver *Plus*.

Yes, EVERYTHING you need to create your own dynamic Personal and Business Web pages Thousands of icons, textures, backgrounds, graphics, templates, and style sheets. Huge library of sounds, ROYALTY FREE! Hundreds of WWW tools. Build your own Hotlist of recommended sites from a database listing of thousands of websites. Instant Internet Access

Knowledge Media ™

http://www.km-cd.com

(800) 78 CDROM   (916) 872-7487 (916) 872-3826 Fax
436 Nunneley Rd., Ste. B, Paradise, CA USA 95969

Complete and Return this Card
for a *FREE* Computer Book Catalog

Thank you for purchasing this book! You have purchased a superior computer book written expressly for your needs. To continue to provide the kind of up-to-date, pertinent coverage you've come to expect from us, we need to hear from you. Please take a minute to complete and return this self-addressed, postage-paid form. In return, we'll send you a free catalog of all our computer books on topics ranging from word processing to programming and the internet.

Mr. ☐   Mrs. ☐   Ms. ☐   Dr. ☐

Name (first) ⬜⬜⬜⬜⬜⬜⬜⬜⬜⬜ (M.I.) ⬜ (last) ⬜⬜⬜⬜⬜⬜⬜⬜⬜⬜⬜⬜⬜

Address ⬜⬜⬜⬜⬜⬜⬜⬜⬜⬜⬜⬜⬜⬜⬜⬜⬜⬜⬜⬜⬜⬜⬜⬜

City ⬜⬜⬜⬜⬜⬜⬜⬜⬜   State ⬜⬜   Zip ⬜⬜⬜⬜⬜ ⬜⬜⬜⬜

Phone ⬜⬜ ⬜⬜⬜ ⬜⬜⬜⬜   Fax ⬜⬜ ⬜⬜⬜ ⬜⬜⬜⬜

Company Name ⬜⬜⬜⬜⬜⬜⬜⬜⬜⬜⬜⬜⬜⬜⬜⬜⬜⬜⬜⬜⬜⬜

E-mail address ⬜⬜⬜⬜⬜⬜⬜⬜⬜⬜⬜⬜⬜⬜⬜⬜⬜⬜⬜⬜⬜⬜

1. Please check at least (3) influencing factors for purchasing this book.

Front or back cover information on book ☐
Special approach to the content ☐
Completeness of content ☐
Author's reputation ☐
Publisher's reputation ☐
Book cover design or layout ☐
Index or table of contents of book ☐
Price of book ☐
Special effects, graphics, illustrations ☐
Other (Please specify): _____ ☐

2. How did you first learn about this book?

Saw in Macmillan Computer Publishing catalog ☐
Recommended by store personnel ☐
Saw the book on bookshelf at store ☐
Recommended by a friend ☐
Received advertisement in the mail ☐
Saw an advertisement in: _____ ☐
Read book review in: _____ ☐
Other (Please specify): _____ ☐

3. How many computer books have you purchased in the last six months?

This book only ☐
3 to 5 books ☐
books ☐
More than 5 ☐

4. Where did you purchase this book?

Bookstore ☐
Computer Store ☐
Consumer Electronics Store ☐
Department Store ☐
Office Club ☐
Warehouse Club ☐
Mail Order ☐
Direct from Publisher ☐
Internet site ☐
Other (Please specify): _____ ☐

5. How long have you been using a computer?

☐ Less than 6 months   ☐ 6 months to a year
☐ 1 to 3 years   ☐ More than 3 years

6. What is your level of experience with personal computers and with the subject of this book?

	With PCs	With subject of book
New	☐	☐
Casual	☐	☐
Accomplished	☐	☐
Expert	☐	☐

Source Code ISBN: 0-7897-0886-8

7. Which of the following best describes your job title?

- Administrative Assistant ☐
- Coordinator ☐
- Manager/Supervisor ☐
- Director ☐
- Vice President ☐
- President/CEO/COO ☐
- Lawyer/Doctor/Medical Professional ☐
- Teacher/Educator/Trainer ☐
- Engineer/Technician ☐
- Consultant ☐
- Not employed/Student/Retired ☐
- Other (Please specify): _____ ☐

8. Which of the following best describes the area of the company your job title falls under?

- Accounting ☐
- Engineering ☐
- Manufacturing ☐
- Operations ☐
- Marketing ☐
- Sales ☐
- Other (Please specify): _____ ☐

9. What is your age?

- Under 20 ☐
- 21-29 ☐
- 30-39 ☐
- 40-49 ☐
- 50-59 ☐
- 60-over ☐

10. Are you:

- Male ☐
- Female ☐

11. Which computer publications do you read regularly? (Please list)

_____
_____
_____
_____
_____
_____
_____
_____
_____

Comments: _____
_____
_____

Fold here and scotch-tape to mail.

ATTN MARKETING
MACMILLAN COMPUTER PUBLISHING
MACMILLAN PUBLISHING USA
201 W 103RD ST
INDIANAPOLIS IN 46290-9042

POSTAGE WILL BE PAID BY THE ADDRESSEE

FIRST-CLASS MAIL PERMIT NO. 9918 INDIANAPOLIS IN

BUSINESS REPLY MAIL

NO POSTAGE
NECESSARY
IF MAILED
IN THE
UNITED STATES

Licensing Agreement

By opening this package, you are agreeing to be bound by the following:

The software contained on this CD is, in many cases, copyrighted and all rights are reserved by the individual software developer and/or publisher. You are bound by the individual licensing agreements associated with each piece of software contained on the CD. THIS SOFTWARE IS PROVIDED FREE OF CHARGE, AS IS, AND WITHOUT WARRANTY OF ANY KIND, EITHER EXPRESSED OR IMPLIED, INCLUDING, BUT NOT LIMITED TO, THE IMPLIED WARRANTIES OF MERCHANTABILITY AND FITNESS FOR A PARTICULAR PURPOSE. Neither the book publisher nor its dealers and distributors assumes any liability for any alleged or actual damages arising from the use of this software. (Some states do not allow exclusion of implied warranties, so the exclusion may not apply to you.)